Relations indigenous dialogue

Relations
indigenous dialogue

JOSEPH M. SANCHEZ & JOHN R. GRIMES
editors

INSTITUTE OF AMERICAN INDIAN ARTS MUSEUM
Santa Fe, New Mexico

INSTITUTE OF
AMERICAN
INDIAN ARTS
MUSEUM
CONTEMPORARY
NATIVE ART

Institute of American Indian Arts Museum
108 Cathedral Place
Santa Fe, NM 87501
505-983-8900

Published on the occasion of the exhibition RELATIONS: indigenous dialogue
organized by the Institute of American Indian Arts Museum, Santa Fe, New Mexico.

RELATIONS has been made possible through a grant from Lannan Foundation.
Additional support has been provided by the City of Santa Fe Arts Commission
and the 1% Lodgers Tax.

Curator: Joseph M. Sanchez

Editors: Joseph M. Sanchez, John R. Grimes

Essays: *At the Thresholds,* Lucy R. Lippard ©2006 Lucy R. Lippard;
Indigenous and Authentic: Hawaiian Epistemology and the Triangulation of Meaning,
Manulani Meyer ©2006 Manulani Meyer

Design: Janice St. Marie, Joseph M. Sanchez

Photography: Sallie I. Wesaw, Joseph M. Sanchez, Kitty Leaken, Othniel "Art" Oomittuk,
Jeane La Rance, Rose Simpson

Printer: Central Plains Book Manufacturing, Athens, Texas

ISBN: 978-1-881396-27-7

Library of Congress Control Number: 2006927938

Cover Art: Joseph M. Sanchez, *W Hole*

Back Cover: Kitty Leaken, *Hole*; Joseph M. Sanchez, *Prayer Offering*

CONTENTS

Bob Haozous, 2006

A WALK WITH BUCKO

This evening I took a walk behind my home with my walking stick and dog, Bucko. The sun had just receded beyond the horizon and the low cloud cover created a sunset that was beyond any verbal description. When I was young my father used to stop the car on the highway and our family would sit on the roadside just to watch spectacular sunsets.

The southwest is renowned for its natural beauty, and the colors of the sunset at dusk are often breathtaking. For some years all of my thoughts have revolved around a RELATIONS type project and this evening is no exception. I wondered if the sunsets of my ancestors compared to the glorious panorama I was enjoying. No words or painting could have communicated the subtle blending of oranges, pinks, yellows, blues and purples that stretched over the Jemez Mountains to the west. What I observed was mine to experience, mine to enjoy, mine to absorb and love. I could easily indulge in idealistic fantasies and pretend that this was the same shared sunset my tribe viewed in the past but I question that pretext. Just as we of today claim to hold the culture of the past, I too could easily pretend to live and maintain an Apache culture that was thriving over 120 years ago. How can that be? The sky with its depleted ozone layer and additional pollution particles, illuminated by refracted sunlight, may offer a more stunning or less attractive sunset than that of our ancestors. My personal cultural identity is an obvious self contradiction with my Anglo, Spanish (plus African Moor?), Navajo, possibly Ute, and N'de or Apache genetics. These genetics are encompassed by endless identifiers of Western man. How do I honestly call myself Indian or contemporary Apache if the only references to my identity are racially or historically based? Today all we need to proclaim our Indian heritage are proof of blood lines and a federal number.

As we go deeper into the RELATIONS project we must constantly remind ourselves of the depth of culture and physical beauty we commonly share. Consecutively, we must honestly acknowledge the residual damage to our contemporary Indigenous cultural reality and claimed identity. The knowledge we share with our children must focus upon a more meaningful and honest portrait of ourselves. That portrait must include the negative. The Apache people of the past had entirely different cultural ways than we have today. Our existence was based upon hunting, raiding, warfare, trade and occasional farming and harvesting. In the harsh desert climate of the southwest our Apache spirituality and communal laws required a strong relationship to nature and tribe for basic survival. I would be remiss to remind my tribe or family of past tribal deities such as Life Giver, Monster Slayer, White Painted Woman, the Twins, the Little People or our creation stories without also including more immediate adopted Western concepts that are the antithesis of Indigenous or Apache beliefs. Even this simple declaration, if made to an all-Christianized tribe whose culture is near totally Westernized, would risk creating serious dissention and possible expulsion from the tribe. Our older ones are all gone and none of our contemporary people experienced the distant times of cultural autonomy. Nor do they understand what a true Apache identity encompassed or what shared cultural responsibilities are required for survival. Unfortunately we have chosen to continually ignore the true reality of our ongoing cultural decay.

Many of us believe that there was and still exists a profound philosophical foundation supporting tribal identity, knowledge and purpose. The weakened contemporary identity we now share is based on a well maintained, historically focused, romantic, and superficial portrayal that is unable to adapt to change while maintaining fundamental cultural values. We have lost the true meaning of being sovereign and Indigenous. We now allow state supervision over our economic ventures and have thereby reduced our sovereignty to little more than a state level commercial business. The philosophical basis of Indigenous people will remain memory and eventually be forgotten unless we expose and challenge the superficial cultural identity that is currently used.

Here is an example of our acceptance of a non-Indian and Western judgment of our arts.

I recently enjoyed the *Changing Hands 2* Indigenous art exhibition at the IAIA Museum. The combination of technique, aesthetics, and the design of the objects curated into the exhibit was amazing. I left the exhibit with the feeling of uneasiness. During the exhibit the museum director reminded me that it was selected by non-Indigenous 'white' curators. That alone could easily give reason to my unrest. There was another equally disturbing aspect to the exhibition in reference to art ownership (i.e., the changing of ownership or hands from maker to owner) that was related to cultural intent and cultural return. (As a side note, my work was included in the *Changing Hands I* exhibit because I protested the original premise of the exhibit and was immediately accepted as a token dissenting voice. At that time in my career it was ok to accept the premise that any exhibit with one's peers was a good exhibit and good for business.) The entire exhibit is visually beautiful but lacked an internal cultural purpose. It seems that our primary artistic statement was "we Indians are world class artisans," plus, "we have obtained our importance by relying on Western viewpoints and economic values."

This non-cultural/non-Indigenous purpose seems to reek of self glorification and 'artist as hero' worship, non-Indigenous laws of supply and demand, Western economics, Western aesthetics and Western romanticism. By focusing our arts toward economic reward we Indigenous Native artists have lost our fundamental responsibility of inspiring or stimulating internal cultural thought and discussion. The non-Indigenous curators assumed the right to determine who the 'Masters of Indian Arts' were and in doing so arrogantly presented their personal perceptions of Indigenous value and aesthetics. 'Give them the tools and let them create, and therefore their art work will be valued by the collector as fine art' was and still is the fundamental belief of modernized Indian art. This trade school belief that reflects the federal assimilation policy is still rooted in the Institute of American Indian Art's mission. The original goal of this school was to provide economic return from our natural talents as craft producers. This is not to say the artworks of *Changing Hands II* and other Indian art isn't exemplary as individual world class art objects or economically valuable. As an artist I was intimidated and totally captivated by the beautiful work and talent of the artists included in the exhibit. I suppose what I am saying is this: there simply isn't any serious attempt or desire to communicate the contemporary humanity, intelligence or life conditions of the Native American artisans through the arts. Little of the artwork in this exhibit told me that this artwork is a true portrait of us a contemporary Native people.

When the group of RELATIONS entered the hole I found myself apprehensive of criticism. At the same time these people I feared took the time to enter and attempt to understand the project. I'm sure each one of us realized that we could easily paint our individual art statements on the wall space in front of us. Considering the combined talent we represented it could be assumed that the end product would have been visually beautiful and undoubtedly economically valuable. Unfortunately, a group of disconnected individual expressions, however attractive or culturally meaningful, would have undermined the purpose of an Indigenous dialogue. Though some may believe otherwise, I don't think we need Westernized concepts of individualism, self ownership, art jargon and production methods to give our art credibility. To verify that statement we must create a language for our contemporary Indigenous identity. Three very important questions must be addressed: "How do we share and accept another's Indigenous perceptions?" "How do we go beyond the 'me' emphasis that is so all-important to Western man and create a 'we' or tribal thought? And of equal importance, "How do we balance group or tribal identity with the individualistic focus of Western man?"

Other questions should be also discussed. Questions such as: "How are we going to make the RELATIONS project more than a survey exhibit based on historic glorification and the contemporary cultural prettiness concepts?" "What are the group's shared purpose and intent behind the RELATIONS: indigenous dialogue exhibition?"

During one of our meetings the dialogue group entered the hole project together. As we were in the hole I wondered what any one of us, as individual cultural representatives, would consider the primary or most fundamental object or idea that represented the most important aspect of his or her culture. In my tribe we still retain great respect for the concept of power. The cattail pollen is extremely important for blessing and protection and is used privately and in tribal ceremonies. The Pueblo and Navajo people hold corn meal in high esteem, perhaps even considering it sacred. I've watched many other people use tobacco, sage, cedar, eagle and owl feathers, woodpecker feathers, hummingbird bodies, lightning struck trees, turquoise, plants, bear, the sun and moon, and a seemingly endless number of culturally important songs, sacred objects and areas. On a social level all people seem to have sacred songs and chants, clothing, war and medicine items, traditional designs, Creator or Life Giver symbols, unspoken concepts and objects, and a list that seems endless. During the 1960's an anthropologist named Frank Waters wrote the *Book of the Hopi* and most people suddenly accepted the place of Hopi people as philosophically and spiritually superior to the other North American Indian tribes. This respect is seemingly bestowed by 'white' people in authority to whichever tribe they deem worthy throughout America. A Hopi man told me that much of the cultural information was intentionally shared as misinformation, and the authentic information remained closely guarded. Does this type of adulation place the Hopi people on Indigenous people's highest chair of respect? Should we go to any specific tribe for a more pure way of thinking? If we located the most powerful or meaningful talisman, concept or substance should we thereby incorporate it into our Indigenous dialogue as substitute for our own conception of the sacred? How do we deal with the difference in creation or eternity concepts? Do we as a group take a vote or individually choose the most pure, historical, logical and instinctive solutions to our contemporary Indigenous questions? And how do we answer the question of specific sacred cultural place? These questions seem superfluous, but unless we can respectfully acknowledge different cultural viewpoints as equal to our own we will never create the basic alphabet to our new Indigenous language. I personally believe that with the 'we as a part of a whole' of the RELATIONS concept our individual tribal uniqueness must be open to revision into a more commonality of thought. In other words, there wasn't, isn't and never will be a purity of thought or culture unless we first use the nature-based instinct and common sense that exemplified Indigenous thought.

Western training also taught us that we must polarize our thoughts; good against bad, for or against, black as negative against white as purity or good, joy as opposed to sorrow, the vertical of Western thinking contrasted to the horizontal dispersion of the Indigenous. We, as a group, or as cultural representatives, cannot allow ourselves to be dictated to by non-Indigenous philosophy. It is the creation of this Indigenous philosophy that gives our group a sense of purpose. It goes without saying that those of us with traditional knowledge must also accept the importance of those who seek honest, healthy or possibly revolutionary change. Conversely those who are challenging the status quo must equally embrace those who maintain our cultural wisdom and experience. With our dialogue we must give equal consideration to the younger participants because they are truly the eyes and backbone of the elders and older ones because of their hands-on knowledge of contemporary issues. If we accept tradition and change as divergent and unrelated concepts we risk neutralizing our dreamers and visionaries. The role of honest cultural observer could easily belong to the arts. One of the most important unifying factors of the group is the need for meaningful and honest cultural change. That is the basis of the RELATIONS concept.

A Native American elder 'of the Indian arts' once challenged me with this question "What are you trying to do, change the world?" In retrospect the answer should have been "Of course!" If we don't challenge or attempt to make serious change to what appears to be an Indigenous and Indian identity that for all practical purposes is cosmetic, our children and grandchildren will inherit an even less clear cultural identity than we experience. We simply must break through the wall or crust of the hole, together if possible, to honestly understand and make the RELATIONS concept meaningful.

I would much prefer describing my own sunset instead of attempting to create parallels or descriptions of the beauty to my father's father's sunsets. My sunset, as with my culture, exists with me today. I would prefer to explain with my art what is of my own experience rather than portray a romantic, Western historic or tribal historic experience that has been reduced to superficial layers of contemporary Indian identity. It need not be stated that without the reliance, knowledge and respect for our traditional cultural foundation of our Indigenous or Indian past we lose the real purpose of our cultural existence and seriously flirt with new age concepts of individualism. We need the constant reminder that our cultural inheritance must serve as the cornerstone of any meaningful change.

I share these ideas with the hope of creating an open dialogue for further talks. This project depends on our ability to work and share in the creation of a renewed Indigenous language for our dialogue. The knowledge base must be an accumulation of all voices of the group, each contributing his or her specific life and cultural experience. We have dug and shared the hole together. Now we must recreate the dialogue that has always identified us as Indigenous.

Bob Haozous, 2006

Rose Simpson, 2006

RELEVANT WORK AND REAL CULTURE:
A Dialogue in Truth

Mitayue Oyasin. "All my relations" is the way I have been taught to address the ancestors as I enter the sweat lodge, as a human being wanting to take care of himself. We are all related. By that I mean all things: we all share the same planet, share the same air and humans even share 99.9% the same DNA. The idea of RELATIONS is not such a foreign idea, but as humans have evolved, the attitude of dominance over all things has placed our environment at risk—the Arctic is full of PCB's, habitats for our brothers and sisters and the other millions of species on this planet are being eroded by the second, with no regard for the future. In my short 50+ years on this planet I have watched the last old growth forest in the Southwest disappear, witnessed the clear cutting of the giant cedars of Canada, the burning of the Rain Forest for soybean fields and the complete disregard for our pollutants in the ocean, sky and earth. Even our local neighborhoods are full of toxins and chemical residues.

As an artist I feel that it is necessary to talk about what is happening to our world and share it with our people. We need to act as catalysts for change by inspiring our young people, our leaders and elders with relevant work that speaks to the issues that face the planet and us as Indigenous people who are her Relations.

Indigenous dialogue is not a new idea. Native peoples have gathered to talk and share for millennia. Today, it is a core group of artists talking and working together as relations in an effort to engage Indigenous artists from around the world to dialogue. To be honest about who they are and the problems they are facing with the creation of their work, its acceptance by their tribal group, family, collectors, museums and public. It is the openness of the RELATIONS artists to discuss difficult issues, and their willingness to share their thoughts freely that makes this exhibition unique and a privilege for all of us to experience. For the past six months the conversation has covered much ground in an effort to ask questions about our existence spiritually and artistically, the relationship of Indigenous artists to the mainstream, the definitions of Indigenous, our identity, as well as our responsibility and purpose as artists. The process of creating together is something that does not happen often. Artists tend to be individuals and our own egos do not allow easy collaboration. But I can say that it has been my pleasure to be a part of the W Hole tribe, as we have come to refer to the group, a group that has worked together, abandoning our ego and self for a far nobler effort, communication and friendship.

It's "the flinging, not the thing you fling," "our future is at risk," "Native prayer will manifest something potent for our people," "we chanted 'it' into being/we can chant 'it' out," "living on the crust…inside is the philosophy," are moments of dialogue we shared and now share with the public in this publication.

The world needs to look to the Indigenous, as Rocky Jensen refers to us, for the knowledge and wisdom to again be in harmony with all our relatives on an Earth in troubled times. Indigenous artists can be a voice to our people about who we are and how we share our cultural knowledge, a beacon to our children living in a Western world focused on individualism, privilege and entitlement to look to their culture and relations for true meanings of life.

The colonial viewpoint remains in much of the workings of the world subsequently undermining our ability to make decisions that have their basis in Indigenous thought. It is our connection to nature and the ability to listen and truly hear what is going on, that we share and will carry into the future if our children are to know who they are. Indigenous artists have a responsibility to share their thoughts with their people and reach as far as possible into that which helps and heals who we are as Indigenous people. We must restore self-confidence in our true selves as opposed to perpetuating a romantic stereotype for economic and ego-centric gain.

I like what Manulani Meyer says, "the thing we have most in common is our difference." It's our difference as Indigenous people, the diversity of knowledge, language and philosophy that is a rich mother lode of hope to our troubled world. Western artists have looked to Indigenous people for inspiration. Western science has looked to us for medicine. The natural world looks to us as custodians of her well-being. Who better to carry the message to our people and to a world about its lost respect and its misguided sense of place in the natural world than Indigenous artists? As Indigenous artists, we are sharing our art with our own people and are striving to go beyond a self-only view of success. The path is long and will have many peaks and valleys—I welcome the challenge we artists of the Indigenous world face.

Our sense of intuition, this nature-based instinct of who we are as beings on this planet, acts as a guide in our relationship to the grand scheme the creator has placed us in. As artists we create from our environment and experience. The Indigenous world is an abundant field to harvest.

The exhibition hopes are simple, an expansion of dialogue with Indigenous peoples to speak to the issues that we face as artists and people; a public awakening of the beauty and quality of Indigenous thought and the right of Indigenous artists to speak to the truth of their work, interpretation and content. This exhibition is designed as an experience, not a survey of trends or artist heros. It is not displayed on white museum walls, properly labeled to fit into the conceived notions of what museums and art are but rather it is an invitation into Indigenous thought and a glimpse into who we really are.

This exhibition and dialogue asks questions. *Who are we? What is our culture? Who are our children and who will they be in the future? What are we leaving them?*

We have been discussing the questions of ego and individualism, community and responsibility, trust and purpose. *What is honesty? What is your relation to your family, your place, your ancestors, your planet?* —questioning colonial supervision/interference of our work, our direction, our culture, our heritage and our truth. These have been great discussions full of honesty and trust and in the best of intentions, in a good way. The artist's conversations have framed their creations in dialogue. They ask questions in new ways, stimulating new answers and reaffirming our traditional instincts.

Can Indigenous artists create art that truly signifies their cultural heritage today? Will a tribe that has no one who knows the songs of his ancestors attract the "relatives" if the songs they sing are the hymns of Christianity? Can Indigenous art have a perspective that is different if the artists continually refer to Western art history as their reference point? Does the critique of Indigenous art have to be referenced through the damaged glass of cultural racism and male-dominated art egotism?

The knowledge we pass to our children—will it be the same old archetypal, archeological and anthropological fantasies? Do we face more relevant and real descriptions of ourselves, bringing them into the future with their eyes open and their cultural self-hatred revealed for what it is? The necessity to pass on real cultural information to our children is imperative to the continuation of real culture. What can we expect from our artists who create from a culture that has been reduced to a trinket/tourist store—such as what the Hawaiian artists have to face with Hilo Hattie: the store of Hawaii—an entire cultural inventory in plastic, portable and without the burden of what it all means or any of its cultural baggage? We must educate our collectors, our galleries and the public to grace their living rooms and halls with who we are today. We are not who we were before we were conquered, colonized and turned into an economic tourist and film attraction. Artists must accept the risk of financial and public criticism. Controversial art has always been in disfavor before collectors realize its value. We as artists of culture have a responsibility to the true portrayal of our peoples and culture, and must not be falsely seduced by success and privilege.

It is a great honor to work with this amazing group of artists who can openly share their thoughts and creative processes—and who call me relations.

This exhibition is an open invitation to all people. We are all relations and by that I mean everything—from the air we breathe to the rocks that make up the mountains to the four-leggeds to the insects to the water that we drink. We are relations. This is our truth.

Mitayue Oyasin.

Joseph M. Sanchez, 2006

W HOLE TRIBE

relations

mitakuye oyasin

selo'tine

stah-we-tyaimesheeh

unnum-tai wa-i   ittapiha

ittapiha

gah^n hee vooi yah

gah^n hee vooi yah

W HOLE TRIBE DIALOGUE

11.15.05

♦♦♦ I need to stress that I fully believe there is no contemporary gap between the mainland Indigenous artwork and the current statement of Hawaiians. I grew up with Indian people and fully acknowledge their intelligence, experience, vision and cultural knowledge. What is missing is the honest self-portrait that kept us in a sense of balance with ourselves and with nature. That honesty is always here. In Santa Fe, if you look for Indian art that is reflective of our real life experience you will only find statements based on an imagined history, romance and decoration, made for a quick economic exchange.

Our market is based on trade and the direction is outward and away from any purpose other than economics. Our cultures have always had an internal focus. Successful assimilation techniques at work, huh?

I believe that art comes from culture. Period!

It is not a play toy for its own art community, externally controlled or to be farmed out to different public venues or museums.

When we inspire our artists to speak to their own people about themselves we will 'create' an art form that has a cultural purpose beyond economics.

Hopefully when that happens the market will come to us as it always should. Highly idealistic and poverty guaranteed, I know, but that is what I feel. I miss a dialogue with my peers that goes beyond pride, blood and history. We are smart people that (in many ways) pretend to be culturally linked. Maybe it is the artist's job to inspire dialogue and link Indigenous cultures. My entire tribe believes that being Apache is measured by different amounts of blood, whereas, I believe the historic and modern identifier is philosophical and environmental. So, my goal is to create the catalyst for change that forces, begs or cajoles our own to begin learning more of our culture and creating artworks of our 'real human condition' today. I was taught that being Indigenous comes from living by nature's laws instead of worshiping man's laws. We can be Indigenous and philosophical at any time. What are the building blocks for that change and how can we become that catalyst for a more honest self portrayal? It's up to us to take the challenge (and feed our families at the same time). Maybe this is too much talk for an obvious problem and solution. I'll look up some of the postings to my own tribe. We need for you to come to Santa Fe and see this IAIA exhibition 'Indigenous Dialogue' subtitled 'Indian Art for Indian People' as soon as possible. Good chili too. ◆◆◆

12.05.05

◆◆◆ *Daanaht'eke* = the relative of all of us. (The following is a long story cut short) A friend of mine was given two eagles from the Federal Government and his beliefs required a sweat lodge ceremony to purify his family and the eagle. I've always steered clear of any direct ceremonial participation but this was an innocent acceptance to something, of which I knew nothing. During the ceremony the friend, a tough Oregon Paiute ex-AIM'ster, taught me the basics of his Lakota style ceremony and eventually gave me the ceremony with the advice to respectfully 'make it Apache' or your own. During the ceremony he taught me the Lakota phrase *mitakuye oyasin.* This phrase generally refers to 'all our relations' and concerns all things of nature that unite Indigenous man and his universe. ◆◆◆

●●● Before you continue your story, allow me to share with you our basic relationship with nature—a word that does not exist in our vocabulary.

Our concept is the belief in the Dual Polarity, consisting of *Haumea* {Terrestrial} and *Wakea* {Celestial}...these two elements are known by other names as well. The union of sky and earth created the Elementals... and being that we are an extremely poetic and pragmatic people, we gave those Elementals faces and names. The Male and Female Principle in Nature then bore us...humans...and we are called *Kanaka Maoli*...we believe that we are Star Children...in that the Maleness and Femaleness within the cosmos gave birth to all that exists...our inter-relationship on a personal and yet cosmogological level complete. The problem that we have today, however, is that most Hawaiian people, believe that the Elementals were human...and in THIS way are kin, rather then understanding that the very chemical and biological makeup of the universe makes us kin. Our two people seem to believe the same! ●●●

♦♦♦ Two months ago a Navajo friend asked me to make an award bronze for an environmental law center that was to be presented to the Navajo tribe for their successful efforts in stopping uranium mining on the Navajo Nation.

After much research I came up with the Apache equivalent to *mitakuye oyasin*, the phrase *Daanaht'eke*.

This phrase itself was inspired by Drew Lacapa, the White Mountain Apache comedian who, years ago, and in one of his performances, used the term *shideekende* or 'my' relatives. ♦♦♦

●●● Although, we believe that we are kin to "nature," we made a distinction from people different than us. That is why we call ourselves *Kanaka Maoli*...the Genuine or Real People...as opposed to others who were unlike us. There are many chants that tell of navigators traveling to distant lands and encountering "people unlike themselves," people, who they say were NOT, *Kanaka Maoli*. Although the ultimate meaning to kinship with the universe would be kinship with all people...customs, traditions and Sacred Law divided us...and still does for that matter. ●●●

♦♦♦ (In my discussions with students I try to remind them that being tribal is holistic. The 'me' word must be less important than the 'we' word or 'our' as opposed to the individualism of contemporary man)

Consequently the term suggested by my cousin, the tribal historian Michael Darrow, is *Daanaht'eke*.

Daanah=all of our and *t'eke*=relatives.

It's very important to make the distinction between the first person and the third person reference as used in the *shideekende* concept.

Since that time (two weeks ago+years of contemplation) I've been spending my time on that concept of changing the 'me' to 'we or our' with the intention of creating a foundation dialogue that includes all Indigenous people's self awareness. ♦♦♦

●●● Within the tribe, however...there was a meticulous communion of spirit and mind. Characteristic Western and Christian individuality did not exist. The '*Ohana*, '*Oiwi*...Clan and Tribe worked as one. A well oiled machine that was interdependent...each supporting and depending on the other to exist successfully...I have always had a problem with our young artists coming out of university...the "I" and "me" thing when it came to art, creativity and function!!! It seems to be a consensus among those Indigenous who are Western trained, that as long as they are Hawaiian, then their creations are Hawaiian...no need to be anchored to a strong foundation...no need to acknowledge Sacred Law...symbolisms that had great meaning for our people. The young are still in a very political mode...their art reeks with anger, resentment and general distortion of past history. Our people worked and created as one...in our ancient art...however, there was room for individuality...there were hundreds of images of our Male Principle *Ku*...and yet there were no two alike...nothing was ever repeated and yet, the work was accomplished by many hands...the harmony by which we lived evident in our having survived the harsh and cruel world for 25,000 years, yet maintaining and retaining our *Maoli* identity. Big guns, however...somehow, throughout the world...that stronger might...never right...made mincemeat of us all. But, we continue to prevail. ●●●

♦♦♦ In fact, I believe this may be the clue to uniting all of us with a common basis. ♦♦♦

●●● I agree!!! ●●●

♦♦♦ We will need that to overcome specific tribal preciousness. ♦♦♦

●●● Explain preciousness!!! ●●●

♦♦♦ More importantly we must unite against the totally unified modern world who has a mankind basis for thought and purpose, with the driving force of the amassment of economic power (eventually you will see my power statement in my exhibit).

When I mention putting everything on the table for discussion I'm referring to those values that come from the self glorified human reference that we Indigenous people have been forced to adopt (all inclusive of all world religions that are based on the human image). ♦♦♦

●●● Yes, yes, and yes!!! As Indigenous, we have been made to adopt many things...from young, I've never adhered to this. This, of course, has always made me strange among my own, who blindly went into the crucible, without flinching. I deplore world religions...religion is the bane of humankind. Our ancient belief, which appears as religion today, is our philosophy...our understanding of life...our acknowledging the Ancestors and All That Is!!! We also had anthropomorphic images that represented that nature that you were speaking of. Explain your meaning further... ●●●

♦♦♦ Commonality: Simon Ortiz. Simon is a westernized Laguna Pueblo man and I a westernized Chiricahua Apache. When you put all our westernization and tribalization on the table I've found that the foundation of the table is basically the same, that being, understanding our interrelationship with nature. We are radically different on the surface. ♦♦♦

●●● Agreed...my exterior, the way I dress...the things and way I eat... the house I live in...those material things that surround me...if this is what you mean by Westernization, then I too have fallen prey!!! However, inside heart and mind...I've always been *Maoli*. This too is a problem in Hawai'i... for the signature is extremely important for Hawaiians to feel Hawaiian... we love pageantry...dressing up in our ancient costumes, walking around with a loin cloth and feather cape and helmet...brandishing weapons... that makes us feel Hawaiian. I'm trying to instill in our young that we need not be the weekend warrior in order to be or feel Hawaiian...that our Ancestral calling is from within. ●●●

♦♦♦ That may be an egotistical statement because Simon has talents and wisdom that are far beyond most of us.

Nonetheless, we seem to be able to function as equals. Historically, according to white historians, we were enemies and Apache is supposed to be a Zuni word for enemy.

We call our self the *Nde* or people so none of that information has any relevance. ♦♦♦

●●● Although, we are now Hawaiians—a name that was introduced in 1845 to define all those Indigenous who live on these eight islands...we were at one time, different island chiefdoms...and even different district chiefdoms within each island...many enemies and many wars...especially in the 18th century!!! We are truly related to one another, genealogically... and yet, we did kill each other unmercifully. ●●●

♦♦♦ I'm now trying to create the foundation for a dialogue through the arts that unites Indigenous people around the earth.

This goal is far from being pan-Indian or pan-Indigenous.

I believe those pan concepts lack validity because the surface sharing doesn't sustain deeper and more profound Indigenous knowledge that is based on nature.

They just feel good and are inspirational. ♦♦♦

●●● Well, there has always been the hope that Pan-Indian or Pan-Indigenous defined exactly that...a profound Indigenous knowledge that was based on nature. To unite...oh boy, that's a hard one...we're still having trouble with the guy who has the key-ring snapped onto his belt...he feels "all that," knows everything...doesn't listen...is his and her own boss!!! There exist such a cultural distortion on these islands, that at best...we can unite those who are ready to unite!!! Those who need only that tiny push...those who are listening and waiting for that sound, that word to bring them over the brink into Enlightenment!!! ●●●

◆◆◆ In the past we somehow maintained our individual cultural identities and philosophies while sharing on other levels. ◆◆◆

●●● With our people there was only one cultural identity and philosophy and the Sacred Law was one...the Westerners introduced the "difference of opinion," that is so prevalent in our culture today! I understand what you mean...on the whole...worldwide, we should be able to bring together those of like "mind." Those who spiritually...from the heart...feel as we do... although our cultural identities and philosophies are quite different. ●●●

◆◆◆ This dialogue or basic statement is a long way from being complete as I brush against new related concepts and thoughts daily but the exhibition at the IAIA Museum could be an important stepping stone. ◆◆◆

●●● I agree!!! ●●●

◆◆◆ I enjoy your emails and learn more every day on our relationship and purpose with this exhibit. ◆◆◆

●●● I too enjoy our long discussions!!! In 1983, we curated an exhibit entitled, "We Are of One People." We invited the artists of Polynesia to participate—the concept being that our genealogical lines emanate from one stem, one source...we are the people who navigated from the Islands of South East Asia...perhaps from the Bay of Bengal...through the Indonesian corridor...through the Bismarck Archipelago...to New Guinea, New Caledonia, across to the Santa Cruz Islands...then that last trek of 500 miles to Fiji, Tonga, Samoa...where the silence of uninhabited islands awaited our voice. The show was spectacular in that we came together as one voice to shout our beauty and power to the world. ●●●

◆◆◆ Although, we do not share the same heritage, genealogy or traditions...I can see a similar worldwide exhibition—sharing those spiritual principles that make us human and sublime. ◆◆◆

●●● In the near future I'm going to propose that we rename the name or focus of the exhibit to 'our relations' to create a basic place for all of us to stand and speak. ●●●

♦♦♦ Any and all ideas are open to be used or dismissed at this point. I look forward to many *kukui* nut lamp meetings with you and yours in the future, either here or there. ♦♦♦

●●● I'll bring the *kukui* nuts and lamp!!! ●●●

12.29.05

♦♦♦ Have we been totally assimilated, are we now white people? No one seems to care or understand our past cultural values. Are we truly white people with Indian Blood (or Fed. number)? What's wrong with letting them (other Apache people) represent us culturally? Our individual welfare checks prove our tribal and cultural validity don't they? Geronimo who? (*Yannie=Goyahkla~*one who yawns?) Don't we all agree that being Apache is something of the past? Could Ruey and Mildred (and the rest of our elders) have fought so hard to maintain what little exists for the purpose of removing our extinction from their own personal records and guilt. Some Apache people from Oklahoma know that there is a contemporary Apache identity available to our children but they are an isolated few and don't seem to care to voice their opinion, share their knowledge, or do the work. "Perhaps we have become lazy" (quote: Wilma Mankiller). What a shame. Where are our tribal council and leadership when we need cultural answers that aren't based upon economic considerations? Does culture mean money? Are we hiding in our closets with a big APACHE INDIAN ON BOARD taped to the door? Someone lead our economic Indian identity into something more meaningful. Please! Our children deserve it don't they? Or do they? Lazy welfare Indians? Wow! If you didn't grow up with a cultural and family sense of responsibility please forgive me for my reminders. A computer button proves wisdom or understanding. Equal voting and other rights can be claimed by idiots in this country can't they? Those rights just provide simple answers that can easily eliminate our incredible cultural wisdom and purpose. Apache—It still exists, believe it or not (unless we, today, don't believe it).

(Now, go ahead, criticize we few for believing in our Apache future and demanding we go beyond a simplistic Indian identity bluff. Our children see right through us don't they? Ask them. Other Apache people await our plea for assistance. They need us too.) ◆◆◆

◆◆◆ I hope things are going well with you and your family (and people). I have an idea for the outdoor space but would like to run it by you before I proceed. I've found 8 lamp posts at 35 ft. each that I am thinking of curving into a 1/4 round shape. These would be attached to the center to make a lodge framework with an inside space height of 25 or so feet and a diameter of 40 or so feet. I don't have the measurements in front of me. This would be the framework we would work from. I thought you could work on the imagery attached to the lodge skeleton or we could work from here. It's more of a challenge than anything visionary but I like to play by instinct and this is a good example of my thought processes. Can you grapple with that idea and let me know if you can take it your direction? It'll look somewhat like a spider when it is done. I'll have to slice and weld the sides of the pipes innumerable times to create the 1/4 round of the lodge framework but I know it can be done. It should be strong enough to support anything we hang or attach to it. It's just a preliminary idea at this point. If you have another idea I'm willing to work with you on any level. Let me know. I hate to see some mall purchase the light posts. I especially hate to see them made into scrap metal by the scrap yard. Happy New Year and I hope to see you soon. ◆◆◆

12.30.05
●●● *Welina mai 'oe e a me!!!* With Greatest Warmth to You All!!! What you propose with the lamp posts has a parallel in our architectural structures. Our homes {*hale*} prominently displayed the Female and Male Principles—the skeleton, of which you speak, inclusive of the posts,

which are the ribs are male...the inside, the womb, is female. Although we did not traditionally work in the round...perhaps we could stretch a point, connecting two semi-circles, which is the Divine Assembly on our temples. Our house structure contained the Ancestral genome!!! In other words, all of the posts held names that applied to direct Ancestral origin...the center of which is the *Pou*...that which is the Foundation of All Things. So, in essence, what I'm saying here, is that I could work with your design—augment it with a central carving that would contain within it both the Female and Male Principle...or, perhaps do four carvings in between the ribs, again designating the Ancestors—or perhaps do both??? I must see your design. I would love this and could see working side by side with you Bob at that time. I like the structure idea...as I've said, it parallels with our own...the other parallel is that Polynesians viewed their world as a cluster of domes floating atop the Ancient Ocean {Pacific}...one dome connecting with the other...that is why we call the world *Honua*—or better *Honu{e}a*!!! The *Honuea* is the Hawksbill Turtle–the back of the Hawksbill is one component of the whole!!! As far as the eye could see, from horizon to horizon is one world...you travel through the Pillars of the Sky in order to enter another's dome. So, we have two parallels that embrace a given people...perhaps peoples throughout the world...it makes for a good simile!!! I like it. Let's continue this dialogue. My family joins me in wishing you and yours the most prosperous and content-filled 2006...with all of us on the same page...we will create a thing of beauty. ●●●

1.23.06

◆◆◆ Welcome to your home on the big island! We have lots of thoughts to share and mull over. Primarily on our sudden group friendship that is based on trust and respect. That doesn't happen often. I've been trying to think of my artistic and social peers who could work together as we four did and I end up with zero. It's a surprise to me that none of us in our project is overly involved with personal egos, and I've met many artists who wouldn't make it through my or our front door, let alone be up to speed on the dialogue. Thanks for the trust and respect. I honestly believe that we can create the slippage (in Islanders terms) beneath what is supposedly real, thereby causing that Tsunami we so desperately need to create cultural renewal. Now we need to tear down the seawall of western arrogance and bigotry that is supported so firmly by our own people.

Also, I want to tell you what you missed this morning at San Ildefonso Pueblo. After seeing the pueblo deer and buffalo dance ceremony I realize how much my concepts are based on theory and desire.

So, here's what I observed. This morning I got up early and was there before sunrise. I seldom venture to the local pueblo ceremonies but our project demands an opening of dialogue and knowledge, so I felt I must attend and report back to the group. Some white lady attendee later mentioned that it was 5 degrees Fahrenheit. (That's nothing to your son Art [again stepson to the white folks].) It was a bit misty and smoky in the dawn light. I stood with a bunch of visitors, mostly whites, and we all looked to these two small hills directly to the east of the village. There was an intermittent shout from dancers emanating from between the hills next to a huge plume of smoke that sounded almost as if they were intentionally herding the deer and buffalo. Suddenly on the top of one hill was the silhouette of a single deer, then others, eventually ending with 7 deer dancers. I was so taken by this image that I didn't notice that on the other hill appeared seven other dancers one at a time. From my bow hunting days I realized that they moved like real deer and not people. This is quite a feat showing an incredible intimate knowledge. Later I realized that the personification of the deer spirit had taken over the dancers identities. This is exactly what is supposed to happen to our Mountain Spirit or *Gan* dancers, even to the point that we are not supposed to speak their names or acknowledge them as people we 'once' knew. This is sacred stuff that is lost to us on that level but available if the tribe demands it. I don't say that lightly being the skeptic I am. They slowly meandered down the hill until they faced a line of the tribal ladies and were being led by a woman with black paint on her face. As I remember all dancers had that black face paint, and each of the ladies in line touched each deer and the lady. In our

Apache ways we also have a time to receive or give a blessing from our medicine people, the dancers or anyone who is considered sacred. Perhaps we could get a pueblo ceremony explanation later from within our group. I looked at the dancers' faces and was amazed at a transformation that made them into the deer beings. It was quite extraordinary. They now walked by the crowds of viewers and guests, a strange mixture of Indians and Anglos, and headed into the main plaza near where we were now standing, accompanied by 8 or so drummers. Then the drum beat changed and they begin to dance in an animalistic movement. This was absolutely beautiful, much like our own Apache ceremonies that I've witnessed, and I was carried away. The dancers were in the plaza dancing when the sun came up and blessed them with its light. I witnessed this same thing with the coming of age (puberty) ceremony we hosted for my daughter (stepdaughter to those white folks) in Oklahoma. During a crucial early morning moment during the ceremony she was suddenly soaked with sunlight. It brought tears to my eyes (something I seldom mention—macho stuff if you know what I mean).

Our tribal members have had two 'girls' ceremonies in Oklahoma with Apache people who politically and economically selected other tribes for their membership, usually for economic reasons but these ceremonies were unofficial to the tribe because of their 'other' tribal affiliations. We don't acknowledge any of those other tribal members even though most of us have other bloodlines and Anglo blood and many of them have more direct bloodlines than many of us. It's a shame that no one in our tribe has any concern for the renewal of our primary ceremonies as of yet, but I can only hope that we eventually expand our experiences and learn to share with other Athabaskan (Apache) before we are truly extinct as a way of looking at the world or lose our cultural distinctness. (Those white folks did an extremely successful number on our group psyche and kudos to them and their ability to transform our focus from the tribe to the individual.) Eventually it ended with the dancers going back to the large building to the West and the family members heading to their respective dwelling.

After this the standard (to them) deer and buffalo dance would continue throughout the day. That dance in itself is full of power and profound cultural purpose. My head was spinning and still is. In our tribal history our mountain spirit dancers also came down from the mountains, accompanied by torch bearers. This ceremony is a reenactment of the *Gans* dancers coming from the earth or cave of which we originated and return to upon death. At one time this dance contained tremendous power and the girl or girls going through the ceremony represented the White Painted Woman (the symbolic mother of our tribe). During this ceremony she was considered sacred and capable of healing and blessings. She was available to bless you at any time she was asked or when someone was in need. I was once told that all Apache ceremony was taken from the Pueblo people during our migration and I've always questioned whether that anthropologist observation was overly simplistic and just some form of white man ignorance. Now, after having the pleasure of meeting you and your Polynesian / Hawaiian ways, plus meeting your son Art, I realize that there is a great amount of parallel cultural knowledge.

I'm referring to the 'sharing of breath' or breathing on the pollen by our medicine men when they use the pollen. I'm so glad that our project is making use of the cultural comparisons with the *hongi* (sp?) or sharing of forehead touching/breath greeting of the New Zealand Maori, the nose touching of the Inuit of Alaska and the blessing/honoring/breathing upon gifts and objects as done by the Pueblo people. I find this to be fascinating stuff to think about, especially in relation to the 'our relatives' concept in the international Indigenous dialogue project that we are attempting. I look forward to our next group meeting and the guaranteed frontal assault with our shared western ignorance. I'm sure our shared humor/ ridicule will keep it on track and keep us laughing. Maybe we will both live to see the young of our people demand more purposeful cultural awareness from our own, much as we have both observed from other Indigenous people. They deserve our efforts.

Good stuff. We all look forward to eventually sharing stories and thoughts with your spouses when they come to the Southwest. ◆◆◆

1.30.06

●●● *Aloha* e John and friends...Lucia and I have not stopped having dialogue of our own, concerning the prospectus...included are some other ideas...I've had epiphany after epiphany...and want to express my inner thoughts about opportunity...the opportunity to present a solution to the pain that our Indigenous people are continuously faced with...so, please bear with me. Having experienced a generation of Indigenous Hawaiian artists, graduating from non-Native institutions, garnering their MFA degrees, going on to teach, expound and share a very individualistic approach to their Indigenous origins...I have had my share of frustration and disappointment. Here, we have a saying among the younger folks, "as long as you have the *koko* {blood}, then anything you create is Indigenous." Well, the problem I find with that is that oftentimes, the artists are creating and sharing from the, personal, individual "I"...and not the tribal "we." I believe that art should emanate from the spiritual "we"...imagery whispered to us from the land of shadows...from the *Wailua,* the Spirit and Soul of our Ancestors. And, instead, we are just regurgitating that which is foisted upon us by non-Native trend-setters!!! You know that edgy New York art. Art that is angry...art that is constantly accusatory, art that defines the wound...and the artist constantly digging at the scab. When does the healing begin? Initially, when our world was young, art was brought into the world to uplift the spirit, to define that ethereal language that allows light to enter the Soul. I believe that we Indigenous folks need a good dose of reuniting with that archaic language...not only defining it to "others," but embracing it ourselves...of course, I realize that each of us has our own artistic style...our own way of projecting the balm that soothes the soul... now is the time to at least come from that place. ●●●

Relations: An Indigenous Embassy

■■■ In addition to its national role, the IAIA Museum serves as a vital hub in global network of Indigenous art and culture. Although Santa Fe is home to an international community of artists, the IAIA Museum, as part of a Native-governed organization, maintains a unique set of connections to contemporary artists and cultural leaders from throughout the Indigenous world - representing communities which face many of the same challenges and share many of the same interests as Native Americans. Therefore, the IAIA Museum has a special responsibility and opportunity to periodically highlight the work of contemporary artists and cultural practitioners outside the Euro-American mainstream.

One such initiative is Relations: An Indigenous Embassy, which will coincide with SITE Santa Fe's 2006 biennial exhibition. The combination of these offerings presents an opportunity for a dynamic juxtaposition and dialogue between Indigenous and non-Indigenous perspectives, visitors, and art critics. Relations will serve as a stimulus for continuing critical and popular discussion, particularly through the "Conversations to Remember," program series. ■■■

●●● Are we indeed going to foster dynamic juxtaposition and dialogue between Indigenous and non-Indigenous perspectives? Will there be those from the non-Indigenous world to offer their side of the Story—or just

those who are somehow related by friendship or by sympathy to the Indigenous way? Essential, but dangerous grounds to tread! Needless to say that most Indigenous are not in tune with our spiritual realm, the non-Native not having a clue! We must somehow allow the exhibition to open the third eye for our own people first, then invite those who are *simpatico* to our cause. ●●●

■■■ Project Background. In August 2005, the IAIA Museum announced a new initiative - a series of biennial projects featuring Indigenous world art, artists, and cultural leaders. The initial phase of the project, since entitled Relations: An Indigenous Embassy, is scheduled to commence in July and continue through September of 2006. The goals of the project are:

1. Through art, to create meaningful dialogue between Indigenous and non-Indigenous worlds, at all levels, including popular audiences, scholars, artists, curators, writers and critics, and cultural leaders ■■■

●●● Ah, my favorite phrase...through art!!! The most ancient of languages!!! ●●●

■■■

2. To establish, for all these groups, a significant benchmark for current and future discussions concerning the meaning and implications of the terms "Indigenous" and "Indigenous art". ■■■

●●● A problem that we are still dealing with in Hawai'i. Our own Indigenous people, those leaders in the political, entertainment and hula communities do not know the significance of the high arts...Because of our temple scenario...Those art were termed "celestial," in that they were created to facilitate the easy transference from the mundane to the divine. So, today, we have fine arts...Very different from traditional or crafts...Those powers that be still make the mistake of putting utilitarian objects in the same category as those from the celestial or "fine" category. Why even the Smithsonian had "wall builders," "*poi* pounders," "flower *lei* makers," etc. as "artists." Although it does take a certain amount of mind and eye coordination and inventiveness to create any-thing...There is a distinction. Because of christianity, our celestial art form is not respected...Not by our people or any one elses. *Kunuiakea*, our paramount male principle is still carved in styrofoam and presented at luaus for decoration, still used as mai tai glasses, coasters, candy...You name it, his image is there...Contaminated...So when I create a *kunuiakea* image...Who is there to pay the respect? Just a very few of our people, I can assure you. I know that the time will come when our own people will return to the fold...Not fast enough for me. However, I never had a prob-lem with my origin or source...Embraced it wholeheartedly at a very young age. ●●●

■■■

3. To expand the inclusiveness and scope of contemporary art in Santa Fe to include a larger array of global, non-western, non-mainstream per-spectives for museum audiences and art critics. ■■■

●●● Yes, yes and yes!!! A long time coming!!! ●●●

■■■ In addition, by synchronizing the IAIA project with other planned contemporary art programs in Santa Fe, the IAIA project, can serve as a "tipping point," that helps Santa Fe gain greater national and international visibility as a significant destination for all forms of contemporary art.

Initial planning, which began in August, included the core team of Museum Director John Grimes, Curator Joseph Sanchez, and artist Bob Haozous. Additional team members have since been added and approxi-mately 20 planning meetings have taken place up to the present time. Additional consultation has taken place with curators and institutional leaders in Santa Fe, Washington, D.C., Venice, and beyond. A large inter-national email database of Indigenous organizations and artists has been compiled, to be used both to identify additional contributors, and to open a channel for communicating project progress.

Project Team. The Project Team will involve the IAIA Museum Director John Grimes, Curator Joseph Sanchez, and approximately 12 to 14 Indigenous artist/ambassadors from the Americas, Africa, Asia, and Oceania. In addition, the project will involve at least 75 (and perhaps hundreds) of additional contributors from throughout the Indigenous world, including contributors of Indigenous spoken language elements, written statements, and short interviews to be included in the exhibition space. The project will invite active participation by local and regional tribal communities. Eight of the Indigenous ambassadors have been selected to date, and have participated in the planning process. They include established artists Harry Fonseca, Bob Haozous, Rocky Jensen, Art Oomittuk, Rebecca Belmore, Simon Ortiz, and Roxanne Swentzell, together with emerging artists Micah Wesley and Rose Simpson. The project team is in the process of identifying 5 to 7 additional established artists, especially from South America, Asia, and Africa. New Indigenous ambassadors will be invited to participate as they are identified by the current members, based on their past work as well as their current interest in the Relations project goals. ■■■

●●● Because we believe in legacy...I want to suggest the inclusion of my daughter Natalie Mahina Jensen Oomittuk to participate on this committee and the exhibition...for she is the chosen one in our midst to carry on the legacy of not only her culture, but the proceedings of *hale naua iii*, Society of Hawaiian Arts. She is renown in her feather work and as a photographer, she has created a wellness where none existed. She is very attached to her heritage, knowledgeable of her cultural art and history and will be an asset to our group...a companion to Rose, who also has received the legacy. ●●●

■■■ Project Purpose. The Relations project is intended to address a number of interrelated issues. It recognizes that still-pervasive stereotypes tend to 1) relegate Indigenous and "Native" art to an inferior status (e.g. craft) vis-à-vis the work of Euro-American mainstream artists; and 2) impose expectations of static adherence to "authentic" forms, styles, and media. As a corollary, Indigenous use of contemporary media and styles are frequently dismissed as "derivative" by the mainstream art establishment, and often, ghettoized in their treatment by museums and the critical press. ■■■

●●● And, I think this is the fault of curators...no offense Joe...but most curators are of non-Indigenous heritage...They don't know our distinctions, so they create survey show after survey show, lumping everything into one bag...*Changing Hands* is a perfect example...you have felt hand bags, next to some subliminally beautiful fine art or celestial pieces...but, this is what they do. I also see that at times, our own people fall prey to the lack of distinction and this has always been a problem with me. Not to say that crafts are of an inferior status, but they are of a separate category...one is utilitarian and the other is ceremonially functional. Even those traditional arts are confused...utilitarian objects that are traditional as opposed to celestial or ceremonial which were traditional. So, we must use our language wisely...I agree!!! ●●●

■■■ The Relations project recognizes that another core problem relates to the meaning of the term "Indigenous" and its resulting implications for those qualities which essentially define contemporary Indigenous art. Neither of these terms (i.e. Indigenous and Indigenous art) is presently well defined nor communicated, even among individuals—including artists—that identify themselves as Indigenous. ■■■

●●● Hallelujah!!! Indigenous art...covers a multitude of sins!!! Indigenous art can be that patchwork quilt, that woven basket, that *kukui* nut *lei,* that *lauhala* hat and that amazing nine foot sculpture!!! Say what??? Indigenous art is not sufficient to describe our intention in relations...we must include the spirituality of our ancient creations...for that is the component that is missing in the recipe that will make our people whole again. That art which somehow defines, translates, displays the spiritual prayer, the ceremony, the ritual, the concept, the philosophy of our ancient people...transferred into art forms, that is the ancient language...that is the imagery, regardless of what medium, that is the Indigenous art that we speak of...so the phrase Indigenous art must come with a disclaimer or additive...Indigenous celestial art might be too powerful...However, if there are those who are against the term "fine," art... I'm not personally...but, we must use another term so that distinctions can be made...not for appreciation of the individual work created, but for the understanding of said work. All work is a prayer if done from the spirit...whether it is a wooden spoon or a huge sculpture or painting, however, one is meant to relate a coded and encrypted message, a language that holds the magic of our ancient people. When you look at the *ku* image...every chisel mark is a story...From the headdress to the clawed feet...a message handed down by ancient carvers...That is what I mean by distinction. ●●●

■■■ Together, these factors force Indigenous artists into choosing from among four possibilities: 1) conforming to outmoded stereotypes; 2) creating art solely with respect to demands of the marketplace; 3) creating culturally relevant contemporary expressions that may not be understood or appreciated by the mainstream art world—or even their own communities; or 4) trying to be assimilated into the mainstream, to be seen and accepted simply as artists, rather than Indigenous artists. ■■■

●●● And, our art movement here, both utilitarian and traditional, inclusive of celestial falls prey to these flaws, leading our artists and artisans to creating inferior work. And, because of the MFA degrees that the white world has somehow demanded of us, in order to be accepted in their mainstream society...our young have fallen prey to creating work that does not stand firmly upon the shoulders of our ancestors. I feel this category the most...I've seen our young ones going by that mainstream, for whatever reason necessary for them to feel accepted...and the *Changing Hands* show is again a perfect example. At the very beginning, Ellen Taubman rejected my work, saying that it was not edgy enough...That it was not out of the box...changing...was the motif desired. But, then, through the anonymous interjection of David de la Torre here, I think, she then desired for me to include my piece. I couldn't understand this posture, because I knew the other Indigenous artists on the list, and their art was "not" edgy, nor New Yorkish in the least...And then to see the catalogue, with sequined sneakers, felt purses, etc., etc., etc. What happened??? There are only a few pieces in the catalogue that I would consider as coming from our celestial place. ●●●

■■■ The Relations project builds on the following assertions, derived from the work of the artist/ambassador team:

• All communities were once Indigenous, characterized by group-centered identity that persists through time and that dynamically integrates the self, society and language with the natural and spiritual worlds. In contrast, the individualism and over-dependence on scientific rationalism in the developed world has fostered ego-centered identities more or less decoupled from nature and spirit. ■■■

●●● Our culture in the pacific did include science and mathematics into the whole...in fact, *kunuiakea* is the patron of time, space and measurement. The difference is that we included science as part of the spiritual world, never differentiating one from the other. The problem that arose from that, however, is that our present day Hawaiians only remember the "fireside version," the metaphor that was our foundation lost to them. The last few generations have had to go back into that scientific process, to delineate, redefine and bring forth that which was our basic foundation. Our leader in this is Professor Emeritus Rubellite Kawena Johnson, our mentor. I do believe we too have a problem with individualism... Something that was not part of our ancient society...And in the arts that poses a problem...Today, we no longer create from the we, but the I... Although, as artists, the I does create the work...For me, I am a conduit for the genius of all who came before. ●●●

■■■

- Indigenous communities are increasingly under threat of assimilation, with a consequent loss of human cultural diversity, including languages, special ways of understanding the world, and being more fully a part of it. ■■■

●●● What do you mean "under threat?" We've been there and gone, my friends!!! What we have remaining today is a fragment of what was...and let us hang onto that fragment for dear life, for if we are further assimilated, even that will leave. We must go back into the past to bring forth all that made our people great...we must bring back the marriage of heart, mind and soul. We must create through ancient glyphs and symbolisms that which will allow our ancestors to speak through our voices. ●●●

■■■

- Indigenous identity is not locked in the past, but can and must exist even in today's complex and rapidly changing world. Indigenous communities offer critical alternative views and approaches to the cooperative management of the earth and its resources, and relations between people. ■■■

●●● Not locked in the past...but the key components, the encrypted message is in the past...if we do not pay attention to that past voice, we are doomed to nothingness...we must hear the voice of the ancestors, and those voices come from the past...perpetuation not preservation!!! We must bring that forward...we must bring that ancient voice into the present, so that our future generations can venture safely, guarded by the spirit of our ancient ones. We have a saying, "You cannot dodge the smoke of the ancestors." And, our Westernized, Christianized society has done just that...encouraged us, assisted us, persuaded us to dodge that smoke...we must walk full face into it, for that is our salvation. ●●●

■■■

- The preservation of Indigenous communities, and thus cultural diversity, is a matter of vital importance to human survival. ■■■

●●● Again not preservation but perpetuation!!! ●●●

■■■

- Preserving Indigenous identity requires an understanding of the ways identity is maintained within Indigenous society, how it is communicated between individuals, and how it is passed from one generation to the next. ■■■

●●● Perpetuating Indigenous identity...passed from generation to generation...my family did just that...both sides...some directly, some indirectly, but all successful...I'm the only one in my family who picked up the gauntlet...and I find myself lucky in that I heard their voice and adhered to their demands...consequently, both Lucia and I trained our children to listen as well and they all follow in our footsteps...with their own signature, of course...But follow they do. ●●●

■■■

- Such understanding can enhance the ability of all people, and particularly Indigenous people, to create stronger communities, with "portable" identities that can be carried into the uncertain cultural and technological landscapes of the future. ■■■

●●● Yes! ●●●

■■■ The essential challenge, in the words of Relations ambassador Roxanne Swentzell, is finding ways to keep intact "the line of where we came from." She goes on to ask the primary question: "How do we tell the next generation who we are?" ■■■

●●● *In ka pae aina* [old name for Hawaiian islands]...we have the benefit of genealogy and the history attached to said genealogy...for generations, some stories going back to the *wa kahiko* which is before we even entered into the Pacific. Our line is aggressively perpetuated throughout Hawai'i...that is not the problem, for the devil is in the smallest details... and it is the detail, that we as artists must define. And through the arts, literature, dance, workshops, lectures, teaching, we can somehow reach the next generation. Lucia tours with her book *Daughters of Haumea*... she brings her audience back to the time of our cultural revolution in 1819, for that was the time of our small death. Going back to that place, she then reconstructs the slow demise, our present day people then understanding what they must return to. So, when our leaders speak of "Hawaiian tradition," my first question is, "What, pre or post?" Post-traditional is tainted with another's flaws. If the cultural story is vague or none existant, we must somehow search our spirit world for the puzzle that fits. We have the right to return things to normal. And, we must!!! ●●●

■■■ The Relations project poses an answer to this question, an answer that reduces its seemingly daunting complexity to the most basic and intimate humane exchange—the exchange of air, of breath, as the essential metaphor, and reality, of all human connection.

Thus, in Native Hawaiian society, individuals traditionally greet with the *honi,* by gently touching foreheads and the sides of the nose. The intent of this so-called "Hawaiian Kiss" is not so much the friendly contact, but more the exchange of breath, or *ha*, which, through its vital force, defines a connection between the individuals, spiritually, emotionally, and physically. ■■■

●●● {I have written about the *ha* in my last missive...Sorry guys, didn't send to all of you!} ●●●

■■■ This moment of immediate, humane connection has parallels throughout the Indigenous world, and like Martin Buber's I-thou relation, it prefigures all meaningful communication, and all real living. Thus, it—the *ha,* the breath, the connection—becomes the foundation of common identity: the breath carries the spoken word, the spoken word carries the prayer, the prayer becomes chant, and together—breath, word, prayer, chant—evoke a shared, interconnected human, natural, and spiritual world —an Indigenous world - that extends across space and time. The Indigenous world is breathed, spoken, prayed, and chanted into being, and must thus be constantly renewed. ■■■

●●● I feel that the *ha* is also dominant in the Inupiat society, you should ask Art to describe their tradition. ●●●

■■■ In the Indigenous world, art is a manifestation of the world, a shared world. It is not primarily the accomplishment of a single ego, or the product of the marketplace. Whatever its form, medium, or style, whether traditional or contemporary, or created for everyday or special use, Indigenous art is an integral part of the cycle of sustaining and renewing the Indigenous world. ■■■

●●● You are right, but remember that in all societies there was a distinction. Remember the distinctions...and define them!!! So there will be no misunderstanding of intention. ●●●

■■■ The word relations, as used in this project, stands for the breath, word, prayer and chant, it stands for the cycle of sustaining and renewing, and it stands for the interconnection of humans, nature, and spirit that define the Indigenous world.

Relations: An Indigenous Embassy is a sovereign outpost of the collective Indigenous world. It is both a sanctuary for Indigenous people, of individual Indigenous nations, and a place for non-Indigenous people to be welcomed as visitors. Among and between all people, it is a place for the negotiation of understanding, for the affirmation of equality, and for crafting the humane accords vital to the whole human future. ■■■

●●● Funny how things happen!!! What goes around comes around!!! The world is in a very, very bad place...and when I study the philosophy of our Indigenous people, I find the answer to how one should go about correcting that problem...but because most of the world is locked into a religious fanaticism...the ancients will not be heard...the solution will not be tested. Unfortunate...perhaps through relations...the growing of relations to include other Indigenous people from around the world, will allow the voice to grow and overcome. ●●●

■■■ The Embassy. Entrance to the embassy begins on sovereign soil, and by the act of invitation. Visitors enter through the Museum's sculpture garden, through a massive installation—a welcome portal—collaboratively created by Bob Haozous and Rocky Jensen. Visitors will be formally invited into the space by Indigenous volunteers (or, by recorded or taped Indigenous speakers, as a secondary means), who will extend an invitation to enter in traditional language, prayer, or chant. ■■■

●●● Yes, the imagery is beautiful...returning to the womb-world. The installation will be the birthing canal...that is predominate in our ritual world. Returning into the womb, in order to be rebirthed whole, sans original sin, for we are not the children of Eve. ●●●

■■■ Admission is free. Visitors receive a printed brochure which serves as an introduction to the embassy, its ambassadors, and to Indigenous nations. Inside the embassy, visitors will encounter the statements of the ambassadors—a series of rooms and environments consisting of installations, texts, sounds, and images. In their statements, the ambassadors will address the essential elements of Indigenous identity—breath, word, prayer, chant, human, nature, and spirit. The installations will encompass other existing works of art, some old, some new, representing the continuity of Indigenous identity across generations. ■■■

●●● You know, I'm having problems with the words embassy, ambassadors...Very *ha'ole*!!! Why can't we come up with words that best suit our culture!!! What are those words...even if they are in English, but somehow translate, interpret our sense of place. Embassy and ambassadors does not. In our native tongue...that place is the *Heiau*, the *paehumu*, the *mala'e*, the *papa*, where one comes to gather. The ambassadors are the *kahuna*...those experts in the field. For this particular project, we cannot use Hawaiian words, but we should use words that somehow cover all Indigenous approaches to that gathering place. ●●●

■■■ The embassy will extend beyond the walls of the museum. As part of the development of the embassy, the ambassadors will be soliciting offerings representing breath, word, prayer, and chant from elders and communities throughout the world. These will be incorporated into the embassy spaces. Within the embassy, internet connections and digital displays will depict—in real time when possible—these ongoing offerings. Visitors will be invited to add their own thoughts. Upon exiting the embassy, visitors will have the opportunity to make a voluntary donation to the help defray the costs of the project. ■■■

●●● My heartfelt hope is that all artists involved create a dialogue and a language that will project the beauty of our individual people. Project a philosophy that encompassed the entire cosmos! Enough of the angry art, for who does it serve? Our main goal as Indigenous artists is to bring back the imagery that will allow the soul to heal from all the pain rendered us in the past 500 or so years. How do we go about doing that? As mentioned above, not by constantly scratching at that scab...but, by finally applying a balm that will heal the wound forever...bequeathing our children that breath of life that will allow for our rebirth into the place created by our ancients. We the perpetuators of that dream are responsible for this charge. ●●●

■■■ Additional Planning. In the next few weeks, the ambassador team will be intensively working to refine the thematic structures, produce a schematic design of the embassy, and develop and execute the specific installations, texts, objects and media. The ambassadors have recently completed an intensive planning session in Santa Fe. During February, the team will be identifying, and conferencing (or teleconferencing) with the 5 to 7 additional ambassadors. Also in February, invitations will be extended throughout the Indigenous world to participate in the embassy, through special offerings, or by sending delegations to the embassy whenever possible. In March, Bob Haozous, John Grimes and Joseph Sanchez will travel to Rocky Jensen's studio in Hawaii to finalize plans for the physical aspects of the embassy. During the period of March to May, texts will be completed for printed matter (e.g. the visa), and, during March to June, the ambassadors will work with museum staff to complete the production of new installation elements, and select existing works for the embassy. Special programming in conjunction with Relations will be finalized during the period February to May, including coordination of speakers, arrangements, advertising etc. ■■■

●●● Looking forward to our next meeting and our next dialogue...I remain friend forever... ●●●

2.2.06

◆◆◆ Rocky: Bravo. Great stuff. I want to update you about the outside lodge shape (including the entire group to share discussions). I managed to purchase 4 instead of 8 light posts for legs. The others were cut up and sold, but an Indian guy working at the salvage yard saved 4 for me. They are square 6" tubes that taper to 3 1/2" tops and are 35' long. The base has a square plate with four holes for attachment to a foundation of some sort. I'm experimenting with the spade-shaped lodge but will let the materials tell me where to go (that and my inexperience with practical math in creating the precise curve). If I'm stuck I'll end up with the half circle (same problem). If you have a definite preference let me know and I'll attempt to create what we need. I suspect either shape will suit our purposes and the curve is stronger. I've yet to design the hub at the top for the four legs to connect and will let that problem solve itself in my studio (a crucial structural problem to say the least). The lodge won't support great weights as planned but will be quite strong (extremely for our usage).

In retrospect I think of our meetings and smile (that means little because I smile when I bump my head). Nonetheless, our dialogue makes me smile. I'm inspired to do something I seldom do, join hands and take up the challenges with others who have like concerns and intelligence. By the way, I've finally gotten a fundamental but inconclusive grasp on the **Hole**. I suspect the entire group knows full well the whats and whys but won't tell me. It may be directly related to the impenetrable seawall awaiting our tsunami-like project. One plus is that the **Hole** is getting mentally deeper as I type.

Powers that be: is there any possibility that others of our group can get funding for the trip to Hawaii? I think we may need the entire group participation and brain power at this fundamental stage. In my rare economic situation I could pay my own way if that enables others to attend the talks.

Rocky: again, thanks for the ideas on John's prospectus. Good stuff. While visiting in Mescalero one of the Apache people called me wild (with no explanation). Not to criticize him individually but the Wild, Angry, Difficult, Out of Touch and Self Serving caricature may be somewhat related to the German concept of untermensch or sub-human (like the Jews, Gypsies and Retarded). Joseph is right in stating that we 'may' or most likely 'will' be severely criticized by all who resist our ideas. A common *"Mister, You are going to Hell"* declaration from our own. Spooky man! I don't think that concept of hell exists to the Apache people. There is only the "Happy Place" and I think it is mentioned as being underground or back to the cave of our origins, perhaps a metaphor for the womb of the earth. ◆◆◆

2.3.06
(Editor's note: following is a forwarded email received during the dialogue)

Honolulu-A federal judge is offering Native Hawaiian groups and the state's largest museum an unusual alternative to settle their dispute over a cache of priceless island artifacts: Sit in a circle and pray. *Hoòponopono,* an ancient Native Hawaiian mediation process meaning "to makes things right," has traditionally been used to solve fights between brothers, disputes over family inheritance and divorce.

This particular fight involves the Bishop Museum and 14 groups, including a state agency that oversees Native Hawaiian affairs. At stake are 83 Hawaiian artifacts that have been missing from the museum since 2000. Hui Malama i Na Kukpuna O Hawaii Nei, a Native Hawaiian group dedicated to the proper treatment of ancestral remains, borrowed the objects from the museum and hid them in a secret cave on the Big Island. They include a human-hair wig, containers with human teeth and carved wooden statuettes of family gods.

U.S. District Judge David Ezra, who already jailed one Hawaiian leader for contempt because he refused to reveal the cave's location, has offered the process as an alternative to the federal judicial system. Federal Court officials said they could not recall a previous instance of *hoòponopono* being used there. It has been used a few times at the state level, mostly in casing pending in family court, said Elizabeth Kent, director of the Hawaii Judiciary Center for Alternative Dispute Resolution.

Hui Malama argues that the objects are funerary and not meant for public display. But two other groups sued in Ezra's court, saying the articles need to be unearthed and properly repatriated under a federal law.

Some observers familiar with the Hawaiian process proposed by Ezra have their doubts whether it will work. If traditional rules are followed, they say, group members would be required to sit in a circle, pray, confess to wrongdoing, apologize and forgive.

"You have to let everything out. You cannot hold anything back. Otherwise, you haven't fully confessed and you can't be fully forgiven," said Keala Losch, a Pacific Studies professor at the University of Hawaii. "I don't think people are willing to apologize or admit they are wrong." In the traditional process, group members will not be allowed to speak to each other, but must direct comments or questions to court-appointed mediators. The process can take hours, weeks--or longer.

The mediators are Nainoa Thompson, a master of navigation techniques used by ancient Hawaiians and a trustee of the all-Native Hawaiian Kamehameha Schools, and Earl Kawaa, site coordinator for a Kamehameha outreach program in the beachside community of Waimanalo. Hui Malama's leader, Edward Halealoha Ayau of Molokai, who was jailed over the issues, said he was hopeful but not optimistic. Ezra released him to home confinement so he could participate in the *hooponopono*. "One thing I learned in prison is not to have expectations, because they may not turn out the way you want it to," Ayau said.

The two groups suing Hui Malama—Na Lei Alii Kawananakoa and the Royal Hawaiian Academy of Traditional Arts—want all 14 claimants to decide on the objects' fate under provisions of the Native American Graves Protection and Repatriation act, a 1990 federal law that governs the repatriation of human remains and artifacts.

But despite its goal of bringing people together, mediation at this time likely won't include all groups. So far, only Hui Malama, Na Lei Alii and the Royal Academy have confirmed participation. This could be another problem, said Naomi Losch, who teaches at the University of Hawaii. "It's going to be difficult to exclude people from the process and try to get a resolution," said Losch. Jodi Yamamoto, legal counsel for the Bishop Museum, wouldn't confirm or deny the museum's participation, saying she was sworn to secrecy by the judge.

At least during initial mediation, the state's Office of Hawaiian affairs, another group claiming the items, won't be present, said Lance Foster, director of native rights, land and culture. Desoto Brown, who's been collections manager of the Bishop Museum's archives department for 18 years, said "the level of disagreement has been very strong" among the Hawaiian groups. But he hopes those involved "will do so with a sense of a new beginning."

Hui Malama i Na Kupuna O Hawaii Nei: huimalama.tripod.com/
Bishop Museum: www.bishopmuseum.org/" and
www.bishopmuseum.org/

2.4.06

●●● Well...that is it in a nutshell. However, the devil is in the details!!! Firstly, still cannot wrap reasoning around the Bishop Museum, "lending," 83 artifacts to this very revolutionary group??? What was the purpose of "lending," them the artifacts? It's like the Louvre lending out the Mona Lisa to a group of people who have no connection with its purpose and intention.

Of course, when the disreputable group did "borrow," the artifacts, there was no question among the Indigenous that they would not return them. Hello, what was the Bishop Museum rep thinking? So, the Indigenous party lied in that they agreed to the "borrowing," knowing full well they would not return the artifacts—they received the artifacts under false pretenses—of course, not caring that they did so, because they do not respect the governing laws and more importantly they do no respect what other Indigenous might think or know on the subject—they have made up their minds to do as they see fit, given the narrow structure of their source... and the Bishop Museum used very poor judgment in turning over the artifacts to a nonqualified organization, who had no proper shelter or protection for them. This done on the sly...on a Saturday, when the staff was minimal and the other participating groups could not interfere.

The Bishop Museum was duped...they were told on that Saturday that the other group involved in repatriation agreed with them—the other group could not be reached for comment, so Betty Tatar, assistant director of the Bishop Museum, who was the only one in position on that fateful Saturday, signed the papers, and that was the last we saw of our artifacts.

Remember that Tatar allowed the transfer with the stipulation that the artifacts would be returned. Again, my question was why did this group want the artifacts in the first place? How do you allow your treasures to leave the safety of their protection to be given into the hands of a group that could not care for them? We live in Hilo...the mastermind behind this and other traumatic events lives in Hilo...we, at one time were very close...we found out afterwards that the artifacts were "housed," in their home in Hilo for a long while before reinterred.

I cringe...as an Indigenous and artist—at an individual who views our sacred artifacts as holding the magic of our Ancients...I believe as do the others in the opposing group that our Artifacts are the key to our future...that they must be protected so that our children can be imbued with their *Mana*...their spiritual essence. There will come a time when the images that were secreted will be needed for this purpose. Repatriation of bones is one thing, we firmly believe that the *"iwi"* of our people should be returned...but there is a question as to some of the artifacts.

In 1819, our Iconoclastic Revolution caused a major anarchy that allowed for a tear in our spiritual fabric...at Kamehameha's death, the last reigning *Ali'i,* his consort wife, sent down the edict that destroyed our temples and burned our images. Our *Kahuna* (priests) in order to safeguard their responsibility hid many of the images in burial caves.

Of course, there is no little note taped to the back or bottom of the images that allow us to see which ones these were, so every image is suspect. And, if one knows the cultural ramifications...the rituals and ceremony...one knows that the images were put into the hands of physical guardians who removed the images twice a year for temple rituals. So, once a chief died, and an effigy was created for him or her...that image was not always kept in the burial place. It was removed!!!

So, now the Hui Malama wants everything Hawaiian removed from every museum that holds "their" things. Just keep in mind that they do not speak for all Hawaiians...I and many like me do not feel as they do.

This travesty did not start there...1993-1994 two very important woven images were "stolen," in broad daylight from the Bishop Museum. The very next day, the young man who stole these images came to my house telling me the entire story. I was mortified in that these two images were the only ones of their kind...two magnificent representations of our high, temple art form...never to be seen again. Not only that, another Indigenous group had allotted funds to have a mausoleum built that would house the effigies...again, a few speaking for the many.

So...this act perpetrated by Eddie Ayau is not seen by all Hawaiians as a courageous act...I find him disrespectful in that he hears the voice of only one elder, while ignoring the voice of many, many other elders. So, as the law goes...Eddie was incarcerated for breaking his pledge to the Museum and to NAGPRA!!! As should be...not only will they not return the artifacts, but they will not divulge where the artifacts were interred.

Of course, here on the island of Hawaii...the conspiracy is well known...and many know where the images are secreted. So, now the judge sent down his edict of *Ho'oponopono*...again a ritual out of context, one poorly understood by the non-Native, let alone our people. Who do they choose, two individuals who are indeed respected in our community, but who know NOTHING about our esoteric culture or the process of *Ho'oponopono*. Hello!!! So, what will the outcome be?

I agree with Naomi Losch in that the outcome will not be favorable... and Judge Ezra will again inherit the responsibility of judgment. The reason why the outcome will not be favorable is because the mediators as they are called, were not mediators in the past cultural process.

In the past, the mediators were really judges...one side told their story...the other side told their story...and the judge delivered sentence... the transgressor accepting the judgment...apologizing...the transgressed, receiving the apology...and all things repaired. In this modern day event, no side will take the responsibility of admitting wrong. Eddie certainly will not...he is being called a martyr as we speak. Our modern day culture is filled with these sort of self-serving incidences of pure drama. As an Indigenous carver...as an Indigenous, descended from those represented in the images...I find him in the wrong.

And, this is what has separated our people. There is a painful wedge... that will not heal. There again, relating back to RELATIONS...as Indigenous we must try to create harmony, not dissension. We must heal the wound...not constantly dig at the scab. And, we must know the facts before we act. ●●●

2.4.06

◆◆◆ Rocky: *Dant'e*. Harmony, not dissention! I agree fully. Thanks for the update and perspective. It has again caused me to rethink the Indigenous code or tendency to blindly support Indigenous brothers and sisters just because they claim to represent their 'relations.' I just gave a tour to some Dinè College students today (Navajo College students) and was informed that my exhibition was full of skulls and bondage, therefore unacceptable to some if not most Navajo people. The informant was fully cognizant of my message and was supportive of sharing this accumulation of messages. This brought to mind Joseph's warning that we would be heavily criticized. I truly hope that our RELATIONS message is understood as optimistic, informative, full of love and respect instead of threatening, challenging and disruptive. I personally have no need to create dissention but must always consider the level of ignorance and assimilation of the non-art viewing public. This often results in statement restriction or censorship though fully I realize that art, in essence, is self censorship. Tomorrow is the last day of my exhibit and some younger 'Indians' are beginning to filter in. Here in Santa Fe a fine art museum personal friend admitted that she hadn't even walked two blocks to see the exhibit. We may be awakening a sleeping monster (Yamamoto-ish?). Apache mythology provides us an answer with our 'monster slayer.' Before that we humans were eaten. ◆◆◆

2.7.06

▶▶▶ just letting you guys know i am reading the emails and it's pretty heavy. i might be off track or in the wrong room...but i don't think art is going to save the world. I'm not going to save the world, but i will help out one person at a time and all the helping i can do...is an arms length around me. An arms length even if i travel about!!

But then again, i'm new to reaching out with my creations and i've yet many things to learn from their impacts. i like Bob's idea of the "cultural scout". Yeah, that's awareness and it's necessary. because i always look at my work as reminders of "hey, this can happen if you don't straighten up!" or "hey, why not?!" i hope this is somewhat understandable...hell, i live at a school, but i sure don't type like it!!

i just feel like this is getting too complicated and i'd like to make some definite stuff to work with. from the first meeting i liked the vibe and i've wanted to expand and help with any input. Joe does have a hard job and i'm willing to help you out, man. Our intentions are good...and yeah, we'll probably piss some people off, but i think more people will dig it. we need to meet again. really, indeed.

Bob, as for the HOLE-- i still think you're digging your own grave and calling it quits!!! hahaahahahaa!! Rocko!! i didn't know all of that was going on in Hawaii. so you guys lemme know if i'm all off or something. ▶▶▶

2.7.06

◆◆◆ Micah: Perhaps you should consult with Joseph concerning the potential of this exhibit becoming another survey show that showcases individual talent, history, a romantic self portrait and individual ego rather than serious group thought. IAIA itself was designed as an assimilations trade school with the motto being "give them the tools and let them create." There wasn't and isn't any reference to cultural return built in to the school's mission statement. I certainly appreciate your levity and concern but keep in mind that most of us have had to confront those demons throughout our lives and I'm quite sure that none of us take offense at contradictory ideas and concepts. We are already too close, much like family, and we all have too much to loose. We are still in the how to phase. Perhaps we will end up with a survey exhibition and that would be just fine, considering the quality of artists participating in the group.

Within our group we have some heavy duty thinkers who carry serious Indigenous concerns. And, no, we are not egotistically attempting to change the world although I think it is safe to assume that we all hope that we can use art to stimulate change. This is a unique opportunity for all of us. Most if not all museum exhibits are western thinking-based to spotlight talent and none seem to be from an intellectual, thinking or concerned core like we have. Most if not all museum exhibitions are funded by outside sources that have no interest in a cultural dialogue or 'Indian Art For Indian People.' Concerning conflict and heavy duty discussions ~ It serves any one of us to promote our own art aesthetic and philosophy at this point. The end result will be strengthened if we talk honestly and directly during the planning stages. The cultural self-hatred we all carry that forces us to westernize and detribalize keeps us from sharing and opening up and seems to preserve light weight identifiers of our cultural identity. I think we were all waiting for you and others to break into the dialogue and your participation is sorely needed. On my own tribal chat group I've found that if I shut up others eventually begin speaking. That may work with this group also. We need everyone's thoughts throughout this foundation building process. Also, I suspect the **Hole** concerns rebirth and not death, but finding the answer eludes me. My mother is 93 and my family has long lifespans. I certainly am not trying to change the cycle by digging a hole. ♦♦♦

2.7.06
NOTES FROM SPOKEN DIALOGUE
❖❖❖ What is our future? ❖❖❖

●●● Core that attracts us spiritually Power/*Mana* Process... The flinging not the thing you fling. Living on the crust... inside is the philosophy. ●●●

▶▶▶ Relatives—I've been there. We all have shared experiences. I am speaking from the urban rez. ▶▶▶

●●● The ancestors will help through ritual/ceremony, it was attracted that way. Attract the familiars—One of our most treasured spiritual concepts is that the ancestors are attracted to patterns and rhythms...hence the drumming...hence the many beautiful graphic designs created in their honor. Actually it is all about sacred geometry...that which we are all part

of. We honor our ancestors by creating things of beauty for them—in turn beauty echoing their essence. ●●●

▼▼▼ The wider approach not for the art world...recreate ourselves know your environment in order to survive. Know your elements to create the element/animals in your spiritual connection. ▼▼▼

●●● Part and parcel of everything...Star Children Remember! ●●●

➤➤➤ We have no sense of history. ➤➤➤

●●● Ask for help—Elders ●●●

▶▶▶ What are symbols all humans relate to? ▶▶▶

●●● As Indigenous Hawaiians history is one of the components that we all adhere to...perhaps that is the most documented portion of our heritage...it is the spirituality that we have a problem with...we have a great sense of history...we don't have a sense of our ancient philosophy and religion. Ask for help of the elders...I think taken out of context...only if the elders are knowledgeable of such matters. ●●●

❖❖❖ Our future is at risk. Our relations? The relations? My relations? Native prayer will manifest something potent for our people. Prayer for change. Artist work is our prayer. Take the power of our history. Healing who we are as a people. Beyond money and the art world, we can change. ❖❖❖

●●● We chanted "it" into being we can chant "it" out. We need the "glitter" that attracts our ancestors. Naturalist ideas. Connections that create relations. We are the stone in the water creating the ripple the carries the message.

Yes, we did chant our reality...and continue to do so with every breath we take. We are the stone in the pond...creating that ripple...the more stones, the more ripples...and perhaps, we can then make people aware of our being...not only the non-Indigenous, but more importantly our own people. ●●●

❖❖❖ Our chant will change the world. ❖❖❖

●●● Our chant should change the world...but reality proves otherwise... it will take some chanting to change the world as it stands today...that is not the point...the point is that we must start with ourselves individually... then the larger circle...then the larger circle...then the larger circle...let us show the world that we can heal ourselves within, before we start trying to heal the world without. ●●●

▲▲▲ How do we have a living exhibition, interactive, current? Does it have the purpose/idea we tried to create? ▲▲▲

●●● Hopefully, if we are very clever...for we are all talented...we can create a dialogue that will resonate in some...and it is the some that we embrace...remember the pebble in the pond??? Our relations-the animate and inanimate. ●●●

♦♦♦ The knowledge is there, we are just lazy. ♦♦♦

●●● Perhaps as a people!!! But individually, we have the responsibility to act as a catalyst for those who are mired in apathy. ●●●

▲▲▲ Indigenous Dialogue—the (breath) to begin
I to Us
Me to We ▲▲▲

○○○ You are the ancestral line. You are the storyline, the relative. Your part of the storyline is not told yet. All the pieces of the puzzle are precious (NOW). ○○○

●●● Intergenerational...traditionally that is our responsibility...unfortunately, as a people, many of us have bought into the world's Westernization...each one of us can be just what he or she wants to be...there is no storyline...each of us is not adding on to what came before. This is what we have to achieve in this exhibition/happening...we must come back to center and create a legacy that we can hand down to the next generation. ●●●

○○○ Speak for my people/Speak to my people. We must keep the line of where we came from intact. Who are we? How do we tell the next generation who we are? We all drive cars, speak English, we breathe in everything in this society, it's part of us now but it doesn't change who we are. Some lines are faint and some lines are strong. We depend on each other for survival. How do we give everyone space but share the exhibition not as individuals but as community/relations? ○○○

●●● Personally...although I drive a car, speak English...I choose what and what not to breathe in. Yes, you are right, it doesn't change who we are...and that is perhaps why we are artists...we have chosen the language in which to communicate this steadfastness. ●●●

▲▲▲ The curatorial/artist ambassadors (core team of the exhibition) must keep control of the message (to avoid defusing its strength, going toward a new age message or individualism)

This is not an individual exhibition-not a survey show-not a group show (no individualism). ▲▲▲

●●● Although you say there is no individualism...just how do we as individuals, representing a cultural heritage, exhibit our message if not individually??? So, how far does this go? There is a certain amount of hands-on creativity that happens in all participation. I stand firmly on the shoulders of my ancestors...therefore, create in their shadow... always have. I still must get a clearer picture of just how we are to communicate this language. ●●●

▲▲▲ We are all the same – we are all different. Some metaphors: We are all in the same canoe...The glass is never empty, it is always full...Body punches not a knockout.

Clues....on how we get "it" back. ▲▲▲

●●● Perseverance, persistence, spirituality, truth!!! Not straddling the fence...focus...found center...chanting the ancestor's name every day... we talk ancestors...but we must identify them. ●●●

❖❖❖ We are creating the catalyst for dialogue. Our relationship to the earth—we are clay. Show our frustration with the way things are. ❖❖❖

●●● I think this has been overdone!!! Here anyway!!! Frustration, hatred, resentment, revenge, rage...I've seen it all in our modern day Indigenous art!!! If our Ancestors are attracted by patterns and rhythms that create harmony...how does the show of frustration help the movement? That becomes a personal place...that is individualism! ●●●

○○○ What makes us relations? What makes us intimate with our environment? It doesn't make a difference about the (objects? materials? in the exhibition) but how we relate to them. How do we connect? How do we get people (public) / us to interact? The world is disconnected – we are disconnected less. It's not about a hierarchy it's about how we are related. *Pohahu*/Breath - *Matu*/Relations

We always see the mask from the outside, maybe we should look from the inside. What does it feel like? What does it feel like to look through the eyes of an animal, a being?

How do we get our elders back? ○○○

●●● Speaking from my Hawaiian place...I must borrow an amazing line from my good friend Bob, "olders are not elders..." and that is the problem that we have here in Hawai'i. Too many olders reciting fireside versions that have adulterated our esoteric philosophy. So...for us, it's not so much getting our elders back...it's for my generation. Turning into the type of elder that will relate the spirituality to benefit our next generation...that has now become my generation's responsibility.

Emphasize the breath...power of the breath. All aspects of breath/breathing/chanting all the way to prayer...

From us all...perhaps examples from different tribes and clans represented in RELATIONS.

The breath of our ancestors (the steam rising off the hot stones [ancestors] when water is sprinkled on them in a sweat lodge).

Chanting ourselves back into existence/relations...(perhaps too easy, too obvious, too new age)

Well, dear friends. We're already here...we must chant ourselves into a better space and place...we must chant for a better future...never new age...who do you think the New-Agers stole this from??? Us!!! ●●●

▲▲▲ Adding everyone's breath to the exhibition, to the "prayer", becoming relations.

The global Indigenous community becomes part of the dialogue by adding their breath via electronic media (video, web, sound). ▲▲▲

●●● Different rituals involving breath??? I'm familiar with the Polynesian and Asian...anyone Asian...anyone else? Art has a wonderful example!!! ●●●

○○○ All the beings from each of us, beings from our souls making a prayer..we hear the prayer in the center. ○○○

▲▲▲ Smells, Voices, Breath surrounding us.

The walk through the museum: Entry through the Sculpture Garden, smelling and feeling the local landscape (sage, cedar, wild flowers & herbs, the smell of clay, pinon), the comfort and reality of the land and sky of New Mexico.

A large lodge (perhaps 35 feet tall) is the entrance into the museum (created by Bob with collaborations of some/all of the artists in the exhibition).

(The concept of the exhibition RELATIONS is more of an Indigenous embassy than a traditional Eurocentric Museum exhibition. The artist/ambassadors are being asked to create work for our people not individual statements.)

On the lodge (*pele,* to cling) or other hanging attached items/collaborations or not.

Passing through the lodge, the visitor encounters the welcome of the greeters; chanting,

Exchanging *breath*, singing?

From the welcome an entry (maybe this is where the *pele* is?), a cave like introduction to the space, with encounters of the word relations in many written languages with individual speakers throughout each with relations, spoken, chanted, sung, whispered by many voices.

Guiding you to the south gallery where you "look inside the mask" and "feel" what it might be like to be the dancer transforming to the animal/spirit.

Leaving the south gallery the participant continues through the cave/like (birth canal) to the center of the museum, (the nadir/apex, a coming together place), installations, work and performance by the artist/ambassadors will be together tied by the "string" of the concept.

Relations. Within this conceptual space of an Indigenous perspective, works of art by elders who paved the way to this place will hang revealing its true meaning to the people. The concept of the elders in the center providing wisdom and guidance is what I would like to achieve in placing painting, sculpture, objects with installations and performance that span generations of information but now have their true meanings revealed in an Indigenous context.

The word/sound language tunnel/cave continues to lead the participant to the north gallery, the Indigenous embassy which will connect the participant to the world of Indigenous dialogue in real time. This is the media place, real time communication and interaction with Indigenous people worldwide. ▲▲▲

2.9.06

◆◆◆ I like what Rox said about us forming a new 'tribe' type group. Perhaps this is time to create or exercise that group/tribe intent and poll individual members concerning purpose and statement. Joseph Sanchez is our exhibit curator. I would trust his abilities to conduct an open poll concerning our statement and express his ideas of how far we can go. I've faced self & internal Indian censorship issues continually throughout my career and don't consider the restriction of my statement to be anything personal. It is just a factual though unacceptable part of being an Indigenous artist. Perhaps our personal Indigenous cultural damage and how we present it could be an important part of our exhibition. Just how far do we want take this Indigenous dialogue or RELATIONS opportunity or statement? Is perceived or actual 'anger' or confrontation even an issue? Maybe we could all write something concerning our own perception of this group exhibit and its mission. I'm sure it would help to formulate a more concrete mission behind the exhibit. This may be an opportunity to unite in ways we've never had available before. I could easily honor the ideology of the group if my ideas are too confrontational or in any way damaging to our group statement. I consider the 4-legged lodge that I am preparing to be nothing more than a generalization or introduction to our statement and even that structure is optional to the exhibit. I like the idea of it becoming a place for all of us to speak, pray or chant, or a place for us to place our creations. It seems we have reached an unnecessary stalemate of some sort. Meanwhile, the **Hole** is getting deeper in many ways. ◆◆◆

◆◆◆ I have a dilemma that requires your thought processes. I've been told that I ask too much from people and I suspect that is the problem. I never ask more from anyone than I ask from myself and the project seems philosophically cut and dried. I'll try to make it simple (no offense because you two are far from simple), perhaps for my simple self to understand. I've been asking for a new approach with the RELATIONS project. Now I find that Rocky is asking for a more conservative and non-confrontational exhibit statement. That had me mystified until I reviewed his artwork. There are two issues that must be brought into perspective. His discomfort at having 'angry' art. And the participatory and communal art statement each artist presents. I'm not really worried about what we come up with as our individual art statement. That is on Joseph's table (thank guut-niss = Pueblo Indian for 'Goodness'). The anger issue that stalemates us seems to be based on outside perception instead of our own acknowledgment that our art is driven by anger. I'm not worried if 'angry' art doesn't reflect well for Indigenous artists. That's a no brainer for me, because I don't consider any of us driven by anger. Passion yes, anger no, though I like both as a means of stimulating art. The other relates to the posting I sent to the group concerning a wisdom keeper who acknowledged that he couldn't produce artwork that challenged the wisdom he was to maintain. That makes sense to me and it was an honest response to our dialogue at the time. The problem I'm facing is parallel in that Rocky is also a wisdom keeper and his art product is usually based on Hawaiian visual cultural history. Our group desperately needs open dialogue on all subjects that are directed toward our own people, especially at this early stage of dialogue. In fact I suspect that non-censorship is why we are all considering this project so important. I don't want to confront anyone (in any way) by demanding that we create our real and contemporary vision of the world, especially when an artistic statement is based on reproducing old concepts of culture. That is his job and it is a respectful 'maintenance' position that must go hand in hand with development. (That is what I learned from the Maori = cultural maintenance is death unless it included cultural development.) That is the crux of the conflict. Joseph mentioned to me in the beginning that the dialogue must drive the exhibit statement, so I'm sure he is as concerned as I am. I personally consider Rocky and Art to be incredible people and gifted artists, but hate to see one's aesthetic or artistic statement dominate our discussions (and that includes mine). That is why I am asking if you think I should 'cut the crap' so to speak and allow our culturally disrupted group to reign in our statement. (I suppose that is a leading, loyalty demanding statement, isn't it? I'm not asking for loyalty, just a bit of common sense that you two seem to have when you aren't joking.) I hope this request makes sense. I just came from the hole and am ready to confront this issue head on. On the other hand maybe I'm asking too much, too soon, and should back off and let Rocky do what he does best.

Am I putting everyone in an awkward position by asking for a rethinking of our identity and art statement? Otherwise~I'm trying to think of a way to incorporate the hole concept into the exhibit because it may be a metaphor for the resistance to something that should be natural. I'm sure you to are wondering if I've become holy. No, not yet. Perhaps another couple of feet and I'll find you know whose toenail. ♦♦♦

♦♦♦ I agree with Rocky in the perceived overworking of Indigenous frustration, hatred, resentment, revenge and rage. And yet the presentation of 'walking in beauty' over honesty, or seeking cultural goals of harmony in design without a clear statement of the disruptions surrounding that perceived beauty doesn't interest me in the least. My role is catalyst creator and shall always be just that. ♦♦♦

●●● I hope I'm not being misunderstood..."walking in beauty OVER honesty, or seeking cultural goals of harmony in design without a clear statement of disruptions surrounding that perceived beauty," doesn't interest me either. The beauty of my people lies in their spirituality...not their face nor form! And it is the spirituality that I try to bring forth in my work...believing as I do that it is the most important message...a message that indeed will heal. Of course, we do have seminars, workshops, lectures and the such, explaining where everything went wrong...going back to unpeel that onion...getting back to 1819 when all went to hell! So, we know from whence the frustration sprang...so, personally, my art then goes back to our source...which is the spiritual metaphor. And, if it is also beautiful, then more power to it. ●●●

♦♦♦ I just went through a wonderful experience this weekend with my cousin and tribal historian that brought to mind my discussion with a Seneca Wisdom Keeper and contemporary artist friend (if indeed that is his tribal position). After much discussion he told me that his position was to maintain cultural knowledge and the role I have taken as my cultural responsibility was not his. My cousin (whom I have great love and respect for) told me basically the same thing but from a white man's written word-based perspective. He holds great knowledge of our people and I have asked him to share his knowledge countless times. He has always provided what I needed to the best of his ability. His position is that 'our elders gave up traditional cultural practices for good reason' and he is personally insuring that we don't resurrect potentially harmful ceremony. Therefore he supports the loss of our girls' coming of age ceremony, the boy to men's ceremony, the naming ceremony, the haircut ceremony, the cradleboard ceremony, warrior training and countless other tribal identity and cultural purpose providing ceremonies. ◆◆◆

●●● I am so grateful that I get to see the day when most of our people have stopped being fearful of "our things." We are also fortunate that we have our ceremonies documented...chants...prayers...and ever so slowly returning some of them to the fold. But, just a few years ago...our elders and olders were fearful of everything...the "brainwash," working double time. So much was pounded into our hearts and minds that our vision of our own path had become occluded. Times are a changing!!! We need ritual!!! It was the glue that held us together in the past and it is the glue that will bring us together in the future. ●●●

◆◆◆ In consideration of the force used on my people to give up life, land, spirituality, language and cultural ways, it is difficult for me to support the decisions given under extreme duress by our olders. ◆◆◆

●●● Yes!!! ●●●

◆◆◆ We have not one 'older' who knew of or experienced life as a free and sovereign people. An unfortunate fact is that our sovereignty is a joke, only useful for economic opportunity over white people and ego enhancement. *(A reminder that my **white man** reference denotes a whitewashing or dominance over nature and not simplistic skin color definitions.)* ◆◆◆

●●● Aside from political definition, I have always believed in my personal sovereign state. And, there again, we return to spirituality. Early on...in my 20s...I first realized that our people actually had a philosophy, researching further discovered that that philosophy was quite sophisticated...it was at that time that I embraced my identity as a *Maoli*. So, it really doesn't matter what titles the world gives or takes...that is what I am...first and foremost. ●●●

♦♦♦ My role as an artist, as Rose mentioned, is to be on the edge. ♦♦♦

●●● My favorite saying is that if you don't live on the edge, you are taking up too much space...I hear you brother... ●●●

♦♦♦ In romantic terms I am a cultural scout who attempts to honestly look upon our people, to the past for guidance and hopefully to help envision and direct our future. From this position I must honestly report what I see. I simply refuse to ignore the frustration, hatred, resentment, revenge and rage that Rocky so eloquently speaks of. ♦♦♦

●●● And I've seen how these very feelings have destroyed generation after generation of my people. So, when does the internecine war stop? When does brother stop fighting brother...husband stop killing wife and children...the abuse, the drunkenness, the despair...? We all have gone through the pain of being ripped from our place in time...I'm just as angry as the next Indigenous...however, I feel that what comes from my hands, mind and soul, must do honor to those who came before. I believe that in this way, those who suffer might be given the ingredient necessary to minimize the trauma. Cultural trauma!!! On another separate project, I am working to better our men, mainly our Indigenous war veterans who carry a double burden. We are trying to get them back to source, to center...how is this done? We are extending this sharing with the domestic abusers as well. Hence the dialogue with our past...these people live that hatred, revenge, anger...they live with

it every day...let us shine some light into their lives...the lives of all our people. ●●●

◆◆◆ I would prefer to see a mature and experienced grappling and dialogue of the problems we are illegitimately married to, perhaps even going overboard in our discourse, than a focus on the good. ◆◆◆

●●● I agree that a good dialogue gets the blood flowing. True! Listen to what you are saying Bob...you would rather regurgitate the problems rather then focus on the good??? I would prefer to see a mature and experienced solution to our problems. We are the communicators... we are the illustrators of those solutions. What are they? Relations are certainly one! There must be others??? ●●●

◆◆◆ That can and will come in due time. ◆◆◆

●●● The time is long overdue for us!!! That is why we are together— that is why we met...that is why we have become friends...to dialogue, document and share that solution. Am I right??? ●●●

♦♦♦ It's only by going beyond the point of balance that we can have a clear understanding of that place we seek (but that's probably just the pseudo philosopher/idealist in me). And, what better place to talk of serious issues than through the arts? ♦♦♦

●●● I agree!!! ●●●

♦♦♦ I have been labeled all of those supposedly derogatory things of lesser human behavior (*untermensch*=sub or below human) but I refuse to believe that those who know me consider me angry or 'difficult' once they work with me. If I am truly presenting those attributes by my behavior than perhaps I need to reevaluate my perceived position to my people (I assume I'm a sub). That is something I must constantly do anyway. ♦♦♦

●●● You've repeated this several times...what gives??? ●●●

♦♦♦ People viewing my exhibition often leave with the impression that it represented native anger, blame or guilt. Their ignorance is understandable because we too believe that of our own native artists. And, I have no problem with others presenting a more positive viewpoint in this exhibit. ♦♦♦

●●● Explanation please? Let me get this straight...your exhibition of going beyond the point of balance—to some that would be anger, wouldn't it? You are saying that that shows the love and commitment that you have for your people? Right? So, the going beyond (or anger) is directed at whom then? ●●●

♦♦♦ I told a collector who labeled me as angry that If he couldn't see the love and commitment the IAIA exhibit gives to all who view the exhibit than perhaps he should reevaluate his understanding of Indian people and the role of some artists. Rocky is right in telling Joseph that he doesn't envy his job. I have learned to trust and respect Joseph to the point of allowing him to have a great amount of control (with a few exceptions) of my Indigenous Dialogue exhibit. What a job that was, and RELATIONS is immeasurably more complicated. He needs our thoughts and guidance desperately and we Indigenous people need to start talking again if only to assist him with the exhibit concept and layout. Our reluctance and apathy is part of our continuing cultural problems. ♦♦♦

●●● Agreed!!! ●●●

♦♦♦ I too find sharing an artistic statement somewhat difficult but am attempting to relearn a cultural role that gives more importance to the **'we'** of relations instead of focusing on the me of relations. Our writings and thoughts are good stuff to read and share. ♦♦♦

●●● Again, I agree! How wonderful it is to bare one's soul so to speak...and, I am honored Bob that you share your intimate self with me. It is exciting...and because I do not know you well...I ask the questions and I probe your deepest thoughts and study your words to find the answers that will allow me to know you better. If you didn't put them out there for all to see, I wouldn't approach so delicate a subject as soul intention!!! ●●●

♦♦♦ Even if the show doesn't receive funding we have done remarkable things to our own thought processes in challenging our perceived identities. Now if others would speak more and stop letting a few olders jabber on and on as I tend to do. (I suppose it has a bit to do with respect.) ♦♦♦

●●● Hello!!! ●●●

♦♦♦ One more story: Speaking of respect, this morning I was in the bathroom looking in the mirror and saw an old, gray haired man glaring back. I yelled at him to get out and let me brush my hair in peace. (Now I feel sorry for the old buzzard because, in retrospect, I'm sure he earned his wrinkles.) ♦♦♦

●●● I do the same! Time did creep up on us didn't it? I lift the same logs and carve with the same stamina and when I'm in a tiff, I mow my half acre...but that night...I hurt like hell!!! ●●●

♦♦♦ And, I still don't have a concise answer for the **Hole**. I suspect that answer is mine to find or not find. I suppose we must dig our own hole. ♦♦♦

2.12.06

♦♦♦ "I think the Spirit, is the one thing we have to rely on. It has been handed to us as a live and precious coal. And each generation has to make that decision whether they want to blow on that coal to keep it alive or throw it away...Our language, our histories and culture are like a big ceremonial fire that's been kicked and stomped and scattered...Out in the darkness we can see those coals glowing. But our generation, whether in tribal government or whatever we find ourselves--Choctaw, Cherokee, Chickasaw, Creek, Seminole--(**Apache?**)--are coal gatherers. We bring the coals back, assemble them and breathe on them again, so we can spark a flame around which we might warm ourselves." Gary White Deer, Chickasaw 1994

FSA'ers: I added the **Apache**. I'm working on a project entitled RELA-TIONS and has as its goal an Indigenous Biennial art exhibit for native Americans and eventually other Indigenous people. It will be here in Santa Fe, NM this summer. One of the observations that has come up is the conflict between traditional thinking and progressive thinking. *We've deduced that tradition becomes stagnant and runs the risk of becoming extinct if it doesn't openly embrace change.* On the other side, innovative or creative change must rely heavily on tradition. Change is a natural part of life and we Apache people have always accepted it in the past. If the people we've become don't have our cultural purpose on a firm and functional traditional foundation we run the risk of performing as 'new agers'. Change is healthy and we can always be ***N'de*** or **Apache**. ♦♦♦

2.13.06

○○○ I wonder if this has always been the dilemma for the "artists"(if we should call them that).......the crux between maintenance of the culture and being eyes for cultural development?   You state it so well, Bob, thank you. Somehow I got caught with the hole you are digging, Bob..... the hole concept.....the "whole concept". We are looking at the past and then trying to see where our future goes.... is this not trying to see the whole picture? And then there's the "present" place......where's that? Is that the hole or is the hole the looking for the past by digging forward? Maybe we need to "fall" into the hole and just experience it in the moment? Wow! I'm sounding pretty way out there....but seriously, this is a "deep" question and you are right there with it Bob. I think it frightens us to really be present with what has happened to us as Indigenous peoples...still hoping to make us come out the other end undamaged.... when we aren't. And to look at the damage without walking around feeling like a poor victim all the time or that we have to "save" what's left or react by rejecting it either.....gee, I think that leaves are not the only things falling in the hole. What's left is us. How do we make a show out of that? What is the rawness of "US"? Maybe instead of "Relations" it should be something that has to do with digging for our souls...........I mean we can't really feel our relations with anything until we are having a real relationship with ourselves. nuh?   Anyway......if you are the asshole, Bob, then I get to be the shit...hee..hee. ○○○

❖❖❖ I would like to express my apologies for my tardiness of response, but I don't believe that all my recent life-efforts have been in vain- it is life, life will teach, and as I live I learn what I need to say.

I recently returned from a trip to Rapid City, South Dakota to perform with my band. We were invited by a pretty well-known punk-rock band called the Reddmen. It is beautiful up there. The show went incredibly well. The Reddmen are a well respected group and there were many people there, white and Indigenous. The group consists of two Lakotas, one Asian and one white guy. They rock.

I am taking a class here at IAIA – "Contemporary Issues in Native Art." I really believe that it would be a good and challenging class but there is one white woman in the class who, I have heard, has come to IAIA to enhance her career in psychology. There is so much opportunity to express some real issues and get past the 'crust' of mental exercise, but it doesn't happen. A friend of mine said that those people are there to give us the experience in making boundaries and being straightforward. I don't want to need that right now. We have work to do. I think I will drop the class, like every one else has, one by one, until all that is left is the teacher and that one white woman.

But I do know that we choose to live in a "white" world, and because of that, sometimes it is easier to convey ideas with the assistance of white people who understand that thought process. But who are we TALKING TO? If it is for us, then why is it at a museum? In Santa Fe? Then if we choose this space to work with, we have the opportunity to reach everyone.

As much as I DO believe that art is a prayer, and that prayer has strength to make incredible change, I have recently found out that, when given ultimate freedom, if we don't have anything to fill it with, the work towards freedom will only be in vain... for fear of what has to fill that hole. (hmmm). I don't think our people are ready for the next stage. And perhaps they are... perhaps, as Bob said, we need "to go beyond the point of balance that we can have a clear understanding of that place we seek"... but I think—like a swing, we have been off balance, we just haven't bothered to turn and look at the swoop. Maybe the first step towards consciousness (cultural survival) is dealing with what we have on our plate.

"Perhaps our personal Indigenous cultural damage and how we present it could be an important part of our exhibition. Is perceived or actual 'anger' or confrontation even an issue?"

It seems incredibly blatant that the trauma that our people live today (drugs, alcoholism, sexual/physical abuse) comes from the repetition or re-enactment of original inflicted pains. And as much as we would like cultural optimism, that pain still beats within our blood stream.

As I scream through the microphone over the wail of the guitar, I need to get it out, or it will fill the hole of my freedom when the time comes. I spoke to Steve Wall about this- what is optimism in the change of Indigenous culture, what is pessimism... he stood expressionless in the door and said "I don't care if it hurts, change has to happen. So is that optimism or pessimism? Change is neither positive nor negative. It is necessary." As we have swung out of balance, there is no other choice but to swing back. I can't wait for it to happen, I pray for the pain of change.

My throat hurts as I scream, and my words are in English, and people are cheering, but my pain is generational, and those consist of Indigenous people.

"We've deduced that tradition becomes stagnant and runs the risk of becoming extinct if it doesn't openly embrace change."

I agree with: "And, no, we are not egotistically attempting to change the world although I think it is safe to assume that we all hope that we can use art to stimulate change." But I think that artists are incredibly egotistical and that is our gift, and it has, and will, change the world.

When I think about self-censorship, I think about my fears. I fear what these artists (that I have respected my whole life) will think of my ideas, so I censor my words. I fear the power of my expression and fear that it will intimidate or conjure fear in others, so I censor my work.

And maybe the purest truth lies within no censorship. I fear people will hate my truth because it will reflect their own.

I know that Bob already knows what the hole means. And it means different things to each of us. Maybe he is digging to find his truth.

At random-I like this quote:"Before that we humans were eaten." ❖❖❖

2.15.06

❖❖❖ It was a great event to see the hero of Canadian Art set of 8 artists, finally making the capital show at the Canadian National Art Gallery. We all knew that one day the sun would shine in our favor. It finally did, 514 years later, the message got through. Good to have witnessed it, the north/south Apache/Denesuline tie renewed.

To have witnessed the Creator giving the other peoples, the Algonki-anic line; renewed singularly by Mr. Norval Morriseau. It was our keenest hour to have beheld. That was a proud day. I have passed the key event unto my Cree friends, that their line of east-west is now established by the Morriseau Show. This man suffered to get this spiritual life to full effect and to complete the east-west line.

It is the business of the Dene Nations to visually recreate by our inner ability to create what was seemingly lost. Our understanding of our own Creator can give us the words of knowledge of our relations. If we will it and turn it over to "all" our ancestors, it will be done by their kindness and love. By virtue of your meetings, we can paint our future from the lost past. It is still in our recessed thought of who we are, the Dene nations.

Through various efforts, by visitors to our great lands; our relations have been tested, but we still are here...to stay! Think hard on the words you have heard our elders state," One day, our children will come back together." These words are as sacred as the day it was originally stated.

The artist will bring back the relations, "all", not just some.

Give best regards to all that you have met with, it is good to have

their talk. It's that the Dene recreate ourselves as Dene. The political side has gone ahead of us, so now we make their words more clear visually. ❖❖❖

2.15.06

◯◯◯ Yesterday after writing I was thinking that it's very important to think about WHO we are doing this for. I appreciate you bringing that up Rose in your wonderful e-mail. I noticed for myself that depending on WHO I expect to see the work....it ever so slightly changes. I would like to be able to not be so influenced but I'm human. I know that when I'm trying to talk to an "outsider" (non-native) person about cultural things, it's very different than with our own. I think because this is a show in a museum that is going to be seen by many kinds of people, it does bring in a strange dialogue because we aren't dealing with just one kind of viewer. This I think makes it that much more important to do it for ourselves because it is impossible to know the outcome of the audience...a good practice to try not to think even about what "they" are gonna think or feel. I suppose that's what we do anyway ultimately as artists when we are being true to ourselves. I still hold the belief that if I was raised in the belief system of my tribe, then that can't help penetrate what I do........so I still hold the idea that if I am a "native person" my art is native art. It can't help but be. I also think that Rocky is right in his belief that the "traditional" images can hold a strong sense of meaning and sacredness that makes one feel whole. That's why those images were manifested to begin with...they held a timeless power. So, I don't really think we are in opposition....I'm just trying to make new timeless traditional creations. I visited an artist friend yesterday and he and his wife were busy with their little art factory. They had a line of canvas/boards(?) ready for gesso or putting the photo images on..then off they went for the background painting and then the final touch painting. I was both horrified/delighted and envious of his discovery and success. What is so interesting to me about what he's doing right now is that I want one in my house and yet it somehow reeks of stolen cultural images that have become clichè. They are captivating because of the traditional timeless images of design and meaning, then he paints (his style) around them to make them look somehow very old but you can get one NOW. I don't know, its reminding me of our conversation about who we are as Indigenous peoples and how we use that or not. ○○○

2.19.06

◆◆◆ **Whole Tribe:** *(This is just a personal, unofficial pet name to keep me smiling)* We have multiple issues to discuss. To name just a few: What is our purpose as a group? What is the purpose of the exhibit? How does this exhibit lead to Indigenous Biennial Two? How do we assist Joseph's curatorial efforts? *(Or, how do we maintain a valuable group advisory position with the exhibit)* How do we or do we not advise or participate with each other's statements? How do we maintain the 'purpose of exhibit' in our individual or group statements? *(Or do we just dump it on Joseph?)* How do we maintain a statement that doesn't digress into another glorification of **W**estern **A**rt **H**istory **I**ndividualism concepts? **WAHI**? = Why? Hmmm? And how do we keep ourselves from showcasing our own personal cultural viewpoint and thereby ignoring plural Indigenous concepts? ~~~Among other issues? Before you dissect, destroy and discard these questions please feel free to add your own unanswered questions. I'm feeling like the bad guy for asking questions and 'pissing in the stew.' Group members, we are the beans of the coffee, the sugar in the cane, the grease of the fry bread, the blubber of the--well, you know what I mean. *(Please)* Let's continue talking to each other. When the exhibit is history we may have re-created an Indigenous dialogue catalyst. What the Hell? What is there to lose? Perhaps that last question of 'What is there to lose?' is the key to our purpose. *(A gentle self reminder: the transition from individualism to tribalism can be ego painful.)* ◆◆◆

●●● You do know!!! My mentor Kumu Kawena once told me so many years ago...that the knowledge of whatever I was looking for would creep slowly into the corner of my eye. That it would manifest itself. And it continues to be like this since I left Santa Fe. ●●●

2.22.06

◯◯◯ Bob, I've been working over at Brett's studio on a large piece. He came back yesterday talking about your "Hole". All he could say is,"it's interesting" over and over again....hee...hee. I like working with those guys. It makes me realize how isolated I get working out here in my little studio all the time (one could go insane in one's own head). I wonder how hard it would be to find a place that all of "the Whole Tribe group" could work on their pieces together for the show??? Sounds crazy but it sounds like then we could talk all we want and work on our stuff too... ummmm we could rent a space for the month before the show and come and go as needed. I mean, if we are a tribe...then we should spend some "quality" time with each other besides having meetings???? Not that I'm opposed to meeting, I'm just wondering what else we could do. I'm just enjoying actually working around other artists and the thought of working around this group would be tremendous. ◯◯◯

◆◆◆ OUR RELATIONS: *(Daanaht'eke* in Chiricahua Apache, *Mitakuye Oyasin* in Dakota, *Ittapiha* in Muskogie Creek, *Inmi ma tiin-ma* in Yakima, and *Pili a Pau)* I hope everyone is well, productive and in good spirits for life and the challenge of cultural sharing and final exhibit that we embrace. Rox made a suggestion to me that we find or rent a space to work together here in Santa Fe, thereby facilitating more honest and intimate dialogues. My studio is open and usually quite available. I would be honored to share it with any and all of the whole tribe *'if we make it work and it fits into my business work schedule* (which it now does).' The studio fully equipped (the blessings of occasional forced bachelorhood) and we can accomplish whatever we dream or scheme in that place (studio). I know because I can produce almost anything desired in this work space. I usually don't share tools and don't teach, but will make the exception for some people if you are persistent, decent to look at, and like coffee. Lets talk (I think I've begged for that from this group and my tribe before). Anything can be done here, I repeat—anything. Rules: Make a mess, clean it! Disrespect: expulsion!

Dangerous habits: absolutely unacceptable. Foul language: what the hell, it's a studio for creativity! What does this Brave New World W**hole** Tribe think? This is just a concept simmering on my front burner. Let me know your immediate gut feelings as this is just a feeler idea. Maybe a neutral place in town would accommodate our egos better. Believe it or not, I'm not difficult to be around (at least not yet). Rocky and Art are assumed to be on the top of the list of this studio's art producers.

Oh yeah, no work on Sunday (Bob exempt from this rule!). Not because of religious ideology, but out of respect for my tolerant, Jesus freak (day of rest and quiet) neighbors.

And to give you an idea what I'm working on for the RELATIONS exhibit—I'm producing the four-legged lodge for the art park (as previously discussed). It will be approximately 23' tall and 45' wide and probably painted black. Nothing fancy beyond being a reference point for other artists. I've also decided (with John and Joseph's blessings) to cast my hole and hang the actual mold of the hole from the ceiling between the museum shop and the main gallery. Obviously I take this **'our relations'** stuff seriously. These pieces may help you decide how to participate with the overall concept of the exhibit. Why don't you share your ideas with the whole tribe? I'm open to ideas, criticism and suggested changes to my work but it is getting late for group input. As I've stated before, it's quite difficult to give up our western based individualism and hero quest habits. ◆◆◆

2.22.06

○○○ Hello everyone, Bob, no need to apologize for anything. Well, my questions are more about how do we come together to do something together? I am liking the Whole Tribe concept and maybe one way to approach it is for all of us to make a list of what we think are the values of this "whole tribe".....and see where and how we overlap or don't??? ○○○

2.23.06

♦♦♦ Rox and group: The studio is here. I am here. Production time is here. If any of you need a space to produce RELATIONS let me know and we'll talk. Also: water is available from a hose by my househole.

I never actually realized that Power is diametrically opposed to powerlessness. I suppose this may relate to cultural apathy. ♦♦♦

2.26.06

●●● Bob has asked me to share the ceremonies of how Hawai'i Maoli handled the placenta and umbilicus. We were lucky that this newly built hospital in Waimea "looked the other way." Culturally sensitive, they explained to us that many Hawai'i Maoli are asking for their child's placenta and umbilical cord. So, the hospital had to make adjustments in that it still is against all health laws to give "body parts," away, even if they are your "body parts." So, what used to happen in the past was that immediately after birth, the male child was taken to temple {male principle} and consecrated to the Patron of whatever season he was born in—either *Lononuiakea* for the rainy season of *Ho'oilo* or *Kunuiakea* for the Hot Season of summer. The same for the female child—taken to the *Hale 'o Papa* shrine and dedicated to the Earth Mother *Haumea* and other female Ancestors. Being that our people believed in *Ola Hou*, reincarnation...there were rituals done by our *Kahuna Pule* {priests} to identify the previous incarnation of the child. Once identified, the child was given its first sacred name, never to be used except in ritual. Immediately after consecration...the placenta {*'iewe*} was sometimes buried, sometimes kept in a gourd to be reunited with the owner after life's journey...it was traditional to reunite all body parts after death.... The umbilical cord was traditionally secreted in nooks and crannies...yes, the same with us, so that rats wouldn't get to the cord. Now, these nooks and crannies were where all the families went to bury their umbilicus. So, the lava fields, or other rocky areas were covered with petroglyphs denoting family, clan and tribe. Afterwards, the women if a girl child, the men if a boy child would have a feast called 'Aha 'Aina Mawa'ewa'e...the "Clearing of the Path," feast...whereby all obstacles we're visualized to disappear...all children born after the primogenitor having a clear field. Our men and women never ate together. Firm believers in the Dual Polarity, from the beginning of our time, we revered the separation...and until 1819, our women lived in their world and our men in theirs. Not one over the other or more superior then the other...it was a reverence of the male and female principle that sculpted our great laws, customs and traditions. Each principle depended on the other for survival and sustenance. So, when we feasted... we feasted separately...there was men's food and there was women's food...the women never cooking...that was for specific men to do. After the 'Aha 'Aina Mawa'ewa'e...the child, male and female was sent to the women's "long house," called Hale 'Aina to be brought up by Guardians of this and that. Sacred children having many of them. The male children were cared for by women until they were weaned, at which time they then were "ka i mua," thrust from the women's house and sent to that of the men. This was their second birth, at which time they were given their second or third name. From that moment on, the male child no longer could enter the women's house, nor eat with them. He belonged to the world of men. So on and so forth....

I can so relate to your rituals, Bob!!! They resonate within me...they are so like ours. And, it makes me happy to see that you are a true believer in our old ways. Sweat lodge...wish that I was there. We too had sweat lodges...high ritual...for both men and women. Another womb...another birth...another death...I love the metaphor. The foundation of our culture is based on metaphor. Dreams! Our people created reality from their

dreamtime. Understood dreams as being the other side of the world of light...*Ao!* Metaphor was the language of the dreamtime, therefore, the language of their rituals. Actually, this birth and death thing happened daily with us. When we went to sleep, we again entered the *Po* and dreamtime...when we awoke, we were again reborn—reminded daily of the process of life and death.

I join you in the sweat lodge in spirit. We're not scattered physically, but spiritually...and I don't know which is worse. Never mind wet feet... it's when you have to enter the stream up to your armpits that worries me...but then...our people were great swimmers. *Mahalo piha* for your care and love. Your brother Rocky...

Aha!!! The hole...finished you say? Did you have an epiphany? Were there omens? What was your conclusion? Congratulations, for some of us dig forever and never find the end. ●●●

3.9.06

♦♦♦ *Relations: Our interconnection, our relationship to everything that exists.* The concept and exhibit RELATIONS: indigenous dialogue is an attempt to communicate with other Indigenous people in understanding, re-acknowledging or recreating a common nature-based connection, now existing in a fragile state, with internal Indigenous discussions and by using the arts as a forum. The phrase 'relations' or 'our relations' is a common Indigenous concept used to reference nature as a holistic part of tribal identity that includes all things that exist. In contrast contemporary western identity is based on mankind's separation from and dominance over nature with a concentration on individual human expression and existence. With the art exhibition RELATIONS we are attempting to create a shared sense of community with artists from various Indigenous cultures. RELATIONS include artists of all ages and gender, traditional elders whose responsibility is the maintenance and preservation of specific cultural knowledge and others not known as traditional elders who bear the equally important responsibility of overseeing cultural change. All participants involved in this exhibit have equal responsibility, voice, and respect from those involved with the project. In addition to contemporary Native American art that is focused and dependent on traditional and historical knowledge, RELATIONS is asking the more relevant questions "Who are our children today?," "Who will our children become?," "Why are we Indian?," "Why are we Indigenous?," and "What is our cultural role and purpose in the future?" And also "How do we as artists create a cultural participation and cultural responsibility through the art media we choose to work with?" Through the arts we seek the retention and in most cases redevelopment of an identity from the culture coding that derives its power from an honest and instinctive nature-based relationship between our cultural and physical environment. The intent of RELATIONS is to inspire each artist to create a more honest portrait of his or her human condition and share a communal Indigenous sense of tribe that evokes a contemporary cultural experience instead of the continual production of outward, market focused and economically driven artwork. Our primary goal with this forum is to inspire an Indigenous art focus taken from and directed toward our own communities or contemporary native experience. ◆◆◆

3.10.06

○○○ I like what you wrote..........all I would redefine are the 'questions'...maybe because they are what MY questions are. ..."Who are we?," "What is being Indigenous (or 'indin')?," "Where are we headed?," and "What is our cultural role and purpose in the future?" and also "How do we as artists create a cultural participation and cultural responsibility through the art media we choose to work with?" ...I think focusing on the "nature-based connections" IS what makes us different from the Western mindset. The bond or relationship we have towards our environment is what makes us "instinct based" instead of "intellectual based." The more we move into the Western world, the more we seem to act from "ideas" instead of what we know instinctively to be right. Our power and our cultural coding came from this relationship to our instincts which ARE nature-based. When we lose this, then all there is left is ideas of being "indin" or whatever. Thank you for being an evolving conscious human being that is truly searching for the truth. I am right beside you. ○○○

3.24.06
THE SIXTH PARAGRAPH: INDIAN ART DEFINITIONS

(1) HISTORIC EXPRESSIONISM

Historic expressionism is a style that remains true to the techniques and design conventions of nineteenth-century tribal art. Themes may change, but these works remain historically rooted. At the same time, they are distinctly individual. A personal use of image and line marks each artist's work as his own. The artists who work in the style of historic expressionism are not copyists or reproductionists; they are re-interpreters of an ancient tradition.

(2) TRADITIONALISM

Traditionalism—known for its flat, two dimensional representations of historic Native scenes—was taught and encouraged by white patrons such as Dorothy Dunn and Oscar Jacobson. Traditional pictures generally portray an idealized version of earlier Indian ways, using areas of smooth color surrounded by darker outlines. Traditional painters have gradually evolved a style that seeks absolute accuracy in historic detail but has become increasingly dramatic in theme and less stylized in form, particularly with the addition of background and perspective.

(3) MODERNISM

Modernism freely experiments with mainstream contemporary techniques, yet remains visually identifiable as Native American art. It incorporates styles as varied as cubism, surrealism, and photo-realism, yet still portrays Indian motifs and themes – themes spanning an enormous range, from realistic portraiture to bitter social commentary. The modernist Indian artist borrows and adapts from all styles and techniques, following creatively where talent and interest may lead.

(4) INDIVIDUALISM

Individualism is not an Indian art style. It is totally indistinguishable from mainstream contemporary art. The artist is Indian, but the artwork is not; at least it is not necessarily recognizable as "Indian." Individualistic Indian artists have a primary allegiance to self, not to a movement or an ethnic group. These artists are frequently criticized for abandoning the Indian tradition in favor of complete artistic freedom. Until quite recently, many critics challenged the right of the individualistic artist to be called Indian. (From: *MAGIC IMAGES—Contemporary Native American Art,* Edwin L. Wade and Rennard Strickland, Published 1981)

(5) THE HUMAN CONDITION

Depictions of the human figure, primarily in the form of stylized or abstracted images, have been important in Native American Art in the Southwest from prehistory to the present. This rich tradition is today paralleled by a large number of Native artists who are examining other aspects of the human condition through the figure. For these artists, the human figure is not distanced and objective but intensely personal and revelatory of self-consciousness and cultural awareness. The artists featured in this section of 'Changing Hands' are engaged with figuration in their work and are able to illuminate social and political issues, express individual or group sentiments, and communicate their reflections on values that give meaning and direction to their lives. Pathos, beauty, humor, and irony are embedded in their presentations of the human body. These artists describe themselves and their world through the figure, but also invite us to see ourselves in these images. (From: *Changing Hands: Art Without Reservation, 1, Contemporary Native American Art from the Southwest*, General Editors: David Revere McFadden, Ellen Napiura Taubman, Published 2003).

♦♦♦ **The Sixth Paragraph:** Searching for a missing identity. To formulate the sixth paragraph we are required to create or redefine our prevailing identity as Indian artists and Indigenous people. Currently this definition relies upon westernized aesthetics, politics, history, religion and economics for its basis and was conceived by writers and scholars of those disciplines. To formulate this new or renewed identity description we must answer these challenging contemporary questions: 'Why are we Indian or Indigenous?,' 'How do we create cultural art that reflects our true human condition?' and 'What is the cultural purpose of our art?' These questions must have realistic and sound answers instead of referring to generic scapegoat references reliant upon pedigrees of genetic purity or a non-traditional numbering process. The five paragraphs defining our identity as artists contain every answer needed from a westernized perspective. Unfortunately they leave a huge void of reality that only contemporary Native Americans can fill. The missing paragraph exists because we Native or Indigenous people carry the heavy load of racial self hatred and cultural trauma. We refuse to confront problems because our ancestors were forced to synthesize our experiences with Western beliefs. We now reject anything other than what is being maintained, even with the acknowledgement that any healthy culture is constantly in transition. The traditional holistic or nature dependent sense of 'we' has yielded to Western concepts of individualism that dismisses the importance of nature or tribe as a valid basis for our identity. Without our addressing the seemingly obvious conflicts of this identity transformation, we are forced to accept the dehumanization that results from being defined by external market demands and non-Indigenous cultural viewpoints. Groupings such as Historic Expressionism, Traditionalism, Modernism, Individualism and The Human Condition have little to do with how we define ourselves. The simplistic suggestion that art should be driven by artistic freedom instead of cultural responsibilities is truly Western and makes our innovators into outcasts with no cultural purpose other than a trickle down economic reward. Any cultural activity must originate from and be intended for our own people and prevail over external non-Indigenous considerations.

The RELATIONS: indigenous dialogue project needs to share internally our intelligence, philosophy, spirituality, knowledge, and true human condition, plus reach to Indigenous people worldwide for further dialogue. Our purpose requires motivation based upon the earnest desire to create change. A deeply ingrained reticence to challenge our superficial contemporary Indigenous identity puts the full blame of cultural extinction on our contemporary shoulders. Indigenous culture is the 'us' of today and not something based purely on history and economics. Our self view cannot be dependent upon the explanation of scholars, anthropologists, historians or others who share none of our cultural rewards, failures or responsibilities. For the sixth paragraph it is our job as Indian people to define an honest and updated Native American or Indigenous identity using the arts as our forum. ◆◆◆

4.3.06

❖❖❖ I am here in the IAIA library, trying to sort through the crust of my life—this existence we deem "necessary."

I had spoken to Joseph and Bob at Bob's birthday party, which was interesting, because it took me out of the "dialogue" box and threw me into real dialogue. Joseph seemed ready to initiate conversation, and I expressed my interest in everyone writing daily, even if it is short, because it is those small things that are important. I don't think we can even attempt to tackle these big issues unless we understand that the small things are important, too.

After everyone was gone except for a few of us, we sat around Bob's metal fire pit and I told him why it is hard for me to feel like I can talk. I am incredibly humbled by these people that I have admired all of my life, and I don't feel all the time that my words are of any use to these 'geniuses.' But that is another of our fears—that is another of our problems, not feeling that we are good enough. We have been taught that we are not good enough and it manifests itself through what we are doing now. I want to believe that we are all important, and that our place within this world should be just what it is, and in that place we are nothing but perfect.

I suppose that is my challenge—that I need to feel that I am worthy of my opinion and my point of view, if I feel it is right within.

Another thing we spoke of is if people don't want to participate,

1. Why? My thoughts: Because they are not ready to face what we are proposing (?) They don't understand the height of the cliff we are about to jump off of, and aren't willing to. It is much easier to build a ladder or to not jump off at all. Or maybe for some the cliff doesn't even exist.

I want to let them know that I believe that letting go and flying is the most powerful feeling ever, if only we would let ourselves.

2. Why are we forcing them? My thoughts: If someone does not want to be a part of something like this, then why are we pushing them?

I understand that it is easier to soften the blow if there are more people to take it, or to make it more understandable to some simply because more people support it. Bob mentioned that he is attempting to encourage 'courage,' but one could suppose that some people don't even want it.

I would like to think that we should manifest this prayer and bring everyone else along, but doesn't the prayer simply include them in its purity?

Do they need to actively participate in order to be a part? Is this exclusive? And if we become inclusive, then aren't we including the whole world? And isn't that the idea?

Does it soften the impact that we are trying to make if the participants don't understand or aren't willing to take that 'leap?'

I was thinking out loud to Jake on the ride home after leaving Bob's, expressing my thoughts and concerns. When I am upset at someone or something, or I feel the absolute integrity of the concept of what we are doing is at stake because of someone or something, I don't feel right expressing it to anyone.

My fear is that I will make someone angry. If they are angry, then they won't like me. If they don't like me, then I will be alone. And that is scary.

I would like to express to everyone that I welcome all views, even if they are negative, because what we are trying to find isn't just pretty, and it comes with a lot of HARD TRUTHS. I am going to try my hardest to find my ultimate truth and express it to everyone, without my fear of being alone getting in the way.

With that said, I will try to write again tomorrow, and hope to hear from everyone soon. ❖❖❖

4.4.06
RESPONSE TO MY WALK WITH BUCKO (PAGE 7)

◆◆◆ *This evening I took a walk behind my home with my walking stick and dog Bucko. The sun had just receded beyond the horizon and the low cloud cover created a sunset that was beyond any verbal description. When I was young my father used to stop the car on the highway and our family would sit on the roadside just to watch spectacular sunsets. The Southwest is renowned for its natural beauty and the colors of the sunset at dusk are often breathtaking. For some years all of my thoughts have revolved around a RELATIONS type project and this evening is no exception. I wondered if the sunsets of my distant ancestors compared to the glorious panorama I was enjoying. No words or painting could have communicated the subtle blending of oranges, pinks, yellows, blues and purples that stretched of the Jemez Mountains to the west. What I observed was mine to experience, mine to enjoy, mine to absorb and love. I could easily indulge in idealistic fantasies and pretend that this was the same shared sunset my tribe viewed in the distant past but I question that pretext.* ♦♦♦

●●● I, too, often contemplate the same when I view what has become of my islands, especially my birthplace of O'ahu! What Have They Done to My Song Ma??? Yes, we still have much beauty in these islands and I do know the places where little is disturbed and only then can I revisit the Ancestor's perspective. Are they indeed idealistic fantasies...or are we echoing the shared experience? My people believe in *ola hou,* reincarnation...renewed life...that which I look upon in that secluded place has been looked upon before and before and before...by eyes that are now mine—and perhaps only in that secluded place, ours to continue to experience, enjoy, absorb and love! The feeling is always in my gut, *na'au,* never my eyes! ●●●

♦♦♦ *Just as we of today claim to hold the culture of the past, I too could easily pretend to live and maintain an Apache culture that was thriving over 120 years ago. How can that be? The sky with its depleted ozone layer and additional pollution particles, illuminated by sunlight refraction, may offer a more stunning or less attractive sunset than that of our distant ancestors. My personal cultural identity is an obvious self contradiction with my Anglo, Spanish (plus African Moore?), Navajo, possibly Ute, and N'de or Apache genetics. These genetics are encompassed by endless identifiers of Western man. How do I honestly call myself Indian or contemporary Apache if the only references to my identity are racially or historically based? Today all we need to proclaim our Indian heritage are proof of blood lines and a federal number.* ♦♦♦

●●● And do we pretend? Truly? Doesn't the truth of our intention lie in our heart of hearts? We do physically live in a world that is vastly different from that of our Ancestors...true! But, but, but...the inside place is the same! My belief and the belief of our people was that each generation carries on its spiritual mission. I try so very hard to live by the responsibility

given us by our Fixed Ancestors, *Akua Kumupa'a*. Although I honor, respect and am knowledgeable of those other cultures residing in this skin...my heart and soul is in harmony with the face that looks back at me in the mirror. "How do I honestly call myself Indian or contemporary Apache if the only references to my identity are racially or historically based?" Sorry, but that bears repeating. I understand totally, because within our Indigenous place, that is a truth that rings so very clear, it hurts the soul to hear—but then, we cannot generalize, for there are those in our midst who do see the truth about their identity and live it as well. This is what RELATIONS is all about, to get out of that "place"...and I totally believe that we in this artistic tribe are out of that "place," that is what we have in common...our togetherness and shared center will communicate this to others and perhaps they can emerge with the Spirit...the Soul...the *Wailua* that is our true Self!!! *Kanaka Maoli*! ●●●

◆◆◆ As we go deeper into the RELATIONS project we must constantly remind ourselves of the depth of culture and physical beauty we commonly share. Consecutively, we must honestly acknowledge the residual damage to our contemporary Indigenous cultural reality and claimed identity. The knowledge we share with our children must focus upon a more meaningful and honest portrait of ourselves. That portrait must include the negative. The Apache people of the past had entirely different cultural ways than we have today. Our existence was based upon hunting, raiding, warfare, trade and occasional farming and harvest. In the harsh desert climate of the Southwest our Apache spirituality and communal laws required a strong relationship to nature and tribe for basic survival. I would be remiss to remind my tribe or family of past tribal deities such as Life Giver, Monster Slayer, White Painted Woman, the Twins, the Little People or our creation stories without also including more immediate

adopted Western concepts that are the antithesis of Indigenous or Apache beliefs. Even this simple declaration, if made to an all Christianized tribe whose culture is near totally westernized, would risk creating serious dissention and possible expulsion from the tribe. Our older ones are all gone and none of our contemporary people experienced the distant times of cultural autonomy. Nor do they understand what a true Apache identity encompassed or shared cultural responsibilities that are required for survival. Unfortunately we have chosen to continually ignore the true reality of our ongoing cultural decay. Many of us believe that there was and still exists a profound philosophical foundation supporting tribal identity, knowledge and purpose. The weakened contemporary identity we now share is based on a well maintained, historically focused, romantic and superficial portrayal that is unable to adapt to change while maintaining fundamental cultural values. We have lost the true meaning of being sovereign and Indigenous. We now allow state supervision over our economic ventures and have thereby reduced our sovereignty to little more than a state level commercial business. The philosophical basis of Indigenous people will remain a memory and eventually forgotten unless we expose and challenge the superficial cultural identity that is currently used. ◆◆◆

●●● And here is where we embrace our differences. I so appreciate your honesty in telling it like it is, for you and your people. "Indigenous cultural reality and claimed identity!" Claimed identity? My Maoli-ness IS my identity! The Voice that spoke to me so many years ago had the face of a Hawai'i Maoli! It is my Hawaiian Great-grandmother Luika who comes to me in Vision! Sometimes, I am judged too harshly for being too honest about our people...not the people of yesteryear, mind you, but those of the present—those who continue to straddle the fence, those who simply give lip service to our heritage and Divine Responsibility. You say, sharing of the negative? For me, there is no negative! What was true of the past was a truth that took 25,000 years to hone...values that were brought forward by stalwart people who built huge sailing ships and traversed oceans to finally come to find their chiefdom in the Pacific. These people bringing with them a fully developed culture that saw to the physical and spiritual survival, preservation and protection of their people, eternally!!! But, the devil is in the details! The GREAT INTERRUPTION stopped all that!!! That is what is the truth! That is when the negative INSINUATED ITSELF IN OUR CULTURE, HEARTS AND SOULS. Hence, the cultural decay! Aptly put! Unfortunately, our people have INDEED adapted to that negative change in a very big way!!! So much that they've forgotten the Spirit and Soul of our Ancient people...they are mere husks with the fancy outer layer...empty inside. We had a Sacred Law called 'Ihi Kapu...a law that governed the physical and the metaphysical...a law that was created over centuries to protect the WHOLE...a law that for some is our foundation to this day. I'm with you on exposing and challenging the superficial... ●●●

♦♦♦ *Here is an example of our acceptance of a non-Indian and Western judgment of our arts. I recently enjoyed the* Changing Hands *Indigenous art exhibition at the IAIA Museum. The combination of technique, aesthetics, and the design of the objects curated into the exhibit was amazing. I left the exhibit with the feeling of uneasiness. During the exhibit the museum director reminded me that it was selected by non-Indigenous 'white' curators. That alone could easily give reason to my unrest.* ♦♦♦

●●● There is "white," and there is "white!" Lucia has been our curator for 30 years! Her sensitivity and keen eye as to the heart and soul of our culture and art has allowed for the most beautifully designed exhibitions in the entire art-history of these islands. But, my dear brother, I hear what you say, for Lucia is unique in that she has spent a lifetime learning my culture, language and way of thinking!!! I don't know of any other like her. ●●●

♦♦♦ *There was another equally disturbing aspect to the exhibition in reference to art ownership (i.e., the changing of ownership or hands from maker to owner) that was related to cultural intent and cultural return. (As a side note, my work was included in the* Changing Hands I *Exhibit because I protested the original premise of the exhibit and was immediately accepted as a token dissenting voice. At that time in my career it was ok to accept the premise that any exhibit with ones peers was a good exhibit and good for business.) The entire exhibit is visually beautiful but lacked an internal cultural purpose. It seems that our primary artistic statement was "we Indians are world class artisans," plus "we have obtained our importance by relying on Western viewpoints and economic values."* ◆◆◆

●●● And that is the very reason I too protested the exhibit!!! But, was asked by my daughter and son-in-law, and especially by Bob De La Torre, to participate in order to honor our Hawaiian place. All of those Native survey exhibitions are exactly alike...even those curated by the Indigenous...Sara Bates, Janeen Antoine, etc., etc., etc. I love these two ladies, but you are right...their well intended idea was to show the outside world that we are as good as they are...and yes, that wonderful exposure I'll get going from city to city, with "one" piece in the show! A piece that is swallowed up by the thousands surrounding it. I've turned down more survey shows than you can imagine...survey shows are out of context...it's like putting a science project together with a beginning and an end, but no middle...a project that in the end, you have no idea how it works. ●●●

◆◆◆ *This non-cultural/non-Indigenous purpose seems to reek of self glorification and 'artist as hero' worship, non-Indigenous laws of supply and demand, Western economics, Western aesthetics and Western romanticism. By focusing our arts toward economic reward we Indigenous Native artists have lost our fundamental responsibility of inspiring or stimulating internal cultural thought and discussion.* ◆◆◆

●●● Agreed! ●●●

◆◆◆ *The non-Indigenous curators assumed the right to determine who the 'Masters of Indian Arts' were and in doing so arrogantly presented their personal perceptions of Indigenous values and aesthetics.* ◆◆◆

●●● Agreed!!! ●●●

◆◆◆ *'Give them the tools and let them create, and therefore their art work will be valued by the collector as fine art' was and still is the fundamental belief of modernized Indian art. This trade school belief that reflects the federal assimilation policy is still rooted in the Institute of American Indian Art's mission. The original goal of this school was to provide economic return from our natural talents as craft producers. This is not to say the artworks of* Changing Hands II *and other Indian art isn't exemplary as individual world class art objects or economically valuable. As an artist I was intimidated and totally captivated by the beautiful work and talent of the artists included in the exhibit. I suppose what I am saying is this: There simply isn't any serious attempt or desire to communicate the contemporary humanity, intelligence or life conditions of the Native American artisans through the arts.* ◆◆◆

●●● It is my place...my *kuleana*...my responsibility to present through my conceptual art...to communicate to the present and future generations, that which best represented our Ancestral past...those things that made us HUMAN...I am a speaker!!! The contemporary humanity, intelligence or life conditions of the Indigenous Hawaiian is all around us! It is what has sucked us into the mire and keeps us there, generation after generation. Many years ago, I asked myself over and over again...what path should I take??? How should I communicate the Voice??? The answer was loud and clear...I must return that which was set aside...I must take up the Way!!! Our University kids have taken up the gauntlet in communicating the contemporary human condition...and I find that IT lacks our Maoli spirit. I cannot see in communicating that which is already known...that which is already being savored and sucking us dry. I feel that in order to bring our people out of the depths...we must encourage a rebirth...we must plant a seed with our most serious works...plant a seed that will bloom into the people that we once were. ●●●

♦♦♦ *Little of the artwork in this exhibit told me that this artwork is a true portrait of us a contemporary Native people.* ♦♦♦

●●● Including mine? Including Art's? Including Natalie's? I think not!!! I agree with much of the art in the exhibition...but you cannot generalize...for there were some truly inspiring pieces...but, again they were all out of context. ●●●

♦♦♦ *When the group of RELATIONS entered the hole I found myself apprehensive of criticism. At the same time these people I feared took the time to enter and attempt to understand the project. I'm sure each one of us realized that we could easily paint our individual art statements on the wall space in front of us. Considering the combined talent we represented it could be assumed that the end product would have been visually beautiful and undoubtedly economically valuable. Unfortunately, a group of disconnected individual expressions, however attractive or culturally meaningful, would have undermined the purpose of an Indigenous dialogue. Though some may believe otherwise, I don't think we need westernized concepts of individualism, self ownership, art jargon and production methods to give our art credibility.* ♦♦♦

●●● I totally agree!!! ●●●

♦♦♦ *To verify that statement we must create a language for our contemporary Indigenous identity. Three very important questions must be addressed: "How do we share and accept another's Indigenous perceptions?"* ♦♦♦

●●● Okay, one thing at a time!!! Being that All Reality is Perception... the underlying component is respect!!! We are all skilled and honed artists...my particular place is my particular place...one that I am attached to because it comes from the Voice of my Ancestors...I must be true to that Voice. I DO NOT REGURGITATE ART!!! I have a suggestion - perhaps we in this forum should explain a bit about each other's creative place? In this way we know more about each other from a creative perspective. Contrary what others might believe, what I create is conceptual...coming from a foundation well grounded in time, but one that is reinterpreted by this latest generational artist—me!!! So, when I look at other's works... remembering that art is relative to one's taste...we share perceptions by sharing ourselves! We accept perceptions by accepting and respecting one another. ●●●

◆◆◆ *"How do we go beyond the 'me' emphasis that is so all-important to Western man and create a 'we' or tribal thought?* ◆◆◆

●●● I've never created from the "me." I am a tool of the Ancestor's Voice...I follow where they lead for I am part of Them. This is what has been so hard in communicating to our Indigenous here...remember that many of my people are still very Christian...this is one thing that they do not want to hear. The youth, however, is making strong headway, perhaps in a generation or two, things will change drastically. We must continue our work and set examples for them to follow. ●●●

◆◆◆ *And of equal importance, "How do we balance group or tribal identity with the individualism focus of Western man?"* ◆◆◆

●●● I don't!!! Ever!!! ●●●

◆◆◆ *Other questions should be also discussed. Questions such as" "How are we going to make the RELATIONS project more than a survey exhibit based on historic glorification and the contemporary cultural prettiness concepts?"* ◆◆◆

●●● You keep mentioning historic glorification and contemporary cultural prettiness concepts...my feelers are up. Do you see anyone in this group who creates from that perspective? And, if so, who? Those who do shouldn't be in this exhibition!!! We should only embrace those who understand the fundamental concept of RELATIONS! Or are willing to learn those fundamentals, as the youth. How else can we get our message across! RELATIONS is not a survey exhibit and that is that!!! ●●●

◆◆◆ *And also: "What are the group's shared purpose and intent behind the RELATIONS: indigenous dialogue exhibition?* ◆◆◆

●●● For the past 30 years, our Indigenous organization, Hale Naua III, Society of Hawaiian Arts has mounted dialogue exhibitions...that is all we do and that is all we'll continue to do...let us share in each other's place. ●●●

◆◆◆ *During one of our meetings the dialogue group entered the hole project together. As we were in the hole I wondered what any one of us individual cultural representatives would consider the primary or most fundamental object or idea that represented the most important of his or her culture. In my tribe we still retain great respect for the concept of power.* ◆◆◆

●●● In ours as well!!! Power is *mana*...a spiritual energy, emanating from the me, that encompasses the we of our Ancestors. ●●●

◆◆◆ *The cattail pollen is extremely important for blessing and protections and is used privately and in tribal ceremonies. The Pueblo and Navajo people hold corn meal in high esteem, perhaps even considering it sacred. I've watched many other people use tobacco, sage, cedar, eagle and owl feathers, woodpecker feathers, hummingbird bodies, lightning struck trees, turquoise, plants, bear, the sun and moon, and a seemingly endless number of culturally important songs, sacred objects and areas. On a social level all people seem to have sacred songs and chants, clothing, war and medicine items, traditional designs, creator or life giver symbols, unspoken concepts and objects, and a list that seems endless.* ◆◆◆

●●● I have come to learn from my many mentors throughout the years that "nothing is sacred," because "everything is sacred..." It took me a while to grasp this dichotomy! It isn't the "thing," that is sacred, but the WHOLE that is sacred...individual objects, concepts and components put aside so that we do not contaminate them through time. And, because we've removed this sacredness...picked and chosen that which is and that which isn't sacred, we've allowed chaos, confusion and the "fairytale" to grow and devour us. ●●●

♦♦♦ *During the 1960's an anthropologist named Frank Waters wrote the* Book of the Hopi *and most people suddenly accepted and placed the Hopi people philosophically and spiritually superior to the other North American Indian tribes. This respect is seemingly bestowed by 'white' people in authority to whichever tribe they deem worthy throughout America. A Hopi man told me that much of the cultural information was intentionally shared as misinformation, and the authentic information remained closely guarded. Does this type of adulation place the Hopi people on Indigenous people's highest chair of respect? Should we go to any specific tribe for a more pure way of thinking? If we located the most powerful or meaningful talisman, concept or substance should we thereby incorporate it into our Indigenous dialogue as substitute for our own conception of the sacred?* ♦♦♦

●●● Okay, here again, one at a time!!! I so hate anthropological crap!!! This has been done to our people as well...one tribe over another, one Polynesian nation over another...one era more civilized than another. Pure crap!!! We Are of One People! But...be forever wary of "our own conception of the sacred." If we are our Ancestor's Voice...this is, of course, if we truly are...I do not want to presume...but, if I personally want to bring that which was honed by our Ancestors into the present, so that the future can reap the rewards, then I must also respect their Spiritual Way... for that was their strength. Not religion, mind you...but a philosophy filled with logic and wonder...a humanness that was filled with metaphor and allegory...encrypted to live eternally! Aha!!! THE GREAT INTERRUP-TION!!! Well, then, it is up to us to bring it out, dust it off, reintroduce it and make sure that somewhere, with someone, it lives again. And for those who create for the purpose of revolutionary change...the same is true! For even that must stand firmly upon the Ancestral Voice...especially if we are truly embracing the "we" concept. ●●●

♦♦♦ *How do we deal with the difference in creation or eternity concepts?* ♦♦♦

●●● Study the metaphor and allegory of your people...unveil the "fireside versions," that have stifled our people throughout the last 200 years. ●●●

♦♦♦ *Do we as a group take a vote or individually choose the most pure, historical, logical and instinctive solutions to our contemporary Indigenous questions?* ♦♦♦

●●● If we are of like mind...the dialogue is where it's at!!! ●●●

♦♦♦ *And how do we answer the question of specific sacred cultural place? These questions seem superfluous, but unless we can respectfully acknowledge different cultural viewpoints as equal to our own we will never create the basic alphabet to our new Indigenous language.* ♦♦♦

●●● These questions are not superfluous...these are the questions that will make us aware of each other's cultural viewpoints!!! ●●●

♦♦♦ *I personally believe that with the 'we as a part of a whole' of the RELATIONS concept our individual tribal uniqueness must be open to revision into a more commonality of thought. In other words, there wasn't, isn't and never will be a purity of thought or culture unless we first use the nature-based instinct and common sense that exemplified Indigenous thought.* ♦♦♦

●●● Okay, let me piece this out!!! "We as a part of the whole," of RELA-TIONS!!! Tribal uniqueness MUST be open to REVISION? Why??? What does commonality of thought mean? I don't much like the term that has "common" in it. I agree that there isn't at present a purity of thought...I do not agree that it NEVER existed. Remember THE GREAT INTERRUPTION??? We believe that our people achieved purity of thought...or at least our *kahuna* did...made manifest by the logic behind the life and death phenomena and their explanation of the Soul Cluster, *WAILUA.* If we are speaking of the Whole of our respective tribal units, then I agree that we must use the nature-based instinct and common sense that exemplified Indigenous thought. That thought that you speak of...is written in our ancient prayers, chants and poetry...a Sacred Place...one that embraced us generation after generation...then in 1820 the Calvinists came and all was thrown into chaos. It was those few Maoli at the top who got rid of the *kahuna* who maintained the "narrow path," opening the door to the "stranger," ending, not forever, but temporarily, the spiritual integrity of our people. ●●●

♦♦♦ *Western training also taught us that we must polarize our thoughts; good against bad, for or against, black as negative against white as purity or good, joy as opposed to sorrow, the verticality of Western thinking contrasted to the horizontal dispersion of the Indigenous. We, as a group or as cultural representatives, cannot allow ourselves to be dictated to by non-Indigenous philosophy.* ♦♦♦

●●● Yes!!! The dialogue must get outside the group, for I believe that those within this group are truly not dictated to. Among ourselves—these dialogues, although, spiritually uplifting, are like preaching to the choir, don't you think? ●●●

♦♦♦ *It is the creation of this Indigenous philosophy that gives our group a sense of purpose. It goes without saying that those of us with traditional knowledge must also accept the importance of those who seek honest, healthy or possibly revolutionary change.* ♦♦♦

●●● Are you speaking of me again??? If these dialogues are meant for those IN OUR group...THEN who creates from traditional knowledge? As I see it, we all do, in one way or another. And, I also believe that we all create from an honest place. I am assuming that you mean that revolutionary change is healthy...I agree! There is more than one way to skin a cat!!! ●●●

♦♦♦ *Conversely those who are challenging the status quo must equally embrace those who maintain our cultural wisdom and experience.* ♦♦♦

●●● Yes! (Smile)!!! I feel that we as Indigenous artists are all challenging the status quo...regardless of medium, style, artistic communicative language...and, I also believe that this particular group also creates from their cultural wisdom and experience. Those whom I know...I go through their work in my mind and see all three places...challenge cultural wisdom and experience!!! Perhaps the younger need more cultural wisdom and experience...but for us advanced in age...I believe we all come from that place. Again, Bob, I ask, do you think there is one among us who is not? ●●●

♦♦♦ *With our dialogue we must give equal consideration to the younger participants because they are truly the eyes and backbone of the elders and older ones because of their hands-on knowledge of contemporary issues. If we accept tradition and change as divergent and unrelated concepts we risk neutralizing our dreamers and visionaries.* ♦♦♦

●●● Contemporary issues!!! And they would be??? Oh yes, those same issues that have been plaguing us for hundreds of years??? Those issues that die hard in our hearts and minds...those issues that are branded in our souls...those cultural wounds that lay bleeding generation after generation? Those issues??? And what of the Spirit of our Ancestors? Isn't that also the responsibility of our young as well? Today, tradition has become a Westernized interpretation of "our way of life." Our way of life and change are divergent because our youth still do not know enough to go about their culture to make a "change," to evolve from the foundation that was set by our Ancestors. None of our cultures were stagnant...there was always change within the cultural genre, generation after generation...yours, mine, everyone's. In our past, nothing remained the same eon after eon...and why should it be that way now. Oh yes!!! THE GREAT INTERRUPTION!!! The powers-that-be freezing us in nineteenth century time for the benefit of the tourist dollar. So, now, we must go back and extract that which made our people Whole...take that knowledge and absorb it...know our Ancestor's thoughts, hopes and dreams...hear their Song of Origin and only then can you create change...for then it won't be an Aberrant!!! ●●●

♦♦♦ *The role of honest cultural observer could easily belong to the arts. One of the most important unifying factors of the group is the need for meaningful and honest cultural change. That is the basis of the RELA-TIONS concept.* ♦♦♦

●●● Meaningful and honest cultural change!!! Meaningful and honest change! Yes...cultural change? I've worked so hard to understand my Ancestor's thought process, why would I want to change my cultural perspective, when it is that spiritual place I'm trying to maintain? Yes, I must change from this Stygian darkness to one of Light...that I will willingly do!!! ●●●

♦♦♦ *A Native American elder 'of the Indian arts' once challenged me with this question "What are you trying to do, change the world?" In retrospect the answer should have been "Of course!" If we don't challenge or attempt to make serious change to what appears to be an Indigenous and Indian identity that for all practical purposes is cosmetic our children and grandchildren will inherit an even less clear cultural identity than we experience.* ♦♦♦

●●● This resonates deep within me!!! I agree totally, that we've become a cosmetic culture! Cultural hostages!!! Most are, anyway! And the others are walking around in the dark. Damn!!! But, little by little...one by one... they will turn towards the Voice from which they emanate. ●●●

♦♦♦ *We simply must break through the wall or crust of the hole, together if possible, to honestly understand and make the RELATIONS concept meaningful. I would much prefer describing my own sunset instead of attempting to create parallels or descriptions of the beauty to father's father's sunsets. My sunset, as with my culture, exists with me today. I would prefer to explain with my art what is of my own experience rather than portray a historic, romantic or historic tribal experience that has been reduced to superficial layers of contemporary Indian identity.* ♦♦♦

●●● "My Ancestor's sunset was beautiful...immortalized in chant and prayer! I recite it often. But, then I compose my work for the sunset of today as well." You have often mentioned the "historic, romantic tribal experience..." You need not worry, Bob, for I doubt very much if any of us will create from that place. You generalize...dumping all of those who create from their cultural truth with all who simply regurgitate their Ancestral iconography. ●●●

♦♦♦ *It need not be stated that without the reliance, knowledge and respect for our traditional cultural foundation of our Indigenous or Indian past we lose the real purpose of our cultural existence and seriously flirt with new age individualism concepts. We need the constant reminder that our cultural inheritance must serve as the cornerstone of any mean-ingful change.* ♦♦♦

●●● Yes!!! ●●●

♦♦♦ *I share these ideas with the hope of creating an open dialogue for further talks. This project depends on our ability to work and share in the creation of a renewed Indigenous language for our dialogue. The knowl-edge base must be an accumulation of all voices of the group, each contributing his or her specific life and cultural experience. We have dug and shared the hole together. Now we must recreate the dialogue that has always identified us as Indigenous.* ◆◆◆

●●● No, you have dug the hole...we have only shared in your experience!!! Remember, I took you to Our Hole here in Hawai'i—the Hole connected to the birthing canal of the Mother!!! The Sacred Space from which All Life Emanates. I do agree that all voices must come together...I only wish that all within this group participate in a "meaningful and honest" way. These amazing dialogues should be recorded...I'm trying to save them all...they should be put in a book and conserved for all prosperity, for I believe that we are creating a history so passionate and overwhelming, that that change you are constantly talking about Bob, will materialize—through all of our endeavors. ●●●

4.5.06

○○○ Well, I just spent my morning reading the dialogue between Bob and Rocky. It was interesting. At first I was trying to get a clear perspective on where each was coming from but, by the end, I found myself dancing between the two of you in an easy way as if my brain was talking out loud. The "gap" between you two had disappeared and I was hearing a hummmm of two voices talking like in a dance...........and I thought, this dialogue between you two should be displayed in the exhibit as an example of "relations" with each other.....maybe next to your creations...as if they are talking to each other...this talk...this exchange with each other. ○○○

●●● A dance? Yes, I agree, it is a dance...or as my people called it, Sacred Movement...a movement of words, creating patterns and rhythms. Oftentimes two perspectives, sometimes one, and yet we are always of one heart – the "gap," seamless. Your e-mail certainly does bring in the very important and essential Female Principle...you and Rose are maintaining the balance. In our Maoli culture, that is as it was and should be... we are making headway...more and more each year, understanding that the yin and yang, that the *Loina Wahine* and *Loina Kane*, that the Male and Female Priniciples, must exist side by side in order for there to be harmony in the world. ●●●

○○○ I keep thinking of my dialogue that I'm working on with my daughter. Our "relation" is one that is more in the non-verbal area.......... which brings up the whole idea of dialogue not just being verbal or written. I'm enjoying the verbal part of this venture but I do want to add the part that "one cannot read." When I think of a dialogue with each one of you words always come much later.......I live in sensations and thus my relations with you all is on that level. That is how I envision this show..... being on the level of the senses. So, I'm reading through what Bob has written and I can feel where he is coming from and I totally "feel" it....... then I'm reading Rocky's response and I feel where he is coming from and I'm right there with him. So maybe I'm fickle. ○○○

●●● No fickleness about you at all!!! Senses – there's that *Loina Wahine* again...that Female Principle that brings our Male physicality front and center...Sensory – sensual – feelings – intuition! All shared, of course, but in some ways that is how women think and are...coming from the Terrestrial level. The Mother is from the Earth – women are from the Earth— connected...grounded. I so welcome your "feelings." I so welcome that which "we cannot read." ●●●

○○○ Besides this........I was caught by something you said, Rocky: "we must encourage a rebirth...we must plant a seed with our most serious work...plant a seed that will bloom into the people that we once were." OK, but I would change the last sentence to say "the people we REALLY are." ○○○

●●● To become aware that that which we once were is that who we really are!!! Forever and eternally...*mai ka po mai!!!* Yes...that is the ticket. ●●●

○○○ I do think there needs to be a kind of rebirth. A birth into a choice. We can't go back to "before the INTERRUPTION"........we have changed because of this and can't be what we were before........but we do have something that makes us US.........a continuum of our story, even our story of being interrupted. ○○○

●●● My philosophy is that in order to do honor to the Ancestors, I must also respect their honing of life – dedicating their place to pre-serve, perpetuate, develop, evolve into the people that finally made us. How can I not be aware of the "time that was," and bring forward into the "now" the perfection of which they were so very adept at. I study their ways, their laws and their techniques and skill as artists...so many of our people cannot come close to their ancient perfection in any of these. It is my hope one day to be worthy of that place. But, yes, we have changed because of the GREAT INTERRUPTION! Unfortunately, the momentum is lost! The evolution transformed, distorted – I'm trying to find the Way Home...I'm trying to regain the "Narrow Path." The US... that grain of Essence that makes us US has THEM IN IT!!! We continue by standing firmly on Their shoulders. They as US continue through Eternity. ●●●

○○○ As you said, Bob, what are our objects or ideas that represent the most important part of our culture? I like that question. I do think my answer to that question would have to be "our relationship to ourselves, each other and the world around us"........"RELATIONS." The INTERRUP-TION we are talking about........isn't that all about an interruption in how we were relating to everything? We have forgotten how to talk to the animals and the clouds because the interrupters told us we couldn't do that...that everything was separate and NOT in relationship to each other. In our old souls, we know that this is not true. Our Indigenous cultures are all about our relation to all that is........the songs, the dances, the meaning of it all is about that connection. ○○○

●●● This philosophy that you speak of is truly the foundation of all that we were and should be. In actuality, we are this "thing," but so many of us are unaware of its existence within us. Through the arts, I've tried to communicate the meticulous relationship that we've always had with the WHOLE...our culture was never piece meal!!! Today, many of the Hawai'i Maoli take only what is palatable to them...what their Christian sense or Western sense, or commercial sense, tell them is acceptable. We have forgotten how to talk to all the Elements! ●●●

○○○ I have been thinking a lot lately about the relationship I have with my own body...which because of Western interruption, I was partly brought up to believe that I was not the "right" shape, size, colour, etc.... thus my body was "against me" instead of my companion. ○○○

●●● Having been born with a Hawaiian face that resembles a "pure blood," I know exactly what you mean. When I went to the mainland at age 16, I suffered my first prejudices...at home here, it isn't the idea of body, color or features that is biased – it is our philosophy, our truth, our reality that is not embraced – and its interpretation by the Western and Asian powers-that-be constantly display a warped judgment that is abysmal and unforgivable. ●●●

○○○ In this Westernized mindset I became disconnected to myself here and have then had to seek out Western doctors to help me when my body is falling apart because of this disconnection. Meantime, I've been learning to undo this thinking and, with it, comes the realization that my body can communicate directly to me and tell me what it needs or doesn't need.....my body is talking to me. Our ancestors knew this without a second thought. Our medicine people knew how to "talk" to bodies so that they would heal – knowing that they weren't "objects" to control separate from us but in relationship to us...as were the animals and clouds and rocks and each other. ○○○

●●● Yes, yes, yes..our Ancestors, both yours and mine, knew this – and, exquisitely developed a wellness that encompassed the Whole. For every-thing that could go wrong with our bodies there was a cure and preven-tive cure in nature – for everything that could go wrong with our minds, there was ancient wisdom and a honed therapy that was never failing. Listen to your inner voice Roxanne...for it brings with it the wisdom of the Ancestors. ●●●

○○○ Again, I stress the whole concept of "relations" within our "Whole Tribe" being the thread that binds us all and will hold not only the Power of Our Ancestors but the prayers that bring to us what we are needing to be whole / strong again........to be children again in a world that isn't disconnected from us...... a rebirth into a world of sacred-seeing. Ummmm? ○○○

●●● *Amama*—the words are spoken! *Ua Noa*—it has been made free!!! *Mai ka po mai 'oiâ'l'o*—truth eternal was before time! ●●●

♦♦♦ Rox and group: I seldom engage Rocky in any direct dialogue on this forum and have always directed my comments to the whole group. If you, Rocky, feel my thoughts are directed at you personally, I apologize. Words are not my medium. My comments are, and have been, self-directed. I too am victimized by the effects of assimilation into Western thought processes through my 'fine art' school training, religious training, language, economics and military training. The artwork that maintains my standard of living and workspace requires non-Apache, non-Indian support for me to continue and that fact alone demands self-censorship. I have difficulty considering myself a direct reflection of my ancestry without wholly embracing the negatives of my personal life, family and tribe. Perhaps we are only the stepping stone for the ancestral awareness renewal for our children. Alco-hol, disease, ignorance, violence and cultural bluff surround me and should be in my artwork. Most of this group are living contradictions with our 'other than Indigenous' mates and Western style analytical thinking methods. We, as a group, are together for good reasons. I suspect that we are all dissatisfied with the restrictive role of Indigenous or contemporary artists and thinkers as currently required by the market and our own communities. If I have an arts philosophy to share it is simply this: What I learn and share must somehow be received by those who I claim to represent. In other words, climbing this mountain alone sucks. We are here today to newly create what is sacred. What an opportunity! What incredible companions. *Daanahteke*. ♦♦♦

○○○ Bob, I understood that you were talking to the whole group. I apologize for making it sound as if you were only talking to Rocky. It's just that the dialogue between you and Rocky is cool...I think. And Yes, I agree that we are all contradictions to our Indigenous roots in many ways. Maybe that would be an interesting topic to journey down some more. Jake, thank you for your input. It feels good to hear from you and what you are saying. Keep talking. ○○○

●●● I too understood the dialogue to be inclusive of the Whole...there were just some things that I felt earmarked my kind of work and my kind of philosophy...and there is no offense taken...this is dialogue...honest and true...how refreshing to be able to talk to each other without ruffling any feathers...I think the first of its kind. I embrace it wholeheartedly. ●●●

4.6.06
●●● *Oiwi Pa'a No'eau*—I've added a suffix to the thought concept... "Whole Tribe"...of what? in our case, our similar skills in interpreting the phenomena of life...hence "artists"...hence *No'eau.*

Although this is for everyone, a continuum in the collection of dialogues...this one IS meant for Bob, my dear friend...words are truly your medium...you might not think it on your end, but I'm sure that all will agree with me that you do create amazing imagery and vision when you write. I also recognize that much of what you say is self-directed...I sincerely appreciate that place of origin, in this and many other ways, we are true brothers. Remember that with our friendship, there is never a need for apology...as I've said before, we are having dialogue...refreshing, stimulating, allowing us a sense of freedom seldom felt...Rose put it well, when she said that she fears to give her opinion because she might make people angry, then they won't like her, then she'll be alone. Well, haven't we all been there at one time or another? I finally got to the place where I didn't give a damn any longer...and hence, ousted from the game. So, the dialogues allow us that sacred forum—one experienced by our Ancestors, yours and mine. What you state about your creative preferences is your *kuleana,* a situation that makes you accountable for everything you are and everything you do. It is your sacred privilege! If you choose to include that which surrounds you, that is your solemn choice...as is what surrounds me and how I "need" to execute it as mine...this dialogue has been created in order for us to share that center, to share that place, and perhaps with the sharing, create a bridge between the wound and the healing. That has always been my goal in my creative thinking...because I too come from that traumatic lifestyle, one that surrounds me still... it is my art and those who love me that have saved me from the abyss—that give me purpose and sanity. Yes, dear friend, climbing the mountain alone sucks...perhaps my most strident war-cry!!! Unfortunately, we do deal with egos, with the individualistic "I" when it comes to almost everything...there again most giving lip-service to those wonderful, wonderful, precepts set down by our Ancient Ones. We are here to continue to create the Sacred...you need not climb that mountain alone Bob...we are all together in this. Companions true. ●●●

4.10.06

❖❖❖ i've been reading the dialogue between bob and rocky and i find it interesting that they trigger each other so much. there are things that are said that "irk" me, sometimes, that i feel are condescending or seem to come from a place of insecurity. i suppose my point of view or my inspirations come from an almost entirely different feeling. sometimes i feel as if the dialogue becomes redundant in its wordiness, and maybe that is why some of us younger people need to speak.

no disrespect intended, i understand that, without those who have come before us, with intuition/intelligence or without, they have made what we have today, be it positive or negative. and sometimes i think that without having hit rock bottom, some of us may not have been able to see how bad it really is. but then there are those who can't see the fly-swatter if it slaps them in the face.

in October i attended a Bioneers conference in California, (Sara went, too), and i had the opportunity to see a film on John Trudell. it was good to see straight forward the crap that has been blatantly done to us (as Native people), and it ignited some flames within me. after the movie was done, there was a question and answer session and i spoke about the amount of cancer within my community simply because it is downwind from Los Alamos National Laboratories. Me included. It didn't seem like anyone there would be able to help, it felt more like i just needed to say it, and let it out. when i spoke it felt like i was actually "throwing up" to all those 'understanding/conscious' white people. after the movie was

over and i was walking out, random people walked up to me with this "I'm sooooo sorry" look on their face and handed me money. i was in shock. i got a follow-up phone call from some guy from that conference who told me that they had organized a group that was going to come to New Mexico and help me with this problem. i told him i couldn't talk.

I think the problem is ours. the problem is for Santa Clara to deal with. and if we can pray hard enough to bring rain, we have the capability to pray hard enough to heal ourselves. and that prayer sometimes IS FIGHT. and sometimes that prayer is art. and sometimes that prayer is KICKING AND SCREAMING. sometimes the prayer is speaking the truth out loud. and sometimes that prayer is simply crying until there is no pain left.

And no one, absolutely no one, can do it for us, but ourselves. I am sure there are enough problems in California that the assistance group can attend to.

i ran into Sara the other night at the IAIA hogan and she seemed confused by this whole thing. i tried to explain to her above the racket, and after i left i felt like her words are incredibly needed to inspire new issues or points of view to work from. ❖❖❖

►►► In regards to the RELATIONS project, I have been spending a lot of my time feeling and thinking about the letters that I have recently been receiving due to my fresh involvement. One notion that I would like to address is our perspective as an Indigenous whole. Where are we looking towards in terms of western logic – are we devolving or evolving? Are we ascending or descending? I was struck by this matter while I was reading Rocky's letter. I quote…"we are trying to put back what has been stripped away from us, aren't we?" I find that to be a good question. I have spent some time researching prophecy of Indigenous peoples. While I don't let these precautions of prophecy devour my life, I definitely take heed. In many ways I see that we are heading for a catastrophic demise, reprise or rebirth. What's to come after, are we going to move to the fourth circle and live in utopia or are we going back to living as hunter-gatherers in mudhouses (from my pueblo perspective) only to repeat history? Coming from Jemez, which is one of the more rural pueblos in the Southwest, I struggle with myself to define what traditional is. The past month, I spent time cleaning the ditches in which one has a lot of time to think to themselves. This year the officials had us clean the less traditional way, in separate groups rather than all in a line, still without a machine. Every year it changes with bigger groups, smaller groups, with a machine, without, all together, with dances, with races. It depends, I guess. But I find it amusing to hear arguments of what is traditional and what we decide to concentrate on. I mean, this was just cleaning the ditches for irrigation, not to mention all the other activities that still take place. Sometimes I ask myself "Why does it matter if we use a machine or not, why don't we use it and move on to more important matters." And then I tell myself "We need to use our bodies to clean out the ditches, for it is the only way our fields will truly grow, if we men plow the mother earth." I am my own worst enemy. Furthermore, I believe that in the process of moving forward, we will put back what has been stripped away from us, but it will never be the same. There will always be that scar, until we can find our intuition and heal. I believe that the goal in sight is discovering our intuition, not getting back what was stripped away from us, although that would be nice. Thus, are we trying to hold onto tradition or are we trying to grow? I am inclined toward growing. I am inclined toward unlearning my logic and learning my real "common sense." I want us to evolve, only because I feel that at this time in history our mother is too beaten to heal to her same old self. People have lost too much of their intuition to even acknowledge a beaten mother. I feel a new mother is to be born and that all we can do, as humans, is pray; pray that people will grow enough to recognize the vanquished world, pray for forgiveness, pray for our people, pray for what is to be born and pray for what is to become dead. This does not mean that I won't uphold my tribal obligations. I just pray for that time when they tell us to sing and dance. Just a thought..... ➤➤➤

✧✧✧ "... With our dialogue we must give equal consideration to the younger participants because they are truly the eyes and backbone of the

elders and older ones because of their hands on knowledge of contemporary issues. If we accept tradition and change as divergent and unrelated concepts we risk neutralizing our dreamers and visionaries..."

Guwaadzi` to all:

First a note about my own involvement in this endeavor: I enter into this humbly.

And I must say--

I am grateful to those elders, and all those among us who have consciously and carefully endeavored to include myself and all the younger participants in this vital discourse and world-altering dialogue.

Rose. You are dear to me. Thank you so much for your words. And for acquainting me a little with what is upcoming, and some of the discourse that has already taken place. Was most unsure of how to properly enter into the dialogue, without much context. But, you encouraged me to just jump in, so with your blessings I now will.

So much of what I really want to share has everything to do with history, language, truth, Indian self-criticism and Native children.

In October, when Rose, rose and spoke--saying and doing what no one in that whole space could--all I could do was cry. For the story we have shared. For the life we are living. As a Native child, in public-school, in the city, at the pueblo, down south among cowboys and rednecks, no matter where I was, I often thought "It shouldn't BE this hard." I wanted to know why my Indian elders, my father in particular, were away

"SERVING THE MOVEMENT"

when I was right there all along. I believe then as in now, though I could not articulate it before, that "the movement" and the real stuff of a continuing and revitalized Indigenous dialogue and world-view is not "out there" somewhere or something we are reaching for:

IT IS OUR CHILDREN.

And, all too often we have forsaken them, in the name of "the movement", progress, the pursuit of attention paid to our "issues", and the rest. Rose and I, are the daughters of such pursuits. For recognition. For self-determination. For freedom. For equality. For life.

And there are many more like us. Too many who are beautiful, terrible, sick and sacred with all their truth. Do you reeeally want to know our story?

This is what I want to say to Harry (for his daughters have known it too), to my own father (and I have many times -- though I'll say it many more), and to a WHOLE GENERATION of Indian artists, writers, activists, and scholars.

I can only speak for myself here (though I'm pretty certain I'm not alone). My heart and mind are often set on kill, these days. A deep and abiding peace washes over me when I think of blood, when I think of an end to all that is terrible, destructive, arrogant, human.

Indians are some of the worst kinds of killers I know. This is part of the new Indigenous thought theory and practicum now.

Wanting the elders to speak to this, somehow.

Somehow. *dahwaaheh`* ✧✧✧

✧✧✧ "Additional" extremely relevant and pertinent Items I'm hungry to speak more on:

"This trade school belief that reflects the federal assimilation policy is still rooted in the Institute of Indian Art's mission. The original goal of this school was to provide economic return from our natural talents as craft producers..."

Indeed. I have known this murderous assimilative principle. And, intimately. I've given over love, life, and breath in the pursuit of this mission that I have made my own-- that I have allowed to enter my blood, and my language, through language. I have learned the lesson well: we say SELF-DETERMINATION THROUGH THE ARTS, instead of ASSIMILATION THROUGH THE ARTS because it just sounds better. It's no different though. In an "eat, or be eaten" economy and socioeconomic paradigm such as the IAIA is, one eats or is eaten.

We don't speak about it, but it's the truth. "The dynasty" and "The privileged," and "The chosen ones" are phrases used at the IAIA nowadays.

And the phrases in and of themselves are not poison. When coming from the mouths of under-served, sad, and angry IAIA students, this is when they are DEADLY. We have been groomed to compete with one another, to cut one another down at every opportunity, and to look the other way when one of our own is struggling, hurting, drinking/medicating themselves to death, and then dying.

Survival of the fittest right? This is the true story of the IAIA. Not the whole story, but so much of that which has not been spoken thus far. And I, among others, are writing it, saying it. But it won't be easy. And we'll most likely be criticized, condemned, and/or killed as a result-- because what we are bringing to light has the potential to effect steady streams of revenue...places once extremely comfortable. Someone might have told me--perhaps an elder--that if I thought I would find ASYLUM at the IAIA, I was dead wrong. They didn't.

Too late now.

". . . Three very important questions must be addressed: "How do we share and accept another's Indigenous perceptions?" "How do we go beyond the 'me' emphasis that is so all-important to Western man and create a 'we' or tribal thought? And of equal importance, "How do we balance group or tribal identity with the individualistic focus of Western man?..."

Just posed this same question to a good friend and colleague of mine, young, a writer, Dinè and headed for the East Coast now. I didn't pose it in quite this way, but emphasized the fact that it's only going to get harder to maintain the balance between group/tribal identity and "individualism" especially for those graduating from the IA this term. He didn't really respond, but I sensed more defense and defensiveness than anything. It wasn't an attack, just something I'm concerned with, especially when it comes to balancing business with Indian identity, and integrity. Especially as we all venture out into "the real world".

". . . What are the group's shared purpose and intent behind the RELATIONS: indigenous dialogue exhibition?. . ."

And furthermore: how can we best cultivate and utilize the individual insights, talents, and POWER inside of each individual participant? How can I make my voice, questions, points of discourse, more readily available for the group to most effectively utilize?

"...We, as a group or as cultural representatives, cannot allow ourselves to be dictated to by non-Indigenous philosophy. It is the creation of this Indigenous philosophy that gives our group a sense of purpose."

Would like to speak more about this. Especially with a specific emphasis on listening to what the younger participants have to say. What exists when "they" (meaning non-Indigenous people) become a "non-issue"? What happens when what they are, or are not, dictating falls away? What energies/resources have been spent on "resisting their philosophies" at the expense of our own communities and children?

". . . If we don't challenge or attempt to make serious change to what appears to be an Indigenous and Indian identity that for all practical purposes is cosmetic our children and grand children will inherit an even less clear cultural identity than we experience. . . "

And we have seen it. My younger Indian/Native/Indigenous identity is not so unclear-- but it is extremely violent, volatile, sometimes disharmonious, painful, terrible, terrifying, rife with hypocrisy, bureaucratic, holistic, beautiful and extremely deadly when misapplied.

Ha`ah. Indeed. Our children need US, more than they ever needed our WORDS. The old English adage goes: Actions speak louder than words. And indeed they do.

dahwaaheh` ❖❖❖

❖❖❖ first: thank you sara for your words. i am going to have to sit down and mull it over for a little while in my head before i can respond. but it was definitely inspiring. and to be a part of IAIA as well...speaking of wording, you make me feel like i have hoofs on this keyboard.

micah, i miss you. i'm trying to find a chance to call you.

i didn't mean to offend anyone by stating that they were being over-wordy, it just seemed like sometimes people get defensive. but it is true, we have been taught that our only importance is how well we can use the english language to defend ourselves, to make our argument valid. or sometimes using our own language to prove something, even if it makes no sense to anyone else. but this all seems irrelevant to the big picture.

and sometimes the english words that we find to express ourselves are beautiful. i understand that it is part of survival. i thought i would include something i wrote for an interview. ❖❖❖

❖❖❖ *What does Indigenous mean to you?* ❖❖❖

❖❖❖ Indigenous. I suppose it is what you make it. Everyone is Indigenous to somewhere, even if it isn't where he or she is at the present. I think Indigenous comes with a deep feeling of belonging, and the confidence within that. Some people seem incredibly insecure about it, or try to make others insecure about it, but I think it is mostly about knowing your own RIGHT PLACE in the world. ❖❖❖

❖❖❖ *What excites you about your present art project/work?* ❖❖❖

❖❖❖ I am really excited to work with people I respect on a higher level, pushing the boundaries of the power that art has, and questioning what we all have done with it. I also have an opportunity to make a piece with my mother, which is interesting because we have a lot of healing to do there. I am at the point that I think a lot of the damage that has been done to the world comes from the initial relationship or loss thereof with the first parent; mother. Healing this gap that, I believe, exists in most every relationship to everything around you; the earth, loss of logical connection with the "natural" world, people, culture, etc... ❖❖❖

❖❖❖ *Write about bringing the elders up to speed.* ❖❖❖

❖❖❖ I don't think that any one generation is more important. I do think that the communication gap needs to be bridged between all generations so that we can all evolve healthily. I think if we all were able to deal with our issues, and let go of our insecurities, there wouldn't be a need to judge either way. If the communication gap were to be opened, I would like to say: Why are you so caught up in yourselves that you haven't been able to make this world something beautiful for all of us to live in? What have you not let yourself be that you have prohibited us from being what we want to be? Isn't that what you would like to say to your own parents? (Who are the young ones here? Aren't we all?)

Prisons are made to house our lost will-to-live. They wanted to fully live at the time of birth and were not given the love or the chance because it was not given to their parents, or their parents' parents. I would say: TAKE SOME RESPONSIBILITY.

And I would be more than open to hear what they have to say. That's where it starts. ❖❖❖

♦♦♦   Good stuff that makes me think. Meanwhile my tribe (as a people who knew why, had purpose and a unique identity) dies while relying on the books for their new instinct. I'm so used to laying everything on the table for dissection that I forget and thereby become wordy and condescending. Oops. ♦♦♦

▶▶▶   Wow...sara. i need to, as rose stated, mull over this some more. i relate to that as well. righty-O, i dig the writing sara. i tend to see a lot of kiddies fading away and native things aren't gonna save them...they just need help!! i don't look down upon anything native or indigenous, cos there is much to be said for survival.

Hey!! and our mommies are lost now! hey!! daddies somewhere else!! hey!! and we love the abuse because it makes us feel like we are needed!! <<too many times this is going on with native people.

i've been thinking and thinking of words to aid in this dialogue. as you can read...words aren't my greatest. sounds and images are things i relate to the best. symbols and recognizable objects i've been trying to gather and see what ya'll think. so far they are negative in nature, yet unthreatening. like...syringes, scissors, beer bottles, can guns, religious stuff, no smoking signs, tattoos, brief cases...yah know, things indians carry or have carried.

i've been thinking of this monster as in a production sense. i used to stage manage and promote music venues...so i was thinking in terms of the visuals, as well as concepts.

i really feel the need to have things that are visually intriguing. in order to convey the sense of RELATING. i know you can define that in all kinds of ways or say the white man dictates the way we shouldn't be relating or blah. but really, at first you relate with what you see, then the conceptual stuff and ideas can be related. that's just me. Like i said before...with no offense to anyone, a shit load of people look at santa fe and IAIA and they just don't get it. and that's fine, you can't please everyone. but really nothing is interesting anymore...it needs too much explaining...it's too minimal. and it sucks cos i see techniques and ideas in people's work i like...but i don't dig the overall. and that's important. ▶▶▶

○○○ Hello Whole Tribe,

Sara, good to hear from you and feel your energy. I was over at the Poetry Jam at the Lensic on Friday because Rose and her band were playing. I don't usually like to go listen to Poetry readings because I find them mostly boring. But this was different mainly because of the young people. Their poetry was alive and vibrant and actually saying something. I left feeling hopeful for the human race (which is rare)........like this coming generation has a good head on its shoulders and we might just be able to change this mess we are all in. I totally agree with your hurt and anger at having been neglected......it is a generational disease that I believe started when the Spanish came into New Mexico and thoroughly abused the Pueblos till what was once a continuum of mostly unbroken people raising unbroken babies was broken. In my family, my grandmother's and grandfather's parents both died in the flu epidemics and thus were orphans who were abused by Catholic Boarding Schools........and with dying grandmothers who left them too soon........thus created a wonderful start for my mother's generation who got totally abused by uncles and their motherless mother, thus creating the next generation of dysfunction that had my generation of ignored, powerless children who were brought up with guilt and shame, trying to find our lost identity while being told we are nothing. So we had your generation......one more step down the rabbit hole....of neglect.....of loss.......of searching. Thus I am sooooooooooo ready to do something different. I AM the product of my cultural story (the good part and the broken part) and as I'm watching my grandchildren come into the world, I am more desperate to have something better for them to hold onto and feel strong about...they are our future. I do not want them to feel as I have felt by my own people...thrown out and unwanted. I am not so angry about it anymore but am seeing how I can/might change this sad story. We and our children are IT.

I was talking to my Anglo husband this morning about "Home". He has a hard time with "feeling at home." He was born in North Dakota, grew up in California, went to school in Arizona, moved to Hawaii for 20 years and is now trying to live here in New Mexico. None of these places feels like home to him although he likes Hawaii the best. He did tell me that when he was in Ireland, he felt very happy (he is Norwegian and Irish descent). I wonder if he would feel good in Norway. Anyway.......this made me think about land base as something that identifies us as who we are.........thus Indigenous to that region. I once watched a show about how all peoples came from Africa and how they migrated in different directions and became all the different races that exist. What caught my attention was that they were saying that it takes 20 generations for a group of people to totally change genetically to fit into a new environment (to become part of their environment). Ummmmm??? I think it's interesting because it fits into my feeling of being connected to the southwest in a genetic kind of way. My genes have adapted through many generations to be "from here." This is another aspect of being "Indigenous." Although, being that my father was of German descent........I just might feel at home in Germany....someday I'll have to go there and see. But this is all saying that "blood amount" is what makes us "Indins".......which I don't believe.....but I am somehow genetically "at home" in the southwest. Anyway....food for thought. ○○○

4.11.06

▲▲▲ Whole tribe, Please email me in your language the word relations and the translation, i.e. all my relations, my relations, our relations, etc. ▲▲▲

●●● Relations?

WORDS

words on relations, Indigenous languages, spoken, sung, chanting All words dealing with different levels of relationship... *Pili* - to cling... therefore close relationships...relatives. *Pilina* - joining...relationships that are joined and fit. *Pilikana* – relationships who are kin. *Pili koko* - blood relations. *Pili 'ohana* - family relations. *Pilialoha* - relationships joined by love. *Pili kâmau* - relationships joined by friendship. *Pili wehena* - inseparable relationship. *Pili mua* - preferred friend or relations. *Pili loko* - closely related. *Pili ma ka hanauna* - relations established several generations previously.

BREATH

breath becomes part of the dialogue, heard, felt, whispers, first breath Breath—*hâ* Spiritual breath—*ea* Breath of life—*mauli ola* Last breath—*hanu pau* Deep breath—*hanu nui* Breathe—*haha, manawaea, puailewa, haluhalu, hapaipu, hapahapai, ehaha, hô, hohô, nae'ôpuakau, nakinaki* Whisper—*hâwanawana.*

SMELLS

sage, cedar, sweetgrass, copal, Hawaiian plants, sense of place Sweet smelling—*'ala, 'a'ala, onaona, paoa, kûpaoa, mâpu, moani, anuhea, waianuhea, kolopua, hô'ala, kâna'e, nae, kaluhea pê, puîa* Fragrance—*'a'ala, onaona* Plants—*maile, laua'e, mokihana,* coconut oil, *kukui* nut oil.

MASKS

Looking inside the mask, transformation interactive with viewer. Hawai'i isn't known for a variety of masks...they only had the gourd helmet/mask, called by the three names below...masks were worn in order not to defile the sacred place of an opposing Calendrical Patron...the priesthood of the opposite season would wear the mask as not to offend the ongoing Patron...worn to hide the priest's identity, allowing him to walk through the opposing calendrical season unscathed. *Makahuna*—face hider *Makaku i ke alo*—mask of confrontation *Ipu Nui*—gourd helmet mask.

LODGE

46' diameter, 26' tall entrance to Relations, steel, performance space. The most famous "sweat" lodge was the *Hale Hâwai*—women used this lodge for transcendential rituals...to distance the men from the living world, to join the world of the Ancestors. In order to return to normalcy, the men then had to be reborn into this dimension by going through the *Hale 'O Papa*. The two most important lodges in a Hawaiian village was the *Hale Mua* for the men and the *Hale 'Âina* for the women.

HOLE

6' x 9' x 8' deep positive casting of the negative space, intuitive creating Because we have a Hole that identifies the Mother...the vaginal opening where the menstrual magma flows through, creating all life...I believe that the Hole created by Bob is his personal journey into his personal awareness. Something very private... something *Kapu* to us.

+HOLE

positive representation of earth removed from hole. *Puka*—is a hole that penetrates all the way through. *Lua*—is a hole that has a bottom.

BEINGS COMMUNICATING

Art communicating to Art, concepts reaching out to the other artists. *Lononuiâkea* is our Sacred Patron of Sound...

BUNDLES

Prayers? Bundles tied to lodge, our spirituality, our prayer? Offerings... bundles were given in offering to a specific ritual or a specific desire, or a specific Ancestor or Elemental. Bundles are called *Pû'olo*...filled with bits and pieces, or specific artifacts that have meaning to the one offering the prayer. The Bundle is the physical that succeeds in giving us satisfaction as to the giving...in actuality it is the "energy," that nurtures the Ancestor or Elemental...our energy in creating the Bundle...the energy of what the Bundle contains...our pureness of heart.

LIVING ON THE CRUST

Honestly speaking to who we are as Indigenous people. Technically, Indigenous defines the first people of any given place... An Indo-European word meaning, "born or produced in a particular place, native." Aborigine—from the Latin aborigines, plural, "from the beginning"—an Indigenous inhabitant especially as contrasted with an invading or colonizing people. The crust or earth is—*honua*, a contraction of *honu'ea*—the hawksbill turtle...the Polynesian saw their earth as a series of turtle shells throughout the Pacific Ocean—you traveled to each by going beyond the horizon. They lived ever so gently on the land of their mother.

PRAYER

Communication with the ancestors Prayer is perhaps the most important component of a Hawai'i Maoli's everyday life, some of which are...*Pule*— prayer, *Pule 'aha, Pule 'ana'ana, Pule hai, Pule hana aloha, Pule he'e, Pule ho'ola, Pule ho'ola'a, Pule ho'omaika'i, Pule ho'omau, Pule ho'onoa, Pule ho'onoho, Pule ho'opomaika'i, Pule ho'ouluulu 'ai, Pule ho'ounauna, Pule ho'owilimo'o, Pule hui, Pule huikala, Pule huahula, Pule ipu, Pule kahea, Pule kahiu, Pule kahoaka, Pule kaholo, Pule kala, Pule kameha'i, Pule kuili, Pule kuni, Pule mahiki, Pule 'ohana, Pule pale, Pule 'umi, Pule wi.*

CORE THAT ATTRACTS US SPIRITUALLY

That which joins us together, nature? Perhaps best put, our core is our Spiritual and Sacred Law which we call *'Ihi Kapu*... And that which joins us as humans, *kanaka maoli,* is the Dual Polarity...the *Loina Wahine,*

Female Principle, and the *Loina Kane*, Male Principle. This joins us with "All of those who came before," The Ancestors, *Akua Aumakua*.

POWER/MANA

Our strength as Indigenous peoples. Despite our personal lives...those events that governed our fathers and mothers and now indirectly or directly govern us aside, that which gives me strength is the fact that my Ancestors are always with me...I try to stand firmly on their shoulders.

POWER OBJECTS

Creating objects of "power." For me objects of power are our *Ki'i*...our images...those vessels that hold the Essence of our Ancestors and our Elementals.

NATURE

Stone, earth, sky, wind, fire, plants, animals, humans, insects, everything. Our cultures believes in the Elementals, that which the missionaries termed as Gods and Goddesses...Because we are connected with all things born by the Mother, we are also connected to nature...and with great respect we revered Her...they too became part of the Ancestral genome. *Kumu honua...Kumulipo*...the history and story of our people and all species born to Mother Earth...make us kin.

INSTINCT

The new art ism...intuitism (you can order your t-shirt today). In our culture, there is no intuition...intuition comes from "All of those who came before," in actuality, it is a dialogue between the Ancestors and our Soul Cluster...unfortunately the missionary wiped our knowing clean of this belief...and we are only now understanding that we must again allow our Spirit and Soul to receive the Voice.

WE CHANTED 'IT' IN

Our words and dialogue will create relations...Because our people believed totally in Creative Visualization...we chanted everything into creation... the great Pô, the dimensional of Ancestral power, the Great Mind... *Mana'o Nui*...allowed for the physical. Our poetry, chants, prayers are filled with the process of Creation, both physical and metaphysical.

OUR CHANT WILL CHANGE THE WORLD

Our dialogue/chant will begin to change the way the world looks at Indigenous. Having said this, our continued chanting will indeed change the world, that is if we agree as to what should be chanted into it. As the saying goes, "careful what you wish for." Of course, all life is an experience, the good and the bad of it...but as Indigenous, I think we've had a good share of the bad...goodness must flow.

RITUAL/CEREMONY-IT WAS ATTRACTED THAT WAY

Remembering where we came from. Spiritually, we come from the *Pô*... *Pulotu*...that place beyond the beyond. Physically, we come from *Nu'umealani*...*Healani*...that place beyond the beyond.

WHO ARE WE

Who are our children? We, inclusive of our children are from the Great Indigenous Construct!!! *Kanaka Maoli*...*Kanaka* describes humans, in all of their very fluid motion...*Maoli*, claims us as true and genuine...that which gives reverence to the Source.

WE MUST KEEP THE LINE OF WHERE WE CAME FROM INTACT

Our line is unbroken. Yes, our line is indeed broken. Not altogether, however...giving us hope that in a generation or two...perhaps, we might return to the Mother...in respect to this land that is quickly decaying and perhaps, our prayer of visualization will allow us to return to the Ancestors...to speak for them. I speak for those who cannot speak.

RECREATE OURSELVES

21st century Indigenous people We are a continuum...each generation bringing their piece to the whole fabric of time...the best of the past, careful to add that which can be honored by Ancestors...our piece of the puzzle added to the Whole. *Pono no*!!!

STORYLINE IS NOT TOLD YET

The future is yet to be determined Of course, the future is yet to be determined, because we have yet to chant it into creation...this is where the careful enters...for we must chant not only what is acceptable to us in this present generation, but that which will sit well with our children and their children...careful to create a world that will be their haven...careful to leave behind the balm that will heal their Souls.

THE WORLD IS DISCONNECTED—WE ARE DISCONNECTED LESS

Indigenous people still have intuition/instinct. We are disconnected because we have stopped listening to the Voice of the Ancestors. this is what we must introduce...the method, the process, the Way!!! *Ke Ala 'Iki*!!!

CATALYST

Our dialogue will be a catalyst for understanding/change. As director of *Hale Naua* III, Society of Hawaiian Arts, over the past 30 years we have mounted well over 150 exhibitions...all with the same dialogue, all with the same message. How to return to our spiritual source, our strength, our identity...physically and spiritually. Our exhibitions have been a catalyst for hundreds of young people, who have not only found the way comfortable and easy to slip into because it is their one true skin, but as artists, it opened new horizons, where their personal dialogue added to the Voice inspired others.

INDIGENOUS

Our definition. Going back to the beginning of our time in the Pacific, say perhaps, 4-5 thousand years ago...we called ourselves *Kanaka Maoli*.

And, because we were seafarers, the land did not hold us restricted. But, since we have lived here in *Ka Pae 'Aina*, The Cluster of Lands Placed in a Row...we are attached. One *hanau*...the islands are known as the Sands of our birth...we became of this place...but, we are from all the places that our Ancestors stepped foot.

Kanaka Maoli..., Kama'aina, Maoli, 'Oiwi, Kupa, Keiki Papa,, ●●●

➤➤➤ the word "relations" is synonymous to "everything" in Keresan. the word is *shoet-nei-khi.* that is as good as i can spell it phoenetically. i don't know the word for relations in Towa, but i will try and find out. i am more fluent in Keresan than Towa, just because it was my first language. hope this is good. ➤➤➤

◆◆◆ Below are a couple of words in Keres, the Acoma language. Other Keres-speaking Pueblos are Santo Domingo, Cochiti, San Felipe, Santa Ana, Zia, and Laguna. Words may vary from Pueblo to Pueblo with colloquial variation although they're generally the same.

Stai-yah-tru-tyaimesheeh=Descendent relatives

Stah-we-tyaimesheeh=Relatives following

Words above are phonetically spelled, and even meanings and pronunciations are "localized." ◆◆◆

◆◆◆ This is what I was given and is probably profoundly simplistic, i.e. grandma's or grandpa's remembrance or something vague from a tribal dictionary. Chiricahua Apache (tribe specific) *Daanaht'eke:* unspecifying what we are related to but basically our relations. Muskogie Creek *Itta-piha:* to be related. *Yakima Inmi ma tiin-ma.* ◆◆◆

❖❖❖ *Selo'tine*—"Our Relatives" in Dene *Suline*. Literal translation: *Sela*—hand. *O'*—from, *Tine*—kin or relations. ❖❖❖

4.17.06

○○○ Well, I don't want to speak for Rose but I will describe what I'm thinking of for the "Mask Room" and also for the "Prayer Room". I am hoping we get a variety of masks for this project. The idea is "relations," or our connection to "others"...be it animals, human, insects, rocks...whatever. The plan is that we have all these masks that people can walk up to but cannot see them unless they put their faces inside the masks and look through the eye sockets to see reflected in a mirror the outside of the masks with their own eyes looking through. This is an attempt to get people to relate more with other beings by visually seeing themselves transformed in the mirror. So, we have this wall of back sides of masks that you have to look through to be able to see the front sides. Does this makes sense???? So when you're making your masks, make sure you can fit it over your heads (as artists we have the biggest heads, so we shouldn't have a problem with others not fitting inside, hee...hee) just kidding. The other room, I'm working out a piece with Rose. We are "re-doing" our beginning with each other.......it is our prayer, as we feel that that is where a lot of the pain and suffering we all feel comes from. I have the clay gathering and set up on a table to begin and, hopefully, I'll start this week making a life-size figure to hold the being that Rose will make and place inside. As I have been imagining this piece, I keep feeling like there is a need for a male presence with it and keep wanting my figure to be leaning up against a post or male symbol of sorts???? Does this intrigue any of our male artists to do???? Just a thought........I like the Whole Tribe creating a "family" in the exhibit (that's what tribes are made up of, huh? families). ○○○

4.20.06

♦♦♦ The hole: The proposed depth, reason for or earth excavation methods were never important. Those who entered the hole expressed personal thoughts and remembrances, sometimes tied to metaphor, at other times actual. Those of us with pervasive Western training considered the hole simply as an individualistic and logical endeavor, sometimes suggested as a metaphor for death.

Others related to the hole as a transition from one perception to another, perhaps as a metaphor for life and change. The decision to make a mold of the hole and suspend the mold in the gallery brought the digging procedure to an end. This ending came with the realization that I could present the hole from the negative, thereby forcing the viewer to acknowledge the hole from beyond the surface of the hole.

The reverse hole: This hole will accompany the suspended hole and will be placed on the gallery floor as juxtaposition. This will probably be a pile of adobe bricks framing the negative space within the hole. The resolution of this image hasn't been reached but will probably be either of a roof of cedar or an open space on top as with the original hole. There is no clear statement as to the purpose of this negative hole other than creating the sense of transition or transformation that is the backbone of the RELATIONS project.

The (diameter of 40 ft., height of 21 ft.) lodge: The framework of the lodge is now nearing completion as I adjust the four legs to a related curve. Previously the lodge legs were not attached but I have recently decided to create a hub in the center for stability. Conceptually the lodge is a place to return to, a place where cultural knowledge is kept and disbursed to those who wished to complete the circle/cycle. The need for all to find that 'lodge' for our own grounding and Rocky's mention that in Maoli (Hawaiian) oral history the circle continues underground gives this structure a purpose in the RELATIONS project.

Mask: For the Rox project, as of yet undefined.

Birth Canal: Question of who does what and personal involvement. ◆◆◆

4.20.06

○○○ Hello Everyone,

I have started my mask and the large piece that I'm doing with Rose. It's all in clay (of course). Feel like we have to meet again and walk the rooms and get clearer on what's what. The meeting the other day ended kinda foggy to me although I thought some really great things were brought up using Harry's photos and Rose's idea of being bombarded with images as we come out of the "birth canal." I like that very much. Also the leaving of all the "ideas" and "images" before we enter the "prayer" room. Micah, thanks for sharing your ideas. I think they would fit in nicely with all we've been talking about. just updating,,,,,, ○○○

4.27.06

▲▲▲ Whole Tribe,

I have been reading a book called *Toward a New Civilization—Why We Must Tame our Instincts to Save the World*...the author almost gets it except that he talks about Indigenous peoples only as barbarians. I like to think that we share our instincts to save the world or at least change it.

"Culture is behavior peculiar to man: it consists of art, rituals, ceremonies, morals and law. It is a movement in the direction of making human life more secure and enduring, following life-sustaining and avoiding life-destroying conduct. Given the same requisites, conventional wisdom identified culture with civilization—a neologism which emerged in 18th century France—but separated the two, although they were for a long time synonymous by associating culture with primitive societies and civilization with developed communities. But culture and civilization have different foundations. The former is dependent upon a general improvement of the mind and behavior; the latter's benefits are conditioned upon a division of society into the haves and have-nots, ie., freedmen and slaves."

Talk to us, ▲▲▲

○○○ Hello Whole Tribe...

I don't have a problem with what you put together to take to NYC... sounds like us. I did have a reaction to the title of that book you are reading, Joseph, and the quote: "Taming our Instincts to Save the World" just made me want to scream. Taming is NOT what I have in mind to do......... that's been the problem all along which disconnected us from nature to begin with and why we don't know shit anymore. Yes, I know I didn't read the book so may not know what he means by that phrase but I took it to mean that instincts are something "bad" that need to be controlled and "tamed". I did not agree to the quote that culture is behavior particular to humans. Culture to me is about anything that works together in groups in a way that nurtures and naturally promotes growth (life)...... this can be found in sourdough bread to plant guilds to flocks of birds to my compost pile. Humans are pretty bad at nurturing these days and thus we are steadily promoting death. I guess I agree that "civilization" is not very "culturally based." I've been slowly working on my mask and piece with Rose. Don't have much more to say. Would like to hear what people are doing also??? anyways........ ○○○

4.29.06

♦♦♦ A Native Embassy in Washington, D.C.

The Mdewakanton Sioux Tribe has suggested that the National Congress of American Indians should establish a headquarters in Washington, D.C and they have suggested an available modern building on the street where international embassies are located. An "Embassy of Tribal Nations" here might improve the national government's recognition of tribal sovereignty; it could also provide a center for tribal leaders who come to Washington for negotiations. This idea has been floating around for thirty years, but now money seems available. For more details see www.indiancountry.com/content.cfm.

Again: Why don't they make an embassy for all RELATIONS that protect a more profound understanding of our existence beyond the me and blood. They already have a warehouse on the mall called the US-NMAI that is awaiting a more useful function beyond the romantic, historic and decorative INDIAN IMAGE, now awaiting further development. But, of course, that Idea may be in the distant (400 yrs?) future. ♦♦♦

5.3.06

➤➤➤ You mentioned the children. I've been wondering how to address that. It seems to me that the work we do is for this generation and those that follow. Let's hope we can create something worthwhile. The red light is flashing not only for Indians but for all on this planet and it seems to me that culture, identity is one thing and just staying alive is quite another. I have no solutions but I do know that whatever the answer may be it just has to include an awareness of this world situation we are in. It's much too brutal and too close to be ignored. And that in itself puts us in another

arena when it comes to identity, brotherhood, and the survival of following generations. Am I making any sense here???? I just think I am rambling on. It's been a long long day. ➤➤➤

◆◆◆ After our meeting on Tuesday I had some thoughts. The reverse sound of Indian music was powerful, haunting and unforgettable and is enough by itself. The thought that the reverse hole should become a meditation chamber or large incense burner horrifies me. I suspect that we are succumbing to linear thinking by creating an answer to the questions we pose. I don't think that we need to explain the music by playing it's interpretation in its correct version and I don't think that the reverse hole needs to be anything more than a pile of mankind's manipulated dirt that reflects the hole itself. The project is going to create a tremendous dialogue with the questions we are posing. We shouldn't be timid at this point and provide answers to viewers who haven't a clue as to our statement. Not yet at least. We have a long way to go (beyond the 59 days till blast off). Let's create the questions in this exhibit. I personally hate the curtains style opening, the spotlights pointing out individuals as heroes (with its silent glorification of acculturation) and the announcer ignoring our cultural loss, pain and apathy. I would hope that my ancestors demand more from me. But, that's my issue, isn't it? ◆◆◆

◯◯◯ I appreciate your wisdom here. Thanks for reminding us to just put it out there and not worry if people are gonna understand it or not. I don't want to "explain" me/us forever either......it's a relief to think of just doing what we feel like expressing and in that there is a true dialogue. To me, this show has opened a door for me to make something that has no thinking of "selling" it to anyone, nor trying to relay a message to people that I'm begging to be understood by, nor trying to do "what's pretty" or "right" or "indin".....it's about my dialogue with myself and with those close to me. I really want feedback about what comes to us when we talk about "birth" (for instance) or "prayer" or "relations?????" I want to know if you thought any more about the piece that Rose and I are creating? Everyone else, I asked Bob if he would add to the piece we are doing because Rose and I thought it needed the male energy part of the picture. I found myself – while working and picturing this piece (a mother leaning back against [?] with her baby) – feeling sad that there wasn't the support of the male energy there. So I thought, why not ask.......I did, no one responded. So I asked Bob directly if he was interested in doing something for her to lean against. He said that he would put his thoughts to it. Thank you. The backwards singing was so powerful and eerie that I left disturbed and excited by it. Here is a piece of this picture that might bring up a lot of stuff in people. I, myself, have a hard time just leaving it backwards without somewhere making it outwards – as in breathing in and then breathing out. We don't have to explain that, but in my own thinking....as with wanting the "hole" to have the inside and outside represented.....I, too, want the song to be both........it finishes the breathing for me. To just breathe in would be death. ◯◯◯

5.4.06

✧✧✧ *Guwaadzi`* group:

Just a note about my involvement in the "dialogue." As is often the case, for elders and younger ones alike, a map (cultural, political, artistic, and otherwise) is needed to be most effective and vital. Coming into the dialogue late, I'm still unclear as to what I, as writer/scholar/ advocate/

younger voice, can really contribute to the discourse and process of reaming/cultivating and erecting the very visual "exhibit".

I'll do what I can--but I need guidance. And I know I'm not alone. I'm not a visual artist, by any means, so I may need more guidance in this particular process than most. My talents are primarily literary and ideological, and I hope you can use them in some way.

Thank you, so much, Whole Tribe--Bob, Joseph, Rose, Micah, Roxanne...EVERYONE. Looking forward to all insights/guidance/criticisms etc. I'm still learning. ✧✧✧

OOO Wow your writing makes me immediately want you present to bounce things off of. Please come to our next meeting?? Thank you for responding. OOO

5.5.06
➤➤➤ Saturday morning. Rox I just read your email you said, "Its about my dialogue with myself and those close to me" I like that. ➤➤➤

5.9.06
➤➤➤ Most of the time it is difficult for me to talk about things that I feel more than understand. But I will give it a try. Our group meeting covered a lot of ground and it seems to me three subjects - change, spirituality, and identity tend to come up a lot.

For a person who never fit in to any place comfortably, change has always been an awareness for me – being of a number of nationalities and having my strongest cultural imprint being the North American white experience followed by my Native American and Hawaiian background. Who am I really?

To look into my identity is a very challenging ride. To begin with, I don't think there is really any conclusion or solid answer. And to know that my identity continues to change daily is hard to wrap my head around.

When it comes to identity and change the only thing I can count on is change.

At times I catch myself talking about transcending culture and I can tell from the response I get some people don't understand what I mean or at times become very fearful. When I say 'transcending culture' I am not talking about denying my cultural background because I am who I am and there's not much I can do about that. However, I can put that in perspective and realize that my world – at age 60 – is a lot different that it was at 25 say. I have learned that I don't have to be this or that or the other to identify myself for someone else's pleasure, curiosity, or comfort.

I think about culture, religion, nationality and identity quite a bit and have learned that when culture is used as a weapon it causes a lot of chaos, evil, violence, greed, hate. And yet, on the other hand, culture can be and often is dazzling. When my daughter Sarah asks me to go to her Hula class, and the room of 20 or so young women start to dance to the chants and the *ipu* gourds, it makes my heart fly away. ➤➤➤

5.10.06

◯◯◯ it's really good to hear from you and refreshing also. I had this dream which has been going around in my head all day.....I want to share it.

Rose and I were on our way to Santa Fe to go to the meeting. At the top of the Santa Fe Opera hill, we took a side trip up the side of the hill to go see "old Pojoaque Pueblo." We had never seen it. At the top of the hill there were mounds of dirt from the old pueblo site, but on top of this were two canons....old and rusty. There was a sign and I went up to read it. It told about how when the Spanish arrived in New Mexico and were attacking Pueblos when they came to Old Pojoaque and were gonna blow them up with canons, but low and behold, the pueblo brought out their own canons and started firing them at the Spanish who were so surprised that they left. Me and Rose laughed and laughed. At this point, Harry showed up and we were still laughing but we went looking for the elevator to go up to the meeting room. We got in the room and no one was there yet, so I went downstairs to check out the show that was going on in the museum.

It was boring and I started back up the elevator. When the doors opened, I saw that the meeting was going on. There was Harry at the far end of the table, Bob halfway, Rose at the end closest to me, and across from her was this older white guy with a pad and pen, writing. Harry was saying some list which the white guy was writing down with enthusiasm. Harry seemed depressed and his words were monotoned. Then this white guy turned to Rose and was telling her that it was her turn. He started telling her what to do and how to do it......and she was suppose to make a list also and repeat it back to him. She looked so uncomfortable and upset. Then she looked over at me kinda pleadingly and I just smiled at her. She then turned back and told the guy that she was not gonna do it. He got upset and told her that she had to. She again said no. He threatened to "tell on her and take her name off the list." She held her ground and said that she didn't care. He got up and left the room slamming the door behind him. I then happily walked to the table and sat down and asked jokingly how the meeting was going. Everyone looked shell-shocked and started trying to defend or explain or uncompromise themselves...etc. Then I turned and asked Rose, "What do you want to do?" She said that she wanted to let people bring pillows into the room and find a nice spot to lay down and go to sleep. I laughed with delight and threw my chair backwards until me and the chair were laying on the ground. My feet were sticking up in the air and I saw that Harry had done the same and his feet were up in the air and we were laughing and laughing. That was the end.

I believe in dreams being the eyes of the subconscious that might tell us things that could help us. So I always study my dreams when I remember them. It's like when someone is dreaming about dancing here in the pueblo......they are needing to bring in the dance because the dance is knocking at their door. Anyway.........so I guess I wanted to share this dream because I think that it's about us looking within ourselves for what we are really about.....not about what "outside" sources might want from us. I liked what you said, Harry, about "going beyond culture." I think that this is what that's about also........yes, we are bound to our specific cultures, but I believe there is a deeper bond than the cultural one. Maybe it would be called "our human instinctiveness." Again, its getting out of the mind and into the senses that makes us aware of the "bigger" picture. That's what makes Indigenous peoples "special," because they practice, or are closer to, that instinctual place than, say, the Anglo Race. But really, we are all children of this Earth and are capable of being part of our environment or not. If culture is not connecting us to this instinctual place, then it is a dead culture. OK, a friend just came over and we had a good talk about all this. He is a good one to talk to. He is a searcher for the reasons behind cultural traditions. To just go through the motions because "that's how its done" or "that's what makes you an indin," without knowing the real reasons why those traditions came into existence to begin with, is just playing out a part with no real essence behind it........no real prayer....empty words. Anyway, I guess I talked long enough........you just got me wanting to gab. See how you are?! ○○○

5.16.06

○○○ [pertaining to DNA] Dear Whole Tribe,

I think that there are some very interesting questions about DNA that are being brought up out there. I am considered half Pueblo Indian and half German, and have thought about this "blood percentage" thing all my life. I did grow up not in my tribal village but very closely connected to it... going "home" every weekend. I grew up dancing in the ceremonies and realizing later that I had the outlook of the world that came from this tribe (or my mother). At 20 I moved into the village and have been here for the last 24 years now. I raised my very anglo looking children here and they participate in tribal affairs and I consider them "pueblos." I have never gotten to visit Germany but have always wondered if I would find it strangely familiar. I have met several Germans who I had this immediate feeling that I understood. I have never felt that with any other "group" outside the Pueblos. So I do think that there is a genetic personality coding that comes with us because of blood, but I would be very careful not to make any judgments about who is what because I also believe that how you were raised makes a huge difference. I helped to raise two almost full blood Pueblo children who were brought up in Los Angeles until they were 8 and 10. If you were to look at them they would appear "Indian," but their actions and their talk were very "LA" and they didn't know simple protocols and ways of seeing that would have been associated to their race. Which brings up the question of whether those "Indian traits" are really what makes one Native or is it the blood and what would that make you want to do or not even if you were given no traditional training?? My son's father left us when my son was born and he had no contact with him. When my son was about 3 or 4, I let him pick out his own shoes at the store. He went straight to the shoes that his father used to wear, which were very odd grey dress shoes. I was shocked that he would have the same tastes as his father without ever having met him. Is that from the blood? I would guess that there are things that come with blood line that are just encoded. You might be able to sense things out in environments that others couldn't just because your genetics have been created to do that over thousands of years. We are truly in very strange mixed-up times........maybe we just need to get used to telling a little longer story when we say who we are instead of one simple thing. ○○○

✳✳✳ My Indianness or Where's the macaroni ??

hello fellow tribe members, I'm happy to finally add to the dialogue:

I was reading about the DNA dialogue submitted, and was struck by the clinicalness of all this. I never really questioned my blood quantum....... the surrounding community where I came from left no doubt in my mind about who I was....

I come from the Peepeekisis, Plains Cree/Saulteaux Nation in southern Saskatchewan, Canada. The name Plains Cree/Saulteaux is in itself a term given to us by the French.

I was recently told by a Parisian friend of mine that Cree, is really Cree' and it means 'to scream,' another version is Cree' meaning 'Creation;' I know, what's the difference in the spelling, none that I can see. Saulteaux is also a French word meaning from 'the Sault St. Marie' which I understand are the famous falls in Ontario Canada (right on the border of the US/Canada) where all the Ojibway once congregated on an annual basis. Whether I have this correct is not important to me as I pretty much know that I am an Oji-Cree and I know we were once allies of the French against the British. This was pointed out to me by a well-known Oneida writer who as fate would have it, had ancestors who allied with the British against guess who.....the Cree.

I identify myself as Cree although my mother constantly points out that I am also Ojibway and that I am more Ojibway than Cree; this argument has gone on for decades. It got more confusing when I started into traditional dancing a few years back. I was adopted by a veteran from the Cheyenne River Nation of South Dakota. So I guess in a nutshell I'm Cree/Ojibway and Cheyenne River Sioux, although now we get into political correctness and we'll correctly (?) name this new addition to my persona, Lakota. The name Deiter....well....we'll come back to that in a later dialogue.....

I come from a reservation that is pretty well known in Canada, probably the US too. In the 70's it had quite a reputation as being a rather rowdy reservation with a lot to watch out for. I was raised on this reservation and had a pretty free life style as a child/adolescent and adult. Even though I was raised on the reservation, I was not raised traditional, not many of us were, we were definitely products of the boarding school experiment. I was not advised to take up my language, our dances or our traditions.....my family were too afraid of the consequences.......Although the funny thing is that I was raised as a hunter from about the age of eight years old. I was hunting for food with a .22 when I was eight, a shotgun when I was 10, and rifles from 12 onward. I never thought of this as traditional but I guess thinking back on it, it was. The men I was brought up around are no longer around. I was taught survival skills that to this day frustrate many who have tried to deny me life's simple necessities, in short, I can live on macaroni and meat, some wild plants and I'm good for the rest of the day.....every day if I have to. You'd be amazed at the many macaroni dishes you can 'chef' up with.

I laugh at this because this mindset is not easy to abandon. The old saying "if life serves you lemons, make lemonade" is actually true......however in my case....if life serves you a raw deal.......find the macaroni...

My family I describe this way, 1/3 traditional, 1/3 Christian, 1/3 don't really give a damn......I was raised in a Christian household, mother was Christian, father was both Christian and traditional. This was on a reservation that was predominately Catholic which, as you can guess, made for some great after-school yard activities. Now combine this with the last name, Deiter, and we now have a full-out brawl or a school yard fight at least once or twice every other month. My question of 'Indianness' was never in question, I was reminded of this not only by my peers, but also my teachers and the white culture that surrounded our reservation. I actually didn't even know I was poor until I was invited to play hockey with a classmate who was white and I went to his house. I was immediately taken back by how much they had, especially the toys in his room stacked from floor to ceiling....the food was so presented and proper, nice people but they didn't have any macaroni.....

My greatest set-back of being Indian was, sadly, that most of the prejudice I received was at the hands of my own people. I was a 'Deiter,' I had a white man's nose, I wasn't good enough.....I even had a Indian teacher who was famous for mistreating his own, he was the hardest on us....we were called 'stupid Indians' by this Indian teacher. He took great lengths to ridicule his Native students for the benefit of the non-Indian students and teachers alike......I thought he was talented as an artist but mean as a wounded badger.

I guess I kind of forgave him, since all I can think of is that he introduced me to oil painting, and in some sort of way I saw his pain. Believe me, I did not arrive at this answer overnight. For many years I wished a lot of things on this man.....today I do not.

I also saw mistreatment from my peers on the reservation and around it. Being a Deiter was akin to being able to fight. In my youth I was stabbed once, looked down too many rifle barrels and drank and drugged and fought and spent nights in cells, and the list goes on.......I was experiencing in my youth with what I call the distorted sense of warriorism; to live this way in my youth was being a warrior......all my cousins did it, so should I........it was definitely a proving ground........my younger brother would play this out with relish.....visiting retribution on those who hurt us, our family, or me.......consequently he spent a lot of time in prison.....today if he even kicks a cat, he's going back to prison........for me, fate would change all that...I find myself at the age of 44 the oldest generation of my family, save for three uncles.....

Any peer of mine on the reservation who were known for pulling knives, pointing guns, or being violent are all gone......none of them survived....not one....well okay..maybe one.

The good people on my reservation were also many; out of respect I will not give their names.....but they know me....they recognize me to this day from my father. My father was a well-respected man, a veteran and in his younger days a bit of a terror.....an old boy as the rednecks put it.......that's another story......funny thing is that at a pow-wow recently, I was all painted up and decked out in regalia, feeling incognito, and out of nowhere comes old 'Charlie,' walks right up to me and smiles then shakes my hand......how the heck did he recognize me..........this happens a lot to me with the older generation, I swear. They can see things you wouldn't see......they have a different vision than us younger folk.

Now on to the gypsy portion of my life.....the Indian guy looking for a job hits the cities......... Vancouver - Venice Beach, CA and all points in between..... ✳✳✳

▼▼▼ Hello Everyone,

As a member of this tribe of Indigenous peoples I would like to introduce myself... I had some trouble attaching a file, an article which explains somewhat about who I am and where I come from spiritually (my people from Tikigaq (Pt. Hope)).... so, here is a site to look up: www.ruralcap.com/aboutrc/pdf/winter2006.pdf. This article has stirred up some controversy amongst my people but it's something that has to be told otherwise we forget about who we are as Indigenous peoples.

I would like to know who the people of this tribe are, through your indigenous language your true identity...*Uvuna* (Myself)..."*Anaqulutuq.*" Many of you know me as "Art" the quiet one.

I am fortunate enough to be born Inupiat and only Inupiat, from the northwest corner of the North American Continent (a gateway to the Americas) from the Bering Straits Land Bridge area.

I feel that this exhibit should honor our ancestors (pre-contact) from our Indigenous point of view and should not be a survey show about angry Indians; there should be no reference to current political situations... How much as Indigenous peoples are we willing to give up...? Let's show people where we come from spiritually.... Bring in that first breath.

When do we know that these Indigenous dialogues work? When we all learn to be around each other like brothers and sisters.... ▼▼▼

5.17.06

○○○ Good to hear from you. Yes, we need to "go back" (the word ancestors has a past reference to it) and feel where we come from, but we are also who we are now.......so how does that fit in? How do these two realities fit together?

I have been having dreams lately of "changing the past." For example one was of me dressing my 2-year old mother, knowing that she was my mother but I was taking care of her as a small child so that she could take care of me better when she grew up. When did time become linear and we turn to the past of Ancestors that were to be looked up to? (Somehow this has a Christian God tone to it.) Was there a "time" that we didn't look up to a "past"? I want to merge time into NOW. Who we are now is who we have been. Maybe it's a matter of reclaiming.

Gotta go reclaim my life.................. ○○○

✱✱✱ It is an Honor to meet you. My respects to you and your people. I may be a bit confused here, my understanding of this exhibit, correct me if I'm wrong, is to address the 'present to the future.' I tangented a bit yesterday with my addition to the dialogue. I should be honest, though, and point out that even though we are all indigenous, each of us brings a different story; some of our stories are angry, some are funny, some are not. My story was rather an introduction to my experiences growing up on a Cree reservation in Canada. I, too, have many ancestors and I, too, come from leaders of my people.

The one thing that I am afraid of is that perhaps we are going down the 'we are the world approach' with harmony and a one-world perspective...... if this is the case then before my peers I would respectfully get off this train. While I am very proud of my people, my ancestors and the land where I come from, I would be remiss to not address some of the very things that to this day are still occurring; I feel that this is my right as an artist.

I was, and I'm pretty sure you were too (given you are from the North), raised in a hunting family. I mentioned that I never really thought of this as traditional, but now that I'm older I can see that it was. My father raised me to pay attention to what the woods tell me, what side of a tree the dust on a poplar is, why the prairie chickens dance the way they do, where to stand when the geese fly, how to track and when to not hunt....I was also taught to give my chair to an elder, when to take my hat off, when to......

I was also taught how to tell what tribes people are from, certain gestures, certain things they wear at pow-wows, certain markings etc, etc....and in regard to land......as you know, a hunter knows a lot about the land upon which he walks........more so perhaps than those who don't walk the many lonely miles in search of the one hunted.

As I mentioned, my experiences also took a shift given the circumstances surrounding my reservation, questions have emerged about our lands.......In regard to the land, I did a piece for an exhibit some time back and one of the questions I addressed to the mainstream community and that catchy little ditty so often song in our schools, 'this land'.

My question was: 'are all men created equal?' 'is this land really for you and for me?' If the answer is yes, then it opens a host of questions about what I and I know others are seeing on 'our' land. and I guess, given this, some of it makes me angry. I got a phone call from home last week saying no one is eating ducks anymore given the health crisis overseas, no one is eating deer anymore, chronic wasting is showing up..............I suspect this same crisis with our game is showing up in many Indigenous communities.....should we be silent or should we say something ?

I feel a lot of respect and connection to the land and people where I come from, but I also feel a lot of laughter, anger and I have a lot of questions....

I cannot sugarcoat what is/has happened to my community, Why, at 44, am I one of the oldest in my generation....? Why, near my homeland, is 80% of the inmate population Native? Why are there two justice systems in Canada – one for the whites, one for the Indians.....guess who always wins? Why are they breaking the treaties with esoteric wording and taking away rights belonging to us, in their words?

'As long as the grass grows and the rivers flow'....

I am angry.....I am affected.....but I also can laugh and learn.

I was recently in New Zealand and stayed with Maori hosts at one of their Maraes. They talked with me and I found out we definitely had a commonality – at that time the Treaty of the Four Shores was being broken, now today it is...........their communities reminded me of mine, good and bad.........I was, on leaving, presented with a song by some of their 'warriors' who stopped by to meet me and my friend from the Northwest Coast, they stopped by with their chaperone from......prison.

I am also afraid that by giving a perspective that all are in harmony and we are all the world, then we are giving the mainstream what they safely want to see, it doesn't question their status quo, rather it continues it....and all go home happy and better for it........not me.

We are indeed as Indigenous people more in harmony with the earth, but honestly, look at what is happening to our earth? Was it us, was it them? Who?

I respect my peers and I have a lot of respect to many of you as artists, but allow me to be honest....to give my experiences, good and bad, funny or not.....otherwise I lie. My respects to all my relations. ✳✳✳

○○○ Thank you for your words. Good things....

We are truly many things and our stories are very different but we all claim our indigenous identities.........what is that? Blood? Life style? I was thinking yesterday about "home".......what makes us feel at home? I have met so many Anglos who talk about not having a place that feels like home. Then I remembered I once heard that it takes 20 generations for a species to adapt to their environment........This would mean that if the average Anglo had babies every 30 years it would take them 600 years to genetically adapt to this environment. We laughed because most indins around here breed a lot faster....according to our calculations, Navajos would adapt to their new environment in 100 years...hee...heee. Anyway.......I wondered if that's why whites don't feel a sense of belonging and home inside themselves, because they have been living in an environment that they haven't had enough time to genetically adjust to? Ummmmmm?..........Could this be part of our Indigenousness???? That we've been around our environment long enough to fit? Your hunting senses are genetically in tuned with your homeland...etc..

anyway............a thought. ○○○

5.19.06

◇◇◇ This New **Indigenous** Dialogue:

is inter-generational inter-tribal, and transcends physical, political, racial, and intellectual boundaries with honesty, integrity, and a provocative vision of a better life for Native and non-Native people.

The boundaries, like our identities and nations, are almost entirely imagined and figurative.

Where does: the "*Apocalypse*" fit into this dialogue?

How, or is it even possible for this exhibition to exist on its own, without our "selling" it? We see that the dialogue, can in fact, function without our selling it, documenting it, or compiling it-- but when it comes to making it known, or our "putting it in the world," this is where business enters. How do we address this?

Ideas:

• How do we "initiate" this specific and non-specific Indigenous Dialogue-- with each other and with the world?

• A specific conscious regard for the sacred, vital, dangerous Thing that Relations is, must be required by all artists.

• The world is listening. What will we say? Re: These words/images/ sounds/architecture and record of the experience/ceremony that RELATIONS is are going to be "out in the world." For better or worse.

• This dialogue: we are engaging in it both verbally, and non-verbally.

"Contextualization and 'Getting It'":

In developing the exhibition and its core construct and concepts/focus we've been required to discuss whether contextualization or whether the audience "gets it" is even important. Questions that come, naturally, after this initial question are: Why? Why not?

After certain discussion (whether we'd like to admit or not):

Yes. We are concerned with the inherent vital issue of contextualization, by Indian artists, and our viewers/readers/those who will receive and experience this distinctly Indigenous Universe and aesthetic as REALITY.

On Writing and the Native Writers/Scholars included in the RELATIONS collective:

As one of the literary artists included in the RELATIONS exhibition, I was required to ask myself about the specific role the writers would play within the specific and non-specific construct of the exhibition, and it seems that:

Native writers, in general and not just as applied to this exhibition, are charged with a brutal and perhaps impossible task in being required to attempt to "apply" MEANING to the Relations exhibition.

However, after much internal and external dialogue and certain reflection, came to the inherent truth of the RELATIONS exhibition that:

"We as artists, both literary and visual, are not 'giving' and/or 'applying' meaning to this exhibition, therefore we are not providing meaning of this exhibition for you (viewer, guest, fellow artists). What we are hoping to provide, through RELATIONS, *for you Native and non-Native alike,* is an intellectual/cultural/political/artistic/spiritual context imbued with our own collective and personal/individual knowingness and "intuitivism" about our own Native experience and experience within our Native Universe, so that you may ultimately access and discover that meaning on your own.

For, we have come to know our Indigenous identity, our Indian-ness, our Indigineity, our Native Being, in this intricate, highly specific, personal, and fluid way."

- Through this profound and vital exploration of Indigenous identity in the 21st century we are practicing: *The Art and Science of Asking Better Questions.*
- This exhibition is intended to Initiate and cultivate dialogue, not end it.
- This exhibition is concerned with doing away with: **ABSOLUTE AUTHORITY, both Native and non-Native.**

The Specific Role of the "Indian Intellectual" in the RELATIONS exhibition:

- What room is there for the "Indian Intellectual" in the exhibition?
- Where do "intellect" and "art for the sake of art" collide, fight, go to war even?

Thought:
We are artists, but we are not just artists. The dialogue that is occurring at all levels, sacred and often silent, between Native scholars/writers and Native visual artists is the dialogue that is being highlighted in this exhibition--the dialogue that is often shared at innate, intrinsic, and non-verbal levels between our most vital Native Voices.

Our distinct mediums do not have to be, and should not be, in opposition with one another. The conversation that our writing and our art is, and has been, having with each other-- our artists should also be having that same conversation. At all levels.

Questions Arisen (to be discussed, but not "solved") in RELATIONS:
- What is Indigenous/Indian/Native/Indignity?
- What is not Indigenous?
- Where do we contradict ourselves at the expense of our life ways, identity, children, and integrity?
- What is "Indian Art"?
- What is *not* "Indian Art"?
- Who seeks to prosper/remain prosperous from the perpetuation of the myth(s) of Indian Art and artists?
- Where does RELATIONS fit into this context? How does it resist it? Does it?
- Who are Indians now, in the 21st century?
- Notion of *"they want us figured out."* We are fluid, in-flux, indetermi-nate, hybridized, and impossible to "pin-down" (but don't call us Post-modern or Postcolonial either)
- Who are our children? What are they saying? What are they doing? What are they creating?

- How do we better "get it", better contextualize and utilize their specific dialogue and language in this discussion of identity, language, social-change through art, self-criticism, prayer, origins, and the ultimate application of this INDIGENOUS DIALOGUE in the 21st century world?
- Where/In what is the future of *INDIGENOUS*?

On criticism:

Dad said to me that I should expect, anticipate, even accept the intellectual and anti-intellectual, sound and unsound criticism that will surely come from my words, my art. And I agreed, even taking it a step further

in saying that we: *must prepare for it. Regard it. For the sacred and vital thing that it is. We must be prepared and equipped to soundly, and comprehensively defend our positions, our "strategic locations." We must prepare for war. And there will be many casualties.*

Not Postmodern, Not Postcolonial:

- We are not postmodern, nor Postcolonial but we are saying: *We as Indian people, our Indian-ness, our Indignity, and our art is not "this" or "that." Our flux is constant. Deal with it.*
- Almost impossible (for Native people/artists themselves): doing away with the comfort inherent in the idea that we must be "this" or "that." And yet we are doing it.
- Specific examples of art/writing, artists/writers who have done just that: hence, the core group of RELATIONS artists.

Saliency/Making the Call:

Questions for Whole Tribe:

- *How were the most seminal, salient, vital, engaging, prominent, and urgent? aspects/points/items for discourse and questions in the exhibition, and its promotional materials, selected? What was the process by which the group chose what was and was not in the final exhibition?*

• *How is this process of deductive and selective reasoning buying into the very ideologies and practices, dominant-elitist-mainstream-western, we have sought and are seeking to move away from?*

Dust:

We are, with RELATIONS, turning all pre-conceived, mis-perceived, ill-conceived and outmoded notions of Indian-ness on their heads, and then-- to dust, for, we **were never that.**

    RELATIONS and this new Indigenous Dialogue also is asking:
How can nothing and everything be sacred at the same time? ✧✧✧

✧✧✧ sending through a poem, and the excerpt that was a major part of my graduation address, from a larger narrative entitled *A New Vision of/for Native Literature.* The poem I am sending along is one I've presented several times. Also sending along to the whole group some general contributions to the dialogue—hope any of it can be utilized in some way:

A New Vision of/for Native Literature

It's absolutely possible to write very beautifully, eloquently and very poorly at the same time. And we have done it. Too often Native writers have chosen acclaim, money, and basic recognition of our voices at the immense cost of a truly collective and representative narrative of 1,001 Native voices. A chosen few have risen to prominence while the rest fell silent and away. The ultimate cost has been our children, our life-ways, our communities, and our dignity-- all the while speaking about how we were saving them. We must write about this now, without flinching or hesitating, and without worrying about who is listening or paying us to do so.

    Articulation and Intellectualization of the profane: how do we do it?

    Strong writing, powerful writing, is less of a review and more of a theoretical and also experiential analysis, less philosophy, less rhetoric, and careful to present more ideas directly and soundly supported by existing text, research, and discourse.

The new American Indian academic/storyteller/history keeper has come full circle, from disconnection, absorption, oppression, and termination, to: return, distinction, resistance, and survival. Where the old, and "recently old" narratives (i.e: Sherman Alexie, Leslie Marmon Silko, Joy Harjo) were concerned with subtle resistance, eradication, and identity loss, the new generation of Indian writers finds redemption, new method, and reaffirmation of identity through neo-creative resistance, and artistic struggle through brand new media and forum.

Younger Native writers are extremely dangerous due largely to the fact of our being dangerously well-equipped, informed by both genocide and ultimate privilege, and due to our existence as the direct result--the children--of the American Indian Movement, the American Indian Rights Age and the so-called American Indian Renaissance. We are extremely dangerous--in both idea and practice--because we represent both the successes and the ultimate failures of those movements and era and their most prominent aspects.

What we must do, and are doing, with poetry now: We are not just speaking, and responding to, the continued slaughter of American Indian people, but of Indigenous people worldwide. We are compelled by a genetic memory and a kinetic essence to speak of the atrocities we have seen, and are seeing, as Indian people...as human people.

We have seen how it is not an impossible thing to use poetry and art to affect recognizable social-change and to realize the true and not just rhetorical self-determination of Indian people. And we must pay a high regard to our elders for this. But we have also seen that the pursuit for self-realization, self-determination, and freedom cannot be wholly dependent upon our narrative and the expression of it.

Sherman Alexie asked me, "What do you love?," as if I was all violence, sex, and hatred. I said then, and I will say it time and time again with my whole-life, until I have none left: this is my love, and it isn't the whole story. And I am not alone.

I am also not alone in saying, to my Nation, to my elders, to those who I love with my terrifying and murderous truth: You better be damn grateful that we're picking up pens when we can just as easily pick up guns and bombs. So many of us are choosing literature and art instead of terrorism, but too many of us are not, and you should not be shocked at all when you see the Red Lakes of the world, in our Indian Country and hearts, becoming more and more common.

We are, and will be in the coming days and years, making the terrifying and startling connections with literature and language about the suicide of our young people, Native women and children, education, the rising use and distribution of Meth, sexual abuse, and terror.

The question is: is our world ready? ✧✧✧

✧✧✧

Active Indianism part I.
Bury my heart at Wounded Knee
feed my eyes to the ghetto
throw my Indian mouth
out to sea.

The Seventh Generation
mis-contorted, distorted
as an infestation
but coming as a
revelation that
annihilation afterall
is sometimes necessary.

Silver rings and
turquoise linings
come to me in dream
but leave with reality
on the underside
of your tongue.

Have you ever seen a real Indian?

Have you ever seen an Indian play the violin?
Have you ever seen an Indian
out of jail?
Have you ever seen an Indian
recite a poem?
Have you ever seen an Indian pick
his nose?
Have you ever seen an Indian
cry?

Have you ever seen an Indian?

When will the crashing cease?
Oh when will the crashing
cease?
Oh when?

Burning
shine
"this white hot light that I'm under
must be the reason I look so sunburned"
History lesson taught
by a man the children know as   Slim Shady.

Indian Sonnett written
by violin's illume.
Dying poet's breath
on my neck
and
I won't be done for some time
no, I won't be done
for some
time.

511 years and counting
511 years
and counting
511 years
and
counting.

Did you think I had
forgotten?

Mercenary for crumbs
fragments and morsels
of light.
Ink blot
looking more and more
like an Indian man
leaving.
Have you ever seen a real Indian?

Have you ever seen an Indian make a pizza?
Have you ever seen an Indian weave a tapestry
out of trash?
Have you ever seen an Indian raise
their
hand
in class?

Have you ever seen an Indian reading Hemmingway at the beach?
Have you ever seen an Indian braid her hair?
Have you ever seen an Indian dye
his hair blonde?
Have you ever seen an Indian explain
American
history?

Have you ever seen an Indian?

And when your hair falls in your eyes
they think you have nothing left to lose
they think you have nothing left to lose
And when your hair falls in your eyes
they think
you have nothing left
to lose.

Red Star
violin native showcase
Ten Little Indians in
army fatigues
E&J in the car.
Lakota Millenium nation
deliver me into
an Indian tomorrow.
She said: "I feel so far away".
Tied her brown hair back
with the strings of my Indian heart.
Watch the Indian marionette show
pay
only 50 cents and a strand of your blonde wig.

I can't escape, but
in my eyes
you can still see
that I want to.

Have you ever seen
an
Indian?

Bury my heart at Wounded Knee.
Feed my eyes to the ghetto
throw my Indian mouth
out to sea.

✧✧✧

5.23.06

✧✧✧

dahwaaheh`
dahwaaheh`
dahwaaheh`

In reciprocity, Bob, Whole Tribe.
Everyone who may chance to read this:

Thank you.
For everything you've shared.
For everything you will share.
For everything you have responded to.
For everything you will respond to.
And, also (this is the hard part) thank you
for that
which you will not respond to;
for that which you will not say.

After much reflection on the dialogue,
I decided to compile my notes thus far--
and present them.

That's all they are. Just notes. Observations.
Fragmentary dialogue. I wish I had more.
To offer.
To share.

This dialogue feels far from stagnant.
Far from static.
Far from un-ambitious.

But screw my "criticism" (while listening
with care and patience).

What is existent here, in this dialogue?
in all the intensive and intricate planning
that has already happened--

is sacred and vital.

We've a long way to go.
And not much time.

Thank you, again, for allowing for my participation
in this ongoing dialogue.

dahwaaheh`
✧✧✧

5.24.06

○○○ Hello Whole Tribe,
Sarah thank you for your dialogue....beautiful and insightful. Bob, I feel
scolded. Joseph, hope you got my stuff........are we meeting next week?
Sorry I couldn't make it this morning...too much...too much. Having to
remember to pace myself. A question to the whole tribe....what is Indin
Time? What is Time to Indigenous us? If we are in relation to our environment......is time different in different cultures? Seems like when we enter
into a sacred space, time is different.......maybe that's why that backwards singing is so powerful.....it takes us out of the Western time frame
and into a nameless time?   anyway.......what do you think? ○○○

6.1.06

✳✳✳ *Aloha Kakou,*

First, I want to say *mahalo nui loa* to John Grimes, Joe Sanchez and Bob Haozous for inviting me to participate in the indigenous dialogues and RE-LATIONS exhibit--I am honored and very much looking forward to being a part of something wonderful--even though frustrating and painful at times!

Second, *kala mai* (excuse me) for introducing myself at the last minute. I know I'm the late comer, but I have been reading everyone's email-- and I've been pretty much aware of what's been going on since my father and husband were there in Santa Fe last. Bob, Joe and John, *kala mai* for not participating in the dialogues while the three of you were here in Hawai'i--didn't realize I was invited so therefore didn't think it was my place. Anyway.....*'O wau* Natalie Mahina Jensen-Oomittuk *ko'u inoa,* I'm Sicil-ian, Native Hawaiian, Danish, French and Irish, born and raised on the island of *O'ahu*--now living on the island of Hawai'i with my husband [Othniel "Art" Anaqulutuq Oomittuk, Jr.] and son [Luciano Anunnayuaq Kaleipuaoka'iouli Anaqulutuq Jensen-Oomittuk].

I was trained since the age of nine in Native Hawaiian featherwork called *kahili*--soft sculpture standards. And then took photography as my major in high school and some college--finally realizing I was bored with the whole western way of higher education learning and thinking. But I was now able to delve deeper into my Native Hawaiian culture, which I did with great passion--learning the cultural beliefs, philosophy and traditions of my Ancestors from 750 B.C. I figure, why fix what ain't broken--just tweak it a little.

Artistically, I've participated in art shows since I was eleven--then started SisterMoon Productions Design and Photography once I left school. I tried doing the commercial thing, even jumping on the Hawaiian theme photog-raphy bandwagon--but I wasn't happy with the results. Instead I was angry (oh yes, I said 'angry') with how my culture was being stereotypically por-trayed by non-Natives from out of town, moving to Hawai'i with a buck or two in their pocket and commercially whoring my culture around--making considerably more than a buck or two back. That's when I was approached by my mom and dad to take over the responsibility of a book project they started work on, called the 'Daughters of Haumea--Women of Ancient Hawai'i'--I, of course, said "YES!" and was forever changed. The 'Daughters' project is very important to me, for it represents everything good, pure and true about the ancient Hawaiian culture and its people.

And that's where I get the inspiration to artistically create--from the stories passed down through my Ancestors--and I don't mean that in a christian/god tone. Ancestors are Ancestors--all those who have come before me. That's how I get my message across, by honoring my Ancestors--through my art. Yup, I'm all about rebirth and that Renaissance shit! It's my way of educating, perpetuating and healing.

So my interpretation of this RELATIONS exhibit, at first it was 'how we relate to each other as Natives'--now it's 'how to have differences yet still relate to each other as Natives.' Which is all good, we just got to realize that and come to terms with the fact that we all will have are own opinions--I thought that what these Indigenous dialogues were for. An expression of one's opinion--not a dictatorship. I'm an individual, I always have been--growing up in Hawai'i I never liked following the norm. But as a Native, relating to my fellow Natives--strongly believe in a 'WE.' Just with bits and pieces of everyone mixed in!

Again, *mahalo nui loa* for the invitation to contribute and participate--sorry if I droned on. I actually meant to keep it short--oh well, I guess I was finally inspired to get off my ass and write! Thank you all for that inspiration!

Me ke aloha pumehana ✳✳✳

✳✳✳ good words....

actually, I'm still on board, talked to Joseph today...sorry about that..........I think I got it now.

anyway, I am compiling a list and will soon have the website up, once I get the names of artists who have sites or areas they want to point to.... images too....about a week for a preview online...

Anyway, my responsibility pointed to you people.....good people.

Struggling with the Native thing myself, I am pretty tied to the land back home, raised that way.......as I'm sure a lot of us are.....I wonder how to balance life teaching here and being there for relatives of mine.....

Some of us have to leave, some to stay.......I know one thing.....they never forget you.

One time I'm out driving in the back country after being away a long period of years, wind blowing the prairie grass and shrubs, I see this guy walking across the prairie about a quarter mile away, looking like a prophet of some sort walking in the distance, away from everything and everybody, miles from nowhere......

after some time......I pull up to him as the wind is whipping his hair and clothes, he looks at me and says......'hi Tony'.......uncanny memory he had since we both looked quite a few years older and different....

The guy lives out in the wild to this day....shows a lot of ingenuity when it comes to living space.......always had, hadn't seen him since grade school.

Technology makes dialogue instantaneous, real time.....that's my vision for this project.....to create the portal through which this is possible....... it's completely possible in a short period of time......

this dialog of us as RELATIONS could be presented both in real time (opening night) via web cam/microphone (hidden) or by web chat rooms (just an idea)...can manipulate the media to give it not such a orthodox 'techy' look........this can be accomplished using virtual and interactive technology, even can change the backgrounds at the same time........... give the illusion of real space......that kinda thing...

My biggest question is what is our identity for the website, what does the space look like, I can model land or environment that is agreeable to all.....maybe it's just a place, a room, anything we can imagine....

I am moving fast on this, so any suggestions or ideas are more than welcome...... ✳✳✳

○○○ Hello Whole Tribe,

Rose and I went to a meeting here at the senior citizen's building (Santa Clara) on the health and concerns of the people living around nuclear sites (Los Alamos). It was interesting. What stuck out to me was a few facts: who came, who didn't, and the over-all feeling of what was said. I wanted to share these with you all because what went on there seemed like a continuation of our dialogue. First....facts: We are fucked. The water in and below Los Alamos has been found to contain a number of chemicals that are very very toxic. The cancer levels in Los Alamos itself is the highest in the country. Even though Santa Clara is upstream from Los Alamos, once the water hits the underground water, it can spread "up hill." The deer and elk that we hunt and eat are drinking from all the areas around waste deposits. They are still dumping waste in unlined ditches in canyons around Los Alamos. The "smoke stacks" from the laboratories contain much contaminates also. The wind direction is right over us......going up the Española Valley into Picuris Pueblo and up into Taos Canyon. The numbers of cancer is very high and also problems with the thyroid is connected directly to some of these chemicals. The people concerned are trying to sue LANL for water pollution and have actually had their lawsuit go through as of the 23rd of May. Who came... who didn't: About four people from the community, including me and Rose. Not a single pueblo official was there. The ones that are supposed to be in a position to care about the community and health of "their" people were not there. I heard later that most of them went home because the computers were down and they had nothing to do. Who spoke: I don't remember names very well but I will tell you about what a few people said that stuck with me. An elder from Taos Pueblo got up and spoke. He didn't want to talk about facts and figures but about what we are doing as indian people. He talked to us as his "relatives." He said, "When you borrow something like someone's car, you don't bring it back scratched or broken or dirty, you clean it and fill it with gas and then hand it back with sincere gratitude. It's the same with our time on this earth. We should care for it the best we can and then hand it to the next generation in good shape or in better shape than we received it." Then he walked up to Rose (she was the youngest one there)......and with tears in his eyes he told her that he was sorry for handing her a world that was so messed up. That we are failing as a people because we are handing the next generation a poisoned world. Louie Henna from Tesuque Pueblo was a wonderful speaker talking about how everything is connected through the patterning of the world and our prayers. We talked with him about the attitudes of the younger generations that have a sense that the world won't last and so there is no future. It's very different from the old view of looking down the road seven generations from now. If there is no future then why work at anything? Why not get what you can out of it all because you're gonna die soon anyway? Rose talked about how she thought she wouldn't live beyond 16 years old. Louie said his son said the same thing. What does this kind of view do? How does it affect the way we live and treat each other and the world around us? How does it make us all feel about ourselves if we are handed a world that is toxic and unwelcoming? How can we feel like life is a good thing and we are, too, if what we see is a world that is quickly using up everything it can use........? There is no future in this. How do we bring back a future and a feeling of hope in a world like this? Then I came home to find one of my turkey hens dead from being raped to death by the tom turkey. Sometimes when they mount the hens they tear open the sides of the hen with their claws. ugh.

anyway.....I'm a bit broken. ○○○

○○○ Hello Whole Tribe,
There is a story I must tell. It's about this dialogue piece I'm doing with Rose and then with the added piece from Bob. Rose and I began this piece with the idea of a prayer in mind. The prayer is about our relationship. Although we have been thinking of our beginnings, it always felt bigger than just us. The story of our births. I worked on this life-size clay figure of a woman half sitting – half leaning back. Her stomach is open to view what is inside. She would lean against (or almost against) a tree of Bob's making. Inside her is a child of Rosie's making. To redo or pray a "new beginning" into being. I finished building her about a week ago. Then the self destruction began. I went to work one day and found her

head lying next to her stomach. No problem........can always fix those kinds of breaks. Finally got her into the truck to load into the kiln at my house. I took off one of her legs in order to fit her into the kiln. Driving through Española, she slid slowly into the side of the tire wrench and broke into several more pieces. No problem....I can glue it after I fire her and use bondo to recreate what is too broken. At this point I thought it was appropriate to have her in pieces that need to be "put back to-gether".......fit the dialogue that seemed to be going on. Yesterday I started firing her slowly trying to be careful not to "take it up to fast." This morning I went to go take a peek look......the kiln was still on! A chair was a little too close to the control panel and blocked the lever for shutting the kiln off at the right temperature. She had been on high all night. I have not looked inside the kiln yet as it's too hot still but I'm sure it is completely melted and might have ruined my kiln also. I went to tell Rose. She was upset......as she has been close to finishing the "baby".....and excited that her baby was getting a "mommy." The melting of the mother has been like a nightmare of the story we have been living in. I hope that she writes her side of this story. We talked about what this means. So I have a major question to add to our dialogue, it may be the most important question I have..........."Now What?" I ask this in all seriousness and sincerity. Rose and I thought that when we can see what the mess is in the kiln and if we can take it out of the kiln at all....maybe we would continue to use it and place this "blob" on the floor with Rose's baby on top of it and Bob's tree next to it. We have a photo of it when it was "whole" and we could lay a picture of it next to it??? It doesn't have an answer just the question of "now what?" Please let me know your thoughts and ideas here.......it is truly a piece in the making/breaking. thank you all. ○○○

❖❖❖   hello all.
i've been working on a mosquito mask that has proven more difficult than i figured. i always do that, though.

    i am also working on a baby, that was supposed to go into the "mother" that my mom spent months working on. i finally felt that someone had made a true place for "me" and cared so much that so much work would go into making it beautiful, welcoming, and comfortable. the baby that i was making was actually happy- something i don't put into my work much and i truly had to find that place within myself to manifest it into the baby. i feel like i am putting a part of myself out there that i have always felt like has been, pretty much, shit on.

it is hard for me to find that part of myself that feels the most vulnerable and put it into this clay.

this piece made a mother that was there to accept and make the world okay and loving for me to be in.

this, in my real existence, didn't quite happen and there was much misunderstanding. first, the INDIAN HOSPITAL botched to the max the first connection that my mother and i could have had. i came into the world thinking that no one was there for me and believing that a steel plate of survival had to be set in place around me- or i would die. this piece was an attempt to re-create that, and maybe allow her to feel like she was there for me and for me to feel that someone was there for me.

this morning mama came knocking on my door and told me that the kiln had fired on high all night. i know what low-fire clay looks like when fired at a high temperature. -sort of like bubbled nuclear waste, and it sticks to everything in the kiln and when the kiln is re-fired it can eat through any kiln shelves and other parts of the kiln like a cancer.

that is what happened to the mom. this strike of fear ran through me as i thought of my little clay baby self that is sitting, waiting in the studio in pojoaque with nobody to be made for, nothing to hold her, and in a panic started thinking of all the things i could make to save her- barbed wire, steel, cactus- some kind of box where no one can see her innocence and vulnerability. then angry- i put myself this ******** far out there and now no one is there? how dare you do this to me AGAIN.

but this time i know the facts. i know that she didn't mean to. i know she worked so, so hard to make something for my piece to belong to, that she kept trying, she kept hoping, she kept thinking that it was going to be okay, there is always a way to patch it up and keep on going. i know, i saw the whole process. i know that she wanted to be there for me, but no matter how hard she tried, she is too broken.

i was sitting with my half-finished painting, paint drying up. staring at the floor as mama told me about the piece. yesterday i was so happy, i had so much hope, i thought i could really be something different. then she said.

"some times looking at the bright side of things can be a denial."

it reminds me of this meeting that we went to a couple of weeks ago, a group that is being started in santa clara about citizens living around nuclear sites. after hearing fact upon fact upon fact that we are doomed, i lost it. the ultimate MOTHER is broken. we come into the world, every single human being, to a mother who is losing it, who is breaking, who can't be there for us the way she was meant to. this incredible hopelessness fell, and frustration, and i really felt like walking out into 85 mph rush hour traffic and just see exactly how insane we have all become. there is no way to pretty up this picture. there is no way to look at the bright side.

what it comes down to, i believe, is that we have to fully go through the realization of exactly HOW BAD it is before we can make the change. we have to make room.

now what if you walk into the big round room- music playing backwards, and you see this baby- ready to be accepted into the world- and all around her, instead of a mother, are those melted pieces of what was supposed to be.

isn't THAT the truth?

maybe what has been labeled as angry indian art hasn't gone far enough to really question WHY. where did these self-destructive indigenous tendencies come from? is it because we, as people indigenous to the land, have our mother (earth) destroyed and then we are lost? maybe we have to recognize and release that loss in order to be healthy enough to come together without REACTING off each other in each of our own insecurities.

i don't want unexplained anger, i don't want unexplained fear, i don't want unexplained hope, i don't want unexplained heartbreak.

i want the raw TRUTH. ❖❖❖

SPOKEN DIALOGUE
(TRANSCRIBED FROM VARIOUS WHOLE TRIBE MEETINGS)

4.12.06

♦♦♦ …transformation is the key to this whole idea of Relations, trying to get back to our relations as "we" rather than as an individual. Instead of that individualism, we need to go back to the concept of sharing our identity amongst ourselves. ♦♦♦

▲▲▲ …basically we're creating an exhibit that's not me saying, "well, I've got three pieces from Bob, two from you, one from you, and one from you;" instead, I'm gonna formulate it in this way: "I've got this new idea." ▲▲▲

♦♦♦ When you say 'transformation,' do you mean, like, transformation as in "change?" Or, say, transformation in terms of "evolution, evolving?" Because transformation, to me, means 'rising from one stage to another.' Or else it can just really mean change. ♦♦♦

♦♦♦ I think that term "evolving" kinda scares me, because in Western society that means getting better and moving forward. But evolving from *my* point of view is where we should have always been. And that is, acknowledging the importance of that concept of relations; it's more than "people." So it's a change, but I don't know how to define it beyond that. But I know that my tribe has lost that ability…we're so individualistic and Americanized that we see ourselves as having individual rights and we *don't* see the tribe as being "us," or the earth as being "us." How do you get that transformation back? How do you inspire the dialogue? It's *not* getting it back…that's one problem I have with this whole show, is that most of us want a product that is "full." I think that we're only offering, we're only cracking the door. And it may be a disruptive crack but we can't backpedal and say "okay that's kinda scary so lets make something that's sweet here," so that when they walk out the door everybody is smiling. We don't want that. That'll come later, maybe next year, two years, four years, as we develop this concept. ♦♦♦

▲▲▲ ...although we've used the word "biennial" it's not what we're creating here. We are trying to start the conversation toward something like that. But this is simply the beginning dialogue. If Indigenous people are going to have exhibitions of their work then they should choose not only how it gets exhibited, but also how it's presented in the community...and not necessarily in that Eurocentric vision of what Indigenous art is. A key point is that there has always been these fixed 'boxes' for the various Indigenous arts. We don't necessarily need to play by that rule. Even though we have been an acting part of this entire strategy in which it has been dictated that "if you're gonna make art it's either gotta be abstract expressionism" or "it's gotta have an ism attached to it." Halfway through one of these conversations, Rose suggested "intuitism." So, we'll create our own "ism" of art and how it's presented. We just want to talk and stimulate people to be honest. Today you said that, "the key words, to me, are honesty and truth in what we're trying to find, and who we are." ▲▲▲

♦♦♦ ...this photograph is a good example. We had a non-Native person – who is very new age – that intellectualized it, photographed it. He wanted Rox and Rose to wear jingle dresses. He couldn't understand why we're dressed like *this*. And so then they want to ask "who *are* these people?" They want the "star." They want the "individual." Even amongst ourselves, we're running into problems understanding who we should be. And we don't have the answers.. ♦♦♦

▲▲▲ We want to share the questions with people, essentially. We want them to come into this space and experience something that's *not* an anthropologist telling them what an Indian person is. That's kind of what they've been used to. You know, they come into the museum looking for that preconceived stereotype. "Where's the baskets?" they ask. That's what Indian art is, for them.

And you know, you'd think that those stereotypes would be over by now. But it's really not. 90% of the public still think that Indians are destined to make only this specific parameter of work. As an Indian artist, you can't say anything about anything else. They don't want you to talk about war, unless it's about patriotism. They don't want you to talk about family unless it's the perfect idealized version, or about being warriors… the Romantic Warrior.

We've been limited by our own acceptance of it, for one thing. It's easy to accept that role, you know. If that role is paying your family's livelihood for years, then it's just that more acceptable. ▲▲▲

◇◇◇ Familiar. Familiar. ◇◇◇

◆◆◆ Well, people know that there's change; but we get confused about what exactly *has* changed. Is it the "thing" that is changing or, is it *we* who are changing? Or is it both? How do we include this as a part of the dialogue that is actually taking place? Can you depict it as a visual representation of that change? Or is it, how we interact and *relate* to the idea? And that's why I ask, "what is this?" When you say transformation, *do* you mean change? Or is it the way that I understand you and transform that information? Or is it moving from one stage to another? So that, it's not above or not below, but just from one place, one stage, one thing to another, transformed. If we want people to interact to the dialogue, then I think we have to make it apparent about what we mean when we state "change in *themselves*." Because we relate to each other kind of statically (seemingly); we actually are relating to each other in terms of, I guess, how *we* put ourselves in *their* place. For example, Sara and I, we actually know our roles. She's the daughter and I'm the father. And yet, when I talk with her, I actually assume – in a sense, in a manner of speaking – that I'm in her place trying to understand me…and she probably does the same thing.. ◆◆◆

◇◇◇ That's one of the challenges of doing this project, especially for those who have no idea about the things that they'll experience. It's gonna be really hard because we're familiar with each other, but for those who are going to be coming in from the outside, it's going to be completely uncharted territory. I'm sort of scared – in my own mind – thinking about how to bring that comfort. We don't want to make them comfortable at *all* levels…but that's part of it. It's not our job to make them comfortable, I know, but… ◇◇◇

◆◆◆ The important part of an exhibition is the creating of dialogue; you try not to turn them off. But maybe it's too soon. That's what I wonder. ◆◆◆

▲▲▲ But if it's too soon, then when is the time? For me it's never too soon. ▲▲▲

◆◆◆ Too soon to make them comfortable? Well, we have the "heartbeat." We were talking about incorporating a heartbeat sound, and I suggested, why don't we get an Indian song and play it backwards. And it was so powerful, it scared us. And so, immediately, they wanted to justify it with a positive, 'cause it's so powerful. And I say no. I say no, let's just shake 'em. Let's hit 'em. They say in their language that Apache means 'head basher;' I think they associate me with that now. ◆◆◆

◇◇◇ Oh man, Apache riff raff. ◇◇◇

◆◆◆ But I'm not Apache. I'm Apache, but at the same time my dad was so gentle that I don't represent my people in that way. Well, this sound is so powerful. You can hear that it's a man singing and you can hear the drum beat. But it's not like he's going [*intake of breath*] and singing the words, it's like he's saying the words and going [*outtake of breath*]. And that's what they were worried about, it feels like you're exhaling and not breathing in. It's unbalanced. And I understand that. It's true. ◆◆◆

◆◆◆ Like those throat singers. They achieve something like that with the throat singing. ◆◆◆

✧✧✧ Well the balance is absent; there's going to be imbalance. It's a challenge and it's hard to write about that. Because so many people— externally – even Native people – they hold tight to that, "well, Native people are balanced." I value balance in my own life, but I am imbalanced you know. And I want to express that in anything that I write or present in this exhibit, as well as the fact that balance is necessary. ✧✧✧

◆◆◆ One of the things that I came up with, is that the difference between us and most 'contemporary man' has to do with time…because we have an ancestral timeframe that *makes* us. Not today. Most of us are very westernized. We think of ourselves as being two-generational, not multi-generational. As "Americans"… even Native people. But there is the other time factor/direction, the generations of the future. So, we don't really own ourselves. And so I think that we have to think of this project in the long run rather than just how do we make an effective exhibition. It's important to think about the audience. But who is, in terms of time, who is our audience? It's us. We have to satisfy ourselves. I like the disruptions. I think that once we create that, the younger people are going to find a way to make it more palatable to our people. I hope so. ◆◆◆

✧✧✧ That's why I put that quote in there. Sherman Alexie was writing comments about my writing and he said, "You're gonna turn a lot of people off with this stuff." And I was like, "And?" But I do know that I have to think about that at all times. I mean, I think about the elders, and I think about the people who I started writing for in the first place. I started writing for Native people when I was fifteen, sixteen, not thinking about what anyone else was going to think. But I know that I'm gonna turn off both Native and non-Native people at times. ✧✧✧

♦♦♦ An elder confronted me during the Venice project. He said "what are you trying to do, change the world?" And I backed away, then said, "Well, of course." And we talked and I said "what can one person do?" Well, we are not one person. Since then I realize that I didn't say that to him then, 'cause I was intimidated. Since then, I realize that that's exactly what our job is. We want to change something 'cause our future, environmentally, is pretty dismal. Maybe. I suspect it's true.

…One of the words we were talking about is *Mitakuye Oyasin,* "Our Relations." I did a ceremony. And the guy who taught me was Paiute, who was conducting a Lakota ceremony. The wisdom of the ceremony was so good – because we *were* talking about "Our Relations." And he mentioned the "breath of the Stone People," and he was talking about the air that you breathe is your relation, and how you are a part of everything. I realized that there is this tremendous wisdom in there. So, I started asking the Navajo what they have for the same word, and I got a *huge* list. It's not just like "our relations" in English, it's very complex. So it's a complex concept that we're trying to put into the whole exhibit. ♦♦♦

♦♦♦ It's a kind of performance? ♦♦♦

▲▲▲ Just about. It sounds like traditional Indigenous singing except that it seems like it's always erasing. It goes [breath intake]. It has kind of a 'sucking' sound that's really spooky. ▲▲▲

✧✧✧ I remember someone writing about that. Where did that come from…the idea…to just play it backwards? ✧✧✧

♦♦♦ Where does the breathing, the song, come in? I kept always thinking of that song. ♦♦♦

▲▲▲ They didn't want it in here, in the prayer room. ▲▲▲

◆◆◆ I think that's wrong. That's the most powerful thing that they have. And that's what the people are going to walk out with, that sound in their head. If you give them the bird sound bytes, I think then that we're very close to just making a performance piece, a plaza-oriented performance piece. And I think we should leave them with that sound. It's just too powerful. Have you heard it? ◆◆◆

◇◇◇ What would the thought be? Why *shouldn't* it be in that space where everybody is going to be? ◇◇◇

◆◆◆ I think that it is inherent in what we're trying to do. We all are so used to coming up with these aggressive thoughts and ideas…and then pulling back. ◆◆◆

[Song playing]

◆◆◆ Yeah, we stood there and listened. We all just crowded around…we couldn't leave. That sound just goes into you. ◆◆◆

◆◆◆ And that's backwards? ◆◆◆

▲▲▲ That's backwards. ▲▲▲

◆◆◆ He said, basically, that this song is their way of seeking balance and that for something like this, he should present the opposite to keep and create the balance. ◆◆◆

▲▲▲ Maybe you should give the audience a rest after hearing this. After you hear this, I think you do need something that's calming. ▲▲▲

◆◆◆ I don't know. Every time I do something in my studio that's really powerful like this – I walk out the door and I take it with me – it's like a blessing. I don't need to calm down. The emotions calm down naturally. ◆◆◆

◆◆◆ …that's part of its' power, you know. There was a song…let's see, I just remember a part of it…[singing]. I don't know if you ever heard that. It's a very powerful song. ◆◆◆

◆◆◆ It's the one we used for my dad's video. It has the same feeling, doesn't it? That song was a warning, or maybe to let people know that you were coming from the distance. That's what *this* song is. But I hate to feel apologetic. I mean, that's not what I do. Anyway, we can solve that in the future. This recording is a group project. And you know, I can understand their logic. ◆◆◆

◆◆◆ But how much liberty do we have that's there to take? I mean, this is already changing it from one direction to the opposite direction. Well, this is also – of course – an example of transformation. We can look at it going from one place to the other, or from one state of being to another state of being. ◆◆◆

▲▲▲ There's something contrary about having it backwards. And there's nothing wrong with contrary. I like this, and I think if we include it we have to justify it within the group. If they feel it's blasphemy, then we probably can't do it…if they are that adamant about it. ▲▲▲

◆◆◆ I think out of respect for whoever did the original recording. ◆◆◆

▲▲▲ He did it for this purpose. ▲▲▲

◆◆◆ He did it for this purpose? ◆◆◆

▲▲▲ Yeah, he recorded it straight so they could play it backwards. They didn't want to use anybody else's material or any other song. They chose the right song to do it with. They knew what they were doing when they did it; they were committed. ▲▲▲

♦♦♦ Well, you know, in that case then, if that's the explanation then, certainly that's the justification. ♦♦♦

▲▲▲ So it's possible. If they have cold feet about it then we just have to work our way through it. ▲▲▲

♦♦♦ Still, I think that they want other sounds in this room. How would that bird sound compare to this? We all know a bird sound. This is just something extremely unique. ♦♦♦

▲▲▲ Then it just becomes more of a diorama exhibit – as opposed to an exhibit that makes you question what you're hearing. And that's what's happening here. It's not a real language, it's a language backwards. ▲▲▲

✧✧✧ I've always had this idea to ask Dad to record some of our language so I could learn it for myself, getting it on tape and saying the words in Keres, and then repeating them back. Because I say the words wrong most of the time. I would say something and I was so afraid in case I got it wrong. So many of us in this generation want to learn the language so badly. But even our own shame and doubt stops it from flourishing. Some of the listeners who come into the exhibition might be able to even bear witness to that process…to be able to get that sense that learning a language is really hard. I'd like to do this recording. ✧✧✧

▲▲▲ Yeah, it's right up there. It's where we're going. We're reaching back to those points where we want to find who we are. Where I grew up we were beaten for speaking our own language in the school. ▲▲▲

♦♦♦ They just told *me* to shut up. ♦♦♦

✧✧✧ And somehow it's found its' way to *us*, where we're kind of afraid. We haven't been beaten, but there's a shame there. ✧✧✧

◆◆◆ I've been thinking, I see a lot taking place, a lot. The diagram you have set right there, the various parts of it…I want to find a trail or road through it. One real idea keeps popping into my brain…It's a map. I mean, the map can be different sorts of things, but one thing that it is—and I think it every time—is sort of an indication of going from one place to another, one time to another, one age to another. And when you go from one place to another, or when something is transformed from one thing to another it's like, not only a structure or something dynamic taking place, but also it's a connection—a connection you know that is necessary. It's not visible, but it can be shown. If the people who see it are going to understand and dialogue with it, then maybe what is taking place with the dialogue is, maybe, not so much words…but a dialogue with their experience as they go from one portion of the exhibit to another. They are interacting by going through that 'map' process. It's like going across the street to the cathedral, or going from here to Tesuque, or going from here to the mountain. There are certain pathways, or roads, that are taken. And we can show this not so much as artists or writers, but actually by *demonstrating* it; demonstrating it so that the person that sees it is actually experiencing the connection…experiencing that map.

So when you come down to right here, then have it be somehow apparent that what they have been following is a route, or a map. How this is shown could be audio or…whether it's language-learning like Sara just gave an example of--one age to another, or the younger to the elder. Or else, it could be shown in written form in the English language. Or it could be both in the Native or Indigenous language as well as the English language, or other languages also. Something that the people – whatever age or whoever comes – can really participate in and participate through…as though they are actually in dialogue with the art…with the project. They are not just dialoguing with us or with each other, but it is actually the art that they are identifying with. Because when I talk to you, in a sense I identify with you. And when you understand me or hear what I have to say, you are in a sense identifying with me. We're exchanging. It's almost like, maybe, overlaying or collaborating our communication skills with one another. It's not like I'm telling you something *so* new and *so* strange that you don't know what I'm talking about. I'm saying things that you already know. And when you listen to me, you – in a sense— enter me and understand me, as you. And so when people are within the exhibit, that same dynamic takes place. When I talk about the map – like I said: place to place, face to face, time to time, age to age, or from infancy to old age, and from beginning and then continuing through say the life stages forever, not just ending but continuing…it would be like journeys from inward, inside of ourselves, inside of each other, or inside the culture, inside our lives…to outward, to out there in the world beyond us. I think when people experience a display we sort of assume that they understand intellectually. But some of that understanding is not intellectual, it's really experiential. It's really psychically. But, if that's too spacey a word, then, use 'imagination' because we rely a lot upon our imaginations. Our imaginations are transposed upon other people's imaginations so that in a sense, your imagination is communicating with my imagination and visa versa. We could do something we can actually touch, hear, taste or smell or act with. And I think the idea of the map could work and be something that's both graphic, audio, experiential— whatever that is, and so forth.

Learning is a kind of an affirmation, or a confirmation and affirmation. I always give credit to people for just being alive. When I leave someplace, what I carry away is the experience of what was positive when I was in that experience. Ten years from now I'd like to be able to remember that place by the experience that I had. And that is a real learning for me. I think it is for most people. How we learn is how we are affirmed.

Well, you know, when Sara was saying Acoma words… when she says it correctly because either I teach her or somebody else teaches her, she remembers it. When she knows, she realizes an experience of saying it the right way so that it's a very positive experience. That's how, then, she learns. That's what she will remember ten years from now, or a hundred years from now. When we look at Indigenaeity then, what is positive as a result of people who have had this experience, who will be confirmed, affirmed of their Indigenous experience? That Indigenousness or Indigenaeity is a positive vibe. ✦✦✦

MARCH 15, 2006

●●● …artists don't see it that way. They just want to get famous. They just want to make money and that's not what our goal is about. It's about creating a stage. It's about creating a dimension. ●●●

▲▲▲ Santa Fe is not that different from Hawaii…it's the number four tourist spot in the world. ▲▲▲

●●● You put the numbers up. But when you go back to the idea of the changes…I mean, that's a very difficult thing. But that was what we were given. We were given that sorry task. Because no one else took it up. There wasn't much that I felt that museums were doing. Museums weren't taking it to that next level. Just like some dances…some dances that we have, they're so geared into doing the same thing because they don't want to be judged or ruled out of the competition. Yet they do it for the competition. The competition does an enormous trauma to them spiritually because they want to win. It diminishes your spirit because you have to deal with all of these other entities that are dancing and competing with you and everybody's cursing you on top of it. *So you think words don't have a meaning or they don't have an affect?* All I'm saying is, you've got to lose, and that starts one thinking. No one here told me "we're gonna lose." But by the end of the week maybe that is going to manifest itself. That is why I want to be very careful with this concept because once you throw it out you can't bring it back in again. So we must be very careful with the words we use.

Santa Fe is a good audience. You have had many experiences there. We have had many experiences here. And our exhibit is just mere decoration. That's what we mean…decoration. Oh, man, I mean the logs started falling down like mad. Everything you mention about what we do here is to the ultimate. We don't spare the horses here. We can't. Then my question was, "did they go through that as well in Santa Fe?" Everyone's been telling me that they came by Santa Fe and they exclaim, "Rocky you should go to Santa Fe." "Why?" "Oh, you'll be amazed." Well, it was during the festival when my acquaintances went through. I went when it was *not* festival. When I came home then they told me, "Oh, you should've gone to the fair." No, what I saw was what I appreciated. Imagine what I would have experienced. I would've been turned 360 degrees all the way around. I would have been so dizzy that I probably wouldn't have even had time to put it all in perspective. Now, that's what they're trying to do here, and that's what we've tried to do for the last twenty-five years, was to create that kind of market. But I wanted to work with a museum like IAIA where you have this in-house scenario and you build upon that in-house scenario. You build upon a foundation, a strong structure, which you guys do have. We don't have that here. The museum is going through a huge problem right now. They have built a new science building and nothing is about the art. No native artists were included in this science building. We've always believed that 1% rule…that for all new buildings 1% of the budget should go towards art. But there is no Native art in this new building. Our huge convention center has no Native art in it. However, non-Native artists took the brush and painted a creation of our culture from their perspective. And all of it was wrong. And again, when you read these magazines that you find in the flap of your airline, most of those stories – what the writer depicts – is what will appeal to the tourists…and, also, there's the "fireside version."

That's what we're talking about when we discuss the "fireside version." We have a lot of that within the culture. The tourist version of our history. It simply does not manifest itself from the historical. Most of our artists are very intimidated by me. I would always encourage them to go into their own history, not necessarily mine, not necessarily the history of the Victorious One, but their own history, their own story. What are the things that your grandparents did, that your great-grandparents did? Remember what they did before they used to go on the Big Journey. Because once you do that, the confidence you build in knowing who you are is the greatest thing. And that's what we *used* to do. When you joined an organization, it helped you to know your own genealogy. Santa Fe is a pocket. I asked Art the same thing. "How was the Heard?" He said, "Well, the Heard is what it is…what it stands for." I said, "Remember, for five years now you've been doing the fair. It's not like Santa Fe."

I don't think it will ever be like Santa Fe. Santa Fe stands on its own. Now, they're catching on to what they need to keep up. Again, they need the dialogue, my friends. ●●●

◆◆◆ Santa Fe's a good market …but it's nowhere near where it could go. ◆◆◆

●●● That's where again you gotta have big shiny balls to take it beyond that. No one knows that without an initial dialogue. You're the only one that's been talking 'dialogue' all these years. ●●●

●○● J.K. Samuels is part Kwakiutl, part Tlingit, and part Hawaiian. What he did was, he told Rocky "if you come to Vancouver we will have a gathering of the tribes…fifteen tribes." People started gathering at twelve o'clock. By the time it came to six o'clock there had to have been twelve hundred people there. The museum set up a wonderful lodge to be an indigenous gathering spot, but when it came time they went, "Ahhh! What do we do! We lost control! What are they doing?" Because we just processed in and tribes were doing their chanting, the Hawaiians did their chanting, and there was ritual. No one was paying attention to the administration and they were freaking out. They were absolutely pulling their hair by the roots. The reception on the invitation read from 6:00 to 7:00…We were still dancing at midnight. ●○●

▲▲▲ That's the thing about Indigenous gatherings. They're very unique in that way. They don't fit into the box… anytime you invite Indigenous people to do something you just throw away the timetable. ▲▲▲

●○● Because I've worked with Indigenous Hawaiians for the 37 years of my life that I've been here, it's something that I know and that I'm accustomed to. So when we go to exhibitions and we see from 6 to 7:30...we *say* from 6 to 9 but we never *leave* at 9. The Hawaiians never leave at 9. We close the lights and we're the last ones to leave the building with our group of people. It's ten, 10:30, 11:00, and we're still there. You see, the museum to me, juxtaposing its reason for being...the reason that they are here is to be caretaker of this Indigenous art. Yet, when it comes to the living people...how do you deal with their generalized view "we love Hawai'i?" Do you love the people? Did you rub shoulders with them? Did you meet any? Now these people, when they advertise the islands, when you see those advertisements on the mainland, you don't see an Indigenous Hawaiian man or woman portraying Indigenous Hawaiian people. It's always a Filipino or an Asian. So they have no idea of what a Hawaiian looks like. ●○●

●●● We talk about "decoration." Indigenous is not part of the decoration. It's too messy. ●●●

♦♦♦ When Roxanne came back, we were talking about the elders and the responsibility of what we're doing. We're really talking about our past. "What about our children?" she asked. ♦♦♦

▲▲▲ ...she's been meeting with her tribe about determining who, among those that have left the Pueblo, can be considered a tribal member. When she went to New Zealand, they asked, "Don't you *know* who your children *are*?" And that just brought it all back. ▲▲▲

●●● That's why she wrote about burying the umbilicus at the doorstep, so that the children would come back and return home. That's the role that all elders always hope that they will be there for, the moment those children come back. ●●●

♦♦♦ That's the lodge. ♦♦♦

●●● Yeah, exactly. That's why the lodge is essential the way it's set up. I hate to put the audience through this, but they have to feel what we feel. It's the frustrations, the fortification of all these things, that make us happy and sad at the same time. They need to feel that as well, because it's a great battle that goes on in our minds and in our spirits. That's some of the things that we can gloss over with a few colors and a few images, but inside it's probably a painful scenario. And you stand back with a glass in your hand and go, "yah I worked hard on it." But you know inside, spiritually, that's not what you wanted to say. You wanted to say "that was overwhelming – spiritually – for me." "I created it for the connection between us, them, and those who came before us."

That's what I love to do, but my wealth is being able to realize that I'm not alone in this bag. Okay, so this is why I'm meeting you guys. And you exchange your thoughts and ideas from one place to another...from one place, from one dimension. It's enormous for us to be standing in these kinds of situations. I'm not afraid to take on a battle. It's...one more notch on our belt, that's about the way I look at it. Basically, people will become more respectful of the place that we come from. I think Santa Fe is ready for this. When talking to Diane, she was just bubbling! You're talking about an art historian that knows art throughout the world. And when we mentioned some of these dialogues, what did she say? "Oh, yeah! There's room for a lot of this!" She's not afraid...she sees that there's something down around the corner ready to happen. And she's made me realize, "you're not gonna just sit there and complain anymore. That's enough. Let's go. Come on." I wanna do something that's gonna really piss them off. And that's what I do. But it's a challenge. That's why we do what we do. And that's what we're going to do...create such an opening that it's going to have to take minds and bodies to figure out how we did it. I've felt this way since you first contacted me about this project.

The world is dying because of it. I mean, I could picture that scenario. And we *have* to picture that scenario...to realize that we've been on this planet for thirty-five thousand years as human beings, and this is as far as we can go? I don't mean technologically, I mean spiritually. You said it the first time. When I started creating one tiki after another, I used to ask myself, "okay not another tiki, right?" …then people started becoming afraid. "Oh, you mean there's not just one?" I said no there's not. "What do you mean, you guys have more?" Yes we have. Teachers were amazed. They didn't understand the difference between the respect for elements and the respect for essence. That's our gods…everything on this planet, we pay them enormous respect and reverence because we are just mere beings. ●●●

●○● I feel that it is very important for the next generation to gain a voice. In the meetings we had at San Diego, we had several of the civic clubs talking about "our kids, our kids, our kids." All the parents were there. Well, you're talking about doing cultural things for your children, yet where are they? … Everyone had children. "Where *are* your children?" I said. They never attend…they're American kids now, they're not interested.. ●○●

▲▲▲ … it's our responsibility to make them interested. ▲▲▲

●○● That's right. That's what it is. It's our responsibility. ●○●

●●● It looks like the word Indigenous is like a Christmas tree. It's what you put on it. It's what is familiar. It's what attracts the audience… ●●●

♦♦♦ And I personally think that we're all Indigenous. ♦♦♦

●○● But you know, it's an awareness. Because when you bring this subject up, there are so many Westerners who – until you mention it, would not think to say, "I'm Indigenous, too." Because they're inclusive of themselves. And of course I, being Sicilian, raised by my dad and my mom, my first language was Italian. Our culture was strictly European even though I was raised in American schools. But my father kept a place for us. Indigenous, or that sense of Indigenous, that no one around me had. So it is up to the parents. It is a responsibility. The parents say "you are going to have that outside of this house. This is going to be part of your wonderful sense of the world."

I could see my father was very disillusioned…we were theatrical people…Within one or two generations they no longer spoke their language, they barely could speak the dialect. But they lost their sense of culture that goes beyond the food eating. And it's like there is no longer any sense of Italian in America. They get together as the sons of the sons of Italy. The community is very, very important. ●○●

●●● I believe that this can happen with IAIA. The tribal effect…it was the program that brought us together. But it is also the program that manifests itself into word. That I use as a very small metaphor. A small window – that's how the communities can be established by that. But basically, it was really an establishment of trust among the community…

When you look at those letters, Bob, that's why I said a lot has happened in just the short months that we've been together and that we've been writing. Even your letters have done a lot for me. But because this is the experimental stage in what we're trying to do, we have to make sure that we cross the T's and dot the I's. That's what I think is essential. But I've always believed that because of what we do, because of the mana we carry within ourselves I think that's what pushes us. 'Cause I get excited just when we talk about this. I get excited even to look forward to the future because that to me is the mana that each of us carries. And these artists, because of their duties, when they do write, I'm always excited to see another perspective from what you write, from what I write, from what John writes. We will set the precedent for this because we did take on this responsibility. And I'm glad people like Roxanne and Rose are starting to feel that. It's like going through the ceremony that evening. We didn't need cameras. But what did appear was something that stayed with me forever. And I said, in spite of the way this was done, in spite of the way it worked, I said, as outsiders we'd probably criticize. We'd ask, "Why can't we take a photograph?" "Why did they just do that?" The questions would come back. "Tell me, I accept all. This is what I did? Okay I understand." Then I would go to him and say, "Explain this to me." Like when I went to the Governor's meeting. "Why did they do that?" I asked. "Because that is the exchange of the dialogue." It made me see so quickly in such a short time. But it needs to be pointed out. If we don't ask these questions we won't know. And these things, these little things that we find very important in our lives might just be overlooked. That's why when I do tell about this type of a thing, it really is not just with the wood-carving project, it has to do with the relationship of the connection of the spirit. ●●●

MAY 16, 2006

○○○ I'm wondering if it would be confusing. Are we going to have clothes there in the exhibit to put on, or take off? It could have the opposite effect. So maybe that's what you do. ○○○

▲▲▲ But that's kind of the truth. Are they there for some people to put on and some people to take off? Our identities are portable identities. That's still the idea, its like a birth canal. And we do have baby sounds in *that* room. We're calling it the birthing canal. ▲▲▲

❖❖❖ The heartbeat or the breath in that first room – so it's the whole circle and it goes all the way through the whole journey from beginning to end. That's what I was assuming, and that the room with the sweetgrass, the sound was gonna be comforting but as soon as you exit that room then it gets real distorted. That's when you have you know, the motorcycle sounds backwards, and the disturbing sounds…with Harry's photographs being projected on you as you walk. ❖❖❖

○○○ I think this area should have the strange noises. This is a very important transition right here.

Yeah, the hard noises. 'Cause this should feel good. And I think Harry's right, I think the clothes rack – if there's gonna be clothes – should be out here, before you walk in. Then you hang up your skin, and go through the birth canal, you get brushed by all the sweetgrass, you walk through here and you have these strange noises. And then you could go that way, or if you go this way you have all the things, the cartoons, and the words. And then you go down to Harry's photograph room.

So you will get just an image or something like that at your feet. But you can also see them on the wall and you'll be walking *through* the projection. ○○○

❖❖❖ We should use our own pictures of our own families, and not just the old black-and-whites but all the way up to now. And if you have one picture, you can crop a lot of strong images out of that one picture. So we wouldn't need hundreds of thousands of them, we would just need a few. ❖❖❖

○○○ When you walk in front of a projector, there's this feeling like something's hitting you. ○○○

❖❖❖ And that's the idea of the crossing images – one hitting the wall here, one hitting the wall here, and one hitting the wall there. I don't know if it will work, but as you walk through you should still be able to see the images ahead of you. But as you walk through they're actually hitting you. ❖❖❖

♦♦♦ Play that sound. To those of you who haven't heard it yet, we have a sound of singing played backward. It's really powerful. I think that maybe it might be a really good introduction to the long range of this project. But I think that maybe we're all kind of afraid to use it, somehow. I suggest that we use it as the theme of the whole thing. When people leave, they'd have that sound in their heads. That might bring them back later on for the continuation of the dialogue. I'm very concerned that we might be making just a pretty show that makes people feel good. I think that this audio is the strongest thing we have going for this whole show. And we can't be afraid of it. I suggest that it be in the main room. ♦♦♦

✳✳✳ It reminds me of contraries. ✳✳✳

◆◆◆ That's kind of what we're trying to do, we're trying to alter something. ◆◆◆

◯◯◯ It is an inside-outside sort of song. ◯◯◯

◆◆◆ That's just my opinion. But I do think that this is the key to the whole show. But that's just my opinion. No, I don't think this thing will compare to the breathing, no matter how we produce it…it's not going to compare. ◆◆◆

➢➢➢ Very hypnotic. ➢➢➢

▲▲▲ It's still peaceful though. It's unsettling, but peaceful. ▲▲▲

◆◆◆ And it could be anybody anywhere in the world. ◆◆◆

▲▲▲ And it could be any language. ▲▲▲

➢➢➢ I find that scary. I like it very much. ➢➢➢

❖❖❖ My question is, are we trying to produce a fear? My fear is that it's so powerful, and that fear is what keeps us from actually looking at things. I'm scared this is going to have an adverse affect, and this prayer is gonna suck our breath and we're not gonna grow because of this. And that fear that maybe we have to go completely backwards in order to find ourselves and heal our people. I was thinking about my cartoons and what I want to do, and I keep going around in my head. I want to take a historic event and change it for the better. To go back in history and say, "no, this isn't the way it happened. We're gonna retell it." But how do you do that? You've gotta reverse and start over from the beginning from the very first family. Relationships, like the piece that we're working on. And I don't want to use the music 'cause I'm scared of what kind of things it could call onto us. And maybe we have to face that scary stuff. ❖❖❖

♦♦♦ It's scary 'cause nobody I know has the slightest idea what we're doing. But we all know its dialogue. It's questions, but that's something really important for our children so they don't have to face this. ♦♦♦

➤➤➤ What if we used this chant but not so loud? ➤➤➤

♦♦♦ I bet you the more traditional would have a problem. ♦♦♦

OOO I think a lot of people would have a problem. OOO

❖❖❖ What we're trying to do with the main circle gallery is that you lose your cognitive sense and you go back to your intuition. And, as you walk through, you're going through the process of releasing your stereo-types and all these "ideals" from your mind. And the idea is to keep that, to keep yourself centered within your intuition in this area so that your breath is constant...and that those ideas of judgments or ideas, placed upon yourself, would be loosened during the process of understanding. Which are where all the cartoons are, and all the words, and the labels that are put on us...and all of it. ❖❖❖

INDIGENOUS AND AUTHENTIC

INDIGENOUS AND AUTHENTIC:

HAWAIIAN EPISTEMOLOGY AND THE TRIANGULATION OF MEANING

Manulani Aluli Meyer
Kanaka Maoli o Hawaiinuiakea - Native Hawaiian
Tamaki Makaurau / Auckland, Aotearoa
On sabbatical from the University of Hawaii at Hilo
Associate Professor of Education

Whether or not you can observe a thing depends on the theory you use.
It is the theory that decides what can be observed.
— Albert Einstein —

Indigenous and Authentic. We must develop new theories from ancient agency so we can accurately respond to what is right before our very eyes. It was Che Guevera, revolutionist extraordinaire, who believed the shackles of ignorance can be snapped via ideas that are indigenous *and* authentic, old *and* new, cycled *and* creative, ancient *and* developed-this-moment. So too with research. Can the idea, then, of duality combine itself into wholeness needed for this time? Dual to non-dual, research to renewal, fragment to whole—yes this is the goal.

This chapter introduces you to indigenous epistemology as viewed by Native Hawaiian mentors, friends and family so that you will understand that *specificity leads to universality.*[1] This is a spiritual principle within ancient streams of knowing. It nests itself within a wider and wider space I now experience as wonderment and truth in deeper and deeper dimensions. This chapter closes with a discussion of the Triangulation of Meaning, an authentic leap into new ways of viewing reality that will challenge current research paradigms based on Newtonian assumptions of space, time and knowing. Indigenous and Authentic. Timeless and Timely. So, put on the tea. Here we go.

HAWAIIAN EPISTEMOLOGY:
THE SPECIFICS OF UNIVERSALITY

But will it also be thought strange that education
and knowledge of the world have enabled us to perceive
that as a race we have some special mental
and physical requirements not shared by the other races
which have come among us?
— Queen Lili'uokalani, 1898 —

All peoples have their own distinct beliefs of what knowledge is and what knowing entails. This idea is an example of epistemology[2] specific to place and people. Applying hermeneutics to politics, education, health, and all modern institutions details why such a simple epistemological truth is often denied.[3] Power, hegemony, colonialization, racism, and oppression are the labels on such acts of denial. I now see these as *unawareness*.

How I experience the world is different from how you experience the world, and both our interpretations matter. *This is an important point* as it links inevitably to transformative policies, awareness, and pathways to liberation via our own articulated epistemology. It expands the idea of what knowledge is suppose to be and in truth is—vast, limitless and *completely* subjective. As ocean people in a warm climate, you bet we have a different way of knowing and thus being. Regardless of the fracas of modernity within our shorelines, we as the first peoples of Hawaiinuiakea have our own uniqueness for how we have approached knowledge / knowing for thousands of years. Our epistemology *still* differs from those who occupy our shores and as we awaken, a revolution of remembering will bring us back to what is valuable about life and living, knowledge and knowing.

The following seven categories help to organize systems of consciousness that are needed to enliven what knowing means in today's rampage called modernity. They are doorways into a space without walls. They are notes in a song my people are singing to you. Do not be put off by its specificity, simple notions and odd languaging. It is merely one group of people finding their way back into meaning—a space we all can share together. Remember, bear witness to your own thoughts now as you delve into these categories of knowing. How will you respond to "exotic other?" Will you see the role of its vitality in your own capacity to see and hear? How will it inform your own ideas of research, knowing and being of service to a world-wide awakening? Be open. Be ready. We have work to do.

Spirituality and Knowing:
The Cultural Context of Knowledge

The question is, Who is the self?
You're not just who you are now. You're aligned with people
who have gone through it lots and lots of times.
— Calvin Hoe, Hakipuu —

Knowledge that endures is spirit-driven. It is a life-force connected to all other life forces. It is more an extension than it is a thing to accumulate. When the Hawaiians I listened to spoke of spirituality with regard to intelligence they were not talking about religion. *These are two completely different ideas.* What was discovered in the thoughts of others and within my own reflection was the intentionality of process, the value and purpose of meaning, and the practice of mindfulness. These ideas accessed via deep and enduring respect for our kupuna, our lands, our oceans, our language, rituals and families became the foundation of a Hawaiian essence. These are *spiritual principles* that if played out as epistemology helps us enter spaces of wonderment, discernment, right viewing and mature discourse. It is an old idea that does not clock answers or place you in special education classrooms because you cannot read at grade level. It is a rich and mature response to life's diversity and brilliance.

The spirituality of knowledge got entangled within the bureaucracy of its form and has been pulled back further and further away from the light of fundamental empirical knowing. It is now often confused with religion and relegated to back room lectures and dismissed by mainstream science. Spirit as knowing is a *real idea* that allows us to ritualize ways to collect medicine, read a text, prepare a meal, or communicate with family. It allows knowing to be an act of consciousness that reaches beyond the mundane into connection and alignment with an essence that finds its renewal throughout the generations. This higher reach of knowing collapsed under the weight of homogeneity and assimilation - around the world. It must right itself through our engagement to secure our survival.

How does the interpretation of knowledge as spirit affect your research? It doesn't. *You do.* It merely points to a frequency that if heard will synergize with your courage when you write without fear after asking questions that search for deeper meaning to an act, an idea, a moment. An epistemology of spirit encourages us all to be of service, to not get drawn into the ego nurtured in academia, and to keep diving into the wellspring of our own awe. In that way our research is bound in meaning and inspired by service to others or to our natural environment. That's an epistemology based on what we refer to as *ea* or animating principles. *Ea* is also our Hawaiian word for sovereignty. And as I believe more in the Nation-Within idea, let it inspire you to develop your own mind within the context of the needs of your own community. Do you see how it can assist you as you begin to formulate the why and what of your work? See your work as a taonga (sacred object) for your family, your community, your people—*because it is.*

That Which Feeds:
Physical Place and Knowing

I am shaped by my geography.
— Hannah Kihalani Springer, Kukuiohiwai —

Indigenous people are all about place. Land/aina, defined as 'that which feeds' is the everything to our sense of love, joy and nourishment. Land is our mother. *This is not a metaphor.* For the Native Hawaiians speaking of knowledge, land was the central theme that drew forth all others. You came from a place. You grew in a place and you had a relationship with that place. *This is an epistemological idea.* Because of the high mobility of Americans, and billboards as childhood scenery, many find this idea difficult to comprehend. Land/Ocean shapes my thinking, my way of being, and my priorities of what is of value. Remember, if knowledge is imbued with spirit, how much more is the where we are inspired in this knowledge making? One does not simply learn about land, we learn best *from* land.[4] This knowing makes you *intelligent* to my people. How you are on land or in the ocean tells us something about you. *Absolutely*. It opens doors to the specificity of what it means to exist in a space and how that existing extends into how best to interact in it. This includes cities, rooms, suburbs and all the many configurations we have found ourselves in.

Land is more than a physical place. It is an idea that engages knowledge and contextualizes knowing. It is the key that turns the doors inward to reflect on how space shapes us. Space as fullness, as interaction, as thoughts planted. It is not about emptiness but about *consciousness*. It is an epistemological idea because it conceptualizes those things of value to embed them in a *context*. Land is more than just a physical locale; it is a mental one that becomes water on the rock of our being. Consideration of our place, our mother is the point here. And she is more than beautiful, or not. *She is your mother.*

How will this inspire your research? Well, to begin with, check your breathing. Is it deep and aware or are you troubled and in a hurry? Land as an epistemological cornerstone to our ways of re-thinking is all about relating in ways that are sustaining, nourishing, receptive, wise. Knowing with land should help you find out more about your own self, and when that process begins as a researcher you start to open your own phenomenological inquiry into *your* origins of space. Was it lined with books or were you in the lap of dandelions? One does not judge here. It's all about *re-cognizing* and finding how space influenced your thinking. Because it has. It does now. And what you bring to your knowing influences all that you do, write and offer to the world. This epistemological category helps us all recover from our childhood traumatic belief that place is never recoverable. With regard to research, our early spaces help create the topic you choose, the questions you formulate, and the way you respond to data. It is all shaped by space. Not time. Conscious-shaping space. Space-shaped consciousness. An epistemological priority.

The Cultural Nature of the Senses: Expanding Our Ideas of Empiricism

I don't think I was taught that! I was hearing it.
— Irmgard Farden Aluli, Kailua —

I surf. My ways of knowing a swell, where to line up for a wave and why Kona winds were perfect for diving (not surfing) in my home waters off Kailua made me a beach rat. It has helped me know my place in the world. It is distinct and based on experiences of place and passion. It differs from yours. You have your own brilliance and priority of knowing. We are uniquely experienced and my sensual history brings my current understanding into a fluid context that extends a modern Hawaiian world view. I am empirically configured by my past and my senses and body were the tools and recording devices in which I retrieved and stored all data. *Our senses are culturally shaped.* This is an epistemological idea. It is not a bad or good thing. It is a fact that for some reason has been misunderstood and developed as a polemic point in most matters of philosophy and basically ignored in research.

Differences at these fundamental levels begin to expand all points of epistemology that will open your mind and keep it open to alternative interpretations of how one hears a song or sees an event. They are the A-B-C's of how and why we engage with others and why we sometimes scratch our head with their renditions of reality. Remember, what we have in common is our difference. It begins first with this, and it is the leaping off point to the beauty of specificity that will bring us to a common knowing. This contextualizes the once static notion of empiricism that believes you and I see the same corn field. It's the maturing of objectivity into subjectivity. It is experience that tells the farmer his corn field is in need of calcium and water as I, the beach rat from Kailua, notice nothing.

Every Native Hawaiian I listened to spoke in terms of their own epistemology, their own empirical understanding of the world. The aroma of a lei pakalana, sunrise pinks splashed in the heavens as Hiiaka, the touch of kalo in cool running waters, the thrill of sound in harmony. All these are aspects of a culture evolving in place, and they all shape the building blocks of knowing—our sensual organs that are culturally configured.

This fundamental idea that our senses are culturally shaped seems almost obvious but it must be understood deeply if you are to proceed into what many may not understand. Keep going. Your relationship to your research topic is your own. It springs from a life-time of distinctness and uniqueness only you have history with. Be encouraged by this! Do not doubt your own capacity to scaffold complex and cultural ways in which to describe the world. It is time to be clear at this very fundamental level.

Relationship and Knowledge:
Self Through Other

How can you be happy in your experiences when others are unhappy?
— Gladys Brandt, Honolulu —

Here is an epistemological category that deepens all other categories. To be in relationship triggers *everything*: with people, with ideas, with the natural world. It was a cornerstone inspiration to the people I listened to. It marked a consciousness of the dialectic, a reckoning with what one brought to other. Relationship gave mentors opportunities to practice generosity with others, harmony with land, and ways to develop their own pathway to an idea. *These are epistemological points.* One was in constant interdependence with others and with natural surroundings. Even in modern Hawai'i, family spoke of awareness of connection and being in right relation with all. Of course this is the ideal that sometimes falls short in reality, but it was a priority most mentors lived out in their lives.

Knowledge was the bi-product of slow and deliberate dialogue with an idea, with others' knowing, or with one's own experience with the world. Knowing itself was in relationship with knowledge, a nested idea that deepened information (knowledge) through direct experience (knowing). The focus is with connection and our capacity to be changed with the exchange. Thus the idea of self *through* other. I believe this is an idea more shaped by our practice of aloha, the intelligence of compassion, empathy and care. It is an ancient idea to heal with all relations, and this included land and ocean. Aloha was a level of consciousness that defined our intelligence.[5] Vivid interconnection was valued. A lived dialectic. After all, did we not bring the endless joy of riding waves to the world?

How does this inspire research? It reminds us that knowledge does not exist in a vacuum. Intelligence is challenged, extended and enriched when viewed in dyad-awareness or group consciousness. Of course this opens doors to the richness of hermeneutics and its inevitable world-wide focus, but first we segue with epistemology. It is the notion that intentions must harmonize with ideas, and ideas form the libretto of our transformational drama. It is all fundamentally done with awareness of other and consequently, of oneself. Will your research bring forth solutions that strengthen relationships with others or will it damage future collaborations? How will your own relationship with self inspire truth and courage to do what will be needed when predictable roadblocks enter your view plain. A knowledge that includes true awareness of other will radically alter research protocols, questions, processes.

Utility and Knowledge:
Ideas of Wealth and Usefulness

Going to the beach for her (mother)
was a place where you would go and gather
and not a place for recreation.
— Pua Kanahele, Panaewa —

Function is the higher vibration of an idea, not the lower. How one defines function is first discovered in its meaning and then its interpretation. Here it is! Here is where the cosmological clashing began, not with the word but with its *meaning*.[6] This is why we go to epistemology and then, inevitably to hermeneutics. This is where Descartes' error comes to light. *Cogito ergo sum*—I think therefore I am—does not divide us from our embodied selves, it can unite us in a wisdom that is embedded in usefulness, awareness and function. This is edging into a universal epistemology. It's all about function. And as aloha is my intelligence, well, I guess this means you can use my board.

Hoaʻe ka ʻike heʻenalu i ka hokua o ka ʻale—show your knowledge of surfing on the back of a wave. Thus one knows. It's not about how well you can quote theory, it's whether those ideas affect how you act. Here is the focus of this entire book: How will you feel encouraged to go forth into the world to alter its frequency? How will you bring robustness to this flat-land knowing literacy keeps un-dimensioned? How will you actualize these principles of being to expand what knowledge is at its core?

Make your work useful by your meaning and truth. I know, it sounds somehow ethereal, but this is the point: knowledge that does not heal, bring together, challenge, surprise, encourage, or expand our awareness is not part of the consciousness this world needs now. This is the function we as indigenous people posit. And the great clarity that I have been waiting to express through the beautiful mind of our beloved kupuna healer Halemakua: *we are all indigenous.*[7]

Words and Knowledge:
Causality in Language

Okay, you give an assignment to a family.
Maybe to that family you'd say: You cook the long rice and chicken.
Come that night it starts to bubble, then you would know
they grumbled. They didn't put their heart and soul in making this
so you can find out who grumbled, I mean, by the taste.
— Florence Kumukahi, Kaipalaoa —

Here is an epistemological category better reflected in Hawaiian literature and historic discussions in text than in the mentors interviewed. It is a subtle category that was clearly repetitive throughout our Hawaiian written history but somehow silent in modern oral descriptions of intelligence. The idea of causality in language is inherent in discussions of spirituality, relationship and utility but the fine-tuned nuance of intention and the agency found in how one languages the world was not readily apparent during interviews. I believe this absence is a sign of where precisely we must lend our awareness.

Hawaiians at one time believed in the causative agency of intention.[8] *Thought creates.* This is why it was seen as negative to even *think* of hitting a child. Negative thoughts then had negative consequences. This whole cycle of reciprocation turns on the integrity and life force of a thought expressed as action. The point here is that effect begins with intention. This is an epistemological idea that helps us mature into a deeper relationship with what action and reality is at its core: *thought*.

The idea that thought creates and intention shapes the observable world may seem far fetched to some but it is now recognized and discussed in depth by indigenous scholars, quantum physicists, mothers, and social scientists, and summarized in many ground-breaking works.[9] Specific to human problems in society, effective research stems from deeply looking into the *conditions* of what may be the cause of specific phenomena. And these conditions are inevitably found in *consciousness*. David Hawkins summarizes it thus: "There are no *causes* within the observable world...*the observable world is a world of effects*."[10] Our thoughts create reality. This is where authentic dovetails with indigenous. This is where standardized tests miss the boat. This is where your research comes in.

What this means is that poverty does not cause drug addiction but rather our *response* to poverty does. My thoughts about the effects of poverty affect how I respond to it. All bets are off, however, if my brain cells are not operable. It highlights the idea that post-colonial for Hawai'i is not first a physical place but a *mental one*. It by *no means* dismisses the physical burden of poverty, oppression and other acts of abuse put on the body, mind and spirit, it simply names what is at the inevitable *core* of anything tangible: *thought*. It also helps us develop a different discourse for solution-making that snaps us out of the level of consciousness it was created in.[11]

The question now may be: What is your intention in doing research? What are your thoughts about your topic? What do you bring to the phenomenon of a moment shared with other? How will you think through the process and product of data collection or how will you respond to experiences and ideas that will be completely new to you? This is not a distant discussion of your bias or of your deductive or inductive realities. It is the pulse of your character that you must name. Understanding causation in intention and language helps us critically self-reflect. It can bring a vibrancy of purpose and truth to your findings and style of writing.

This is not objectivity we are discussing, it is fully conscious subjectivity and it holds the promise of being effective in a radically different way if you understand its meaning and prioritize it at all levels of your research. It is called meta-consciousness. To be more than a woman of my word. To be a woman of my intention. Write about it. Put your thoughts in a Prologue or in an Appendix. It can be done.

The Body/Mind Question: The Illusion of Separation

Without heart we don't have sense.
— Keola Lake, Kahala —

Here is the capstone of Hawaiian epistemology and its sharpest sword in this duel with mainstream expectations of what it means to know something. The separation of mind from body is not found in a Hawaiian world view. It was not apparent in any interview, in any body of literature, in any dreams that arrived to be of service to this unfolding reflection. Indeed, intelligence and knowledge was embedded at the core of our bodies—the stomach or na'au. The na'au for Native Hawaiians is the site for both feeling and thinking. Wisdom, na'auao, also translates as heart, emotion, and intelligence. Modern Hawaiians are trained to dismiss these tuggings of ones embodied knowing for the objective, unfeeling one. Clearly, if one succeeds in this way, culture erodes and wisdom becomes a flimsy caricature of its potential. The divorce of thought from feeling, however, is not part of a Hawaiian view of intelligence.

Body is the *central* space from which knowing is embedded. It was not merely a passing idea but basic to all interviews. Our body holds truth, our body invigorates knowing, our body helps us become who we are. This was not simply a metaphoric discussion of union with sensation and conceptualization. Our thinking body is not separated from our feeling mind. *Our mind is our body. Our body is our mind.* And both connect to the spiritual act of knowledge acquisition. It is part of what we will discuss further as an integral space in the triangulation of meaning.

> Liver is where you digest the powers of perception. Digestion is not purely physical. I have "fed" on knowledge. It is an internal digestion. If I have digested a book, I have eaten it, digested it. This is where we separate epistemologies—in digestion and vital organs. Rubellite Kawena Johnson, Scholar / Educator

But that's what *na'auao* is. It's a cosmic center point. It has to do with your ancestors coming together with you. It has to do with your spiritual being coming together. It has to do with our physical being.

—Pua Kanahele, Kumu Hula / Educator

Knowing there is intelligence to feeling and feeling in intelligence begins the long turn-around from an isolated thinking self void of the potential messiness of subjective realities found in all versions of the world. It brings us back into ancient sensibilities that recognize the strength found in conscious subjectivity and clearly stated origins of thought found in empirical, objective recognition. Objectivity is not the evil here. It does not serve a more awakened future to argue one is better than the other. In our evolving future, both are needed, both are useful, both will find their way to harmony. It is the bullying found in unconscious world-views that would deny that subjectivity is actually a maturing of objectivity, not a dumbing down. Here is where indigeneity and authentic synergize.

HAWAIIAN EPISTEMOLOGY:
IMPLICATIONS FOR RESEARCH

Aloha is the intelligence with which we meet life
— Olana Kaipo Ai —

True intelligence is not described by an SAT score. Here is the point to all this detail on what it means to be intelligent to my people. What are the implications these seven categories of knowledge-making and knowing have on *your* research mind? Did you feel a *remembering* with these ideas? It has become clear to me that the specificity of these Hawaiian epistemological categories is indeed endemic to islands in the middle of the Pacific. But they also offer a way to organize universal truths you may wish to consider:

> Knowledge that endures is a *spiritual* act that animates and educates
> We *are* earth and our awareness of how to exist with it extends from
>   this idea
> *Our senses are culturally shaped* offering us distinct pathways to reality
> Knowing something is bound to how we develop a *relationship* with it
> *Function* is vital with regard to knowing something
> *Intention* shapes our language and *creates our reality*
> *Knowing is embodied* and in union with cognition

I arrived at this view-plain through the specificity of knowing my ancient self—spaces we all can recognize because we all have. True intelligence it ends up *is* self knowledge.[12] Self-inquiry helped shape my own understanding of knowing and put in the light bulbs on a path leading to wider application. It ends my feelings of inferiority and disconnection. It helps discern the glaring difference between uniformity and universality. It is best summarized by Nobel laureate Rabindranath Tagore: *Man's individuality is not his highest truth, there is that in him which is universal.*[13]

So, if specificity leads us into universal truths, how does *that* help us right what is so clearly wrong with our systems and thought patterns? How do we begin to effectively debate entrenched practices that do not recognize a more enduring way to engage in knowledge or a more enlivened way to live in harmony with all things? Why can't we approach research, scientific inquiry and policy-making with integral beliefs that honor and develop fractal approaches to intention?[14] Why do we not engage dialectically with those who oppose us? How are we to develop tools of self-reflection so that we become more capable agents of change and transformation? Here are questions that an expanding epistemology challenges us to think through. Perhaps as we enter the Triangulation of Meaning we are heading into parts of how they will be answered. Indigenous and Authentic, remember? Yes, yes. Let's continue on. We've still got lots to do.

THE TRIANGULATION OF MEANING: BODY, MIND AND SPIRIT

Triangulation, three intimations of one idea,
should be noted as a guide to edifying
coherence among associations.
— Zach Shatz —

Here we go! Here is the authentic part of this chapter. It is a set of ideas that may bring you back to *remembering*. It extends indigenous epistemology into a context of world awakening. It is daringly simple but then again words only point to the truth. *Genuine knowledge must be experienced directly.*[15] It is meant to help you organize your research mind and give you the courage to do so with the rigor found in facts, logic *and* metaphor. It is offered now because it organized my own thoughts and oiled the tools needed to dismantle the Master's House found in perfect order *in my own mind.*[16] We as researchers can now become architects of meaning shaping spaces as yet unseen. Here is the challenge. Here is a floor plan.

Let's begin with the idea of *triangulation*. Wilderness education teaches that if you wish to find your place on a topographical map, one need only locate two geographical distinctions on land and with the use of a compass and pencil, the third and final spot - your location, can then be found. The use of three points to discover one's location in both two and three dimensions is the art and science of "triangulation" and I have always thrilled to its use and implication. Thus the metaphor of *triangulating our way to meaning* with the use of *three* points. These three points? Body, Mind and Spirit.

Using Body, Mind and Spirit as a template in which to organize meaningful research asks us to extend through our objective/empirical knowing (Body) into wider spaces of reflection offered through conscious subjectivity (Mind) and finally, via recognition and engagement with deeper realities (Spirit). Finally we are defining places science can follow into but not lead or illuminate. Other ways of knowing something *must* be introduced if we are to evolve into a more enlightened society. It will not occur with scientific or objective knowledge only. Nobel Laureate Werner Heisenberg puts it more succinctly: *Physics can make statements about strictly limited relations that are only valid within the framework of those limitations.*

So, before we begin this discussion please understand that your schooled mind has been shaped by mostly one point in the triangulation—body. Body is a synonym for external, objective, literal, sensual, empirical. Change-agents, indigenous researchers, cultural leaders, and transformational scholars are now working together to help this idea grow up. So, take a breath. Keep your mind open.

To begin, mahalo to Ken Wilber for his capacity to see patterns in philosophy and research that brought this idea to the world.[18] I have simply extended his preliminary list into trilogies that make sense to me and the needs of our focus. It was my wilderness education experiences that brought forth the idea of "triangulation" as I have experienced the beauty of its practice and utility. We are poised to use three points in our experiencing of life and research to find our way home. Not two. Not one. Three.

THE NUMBER THREE

The Tao gives birth to One.
One gives birth to Two.
Two gives birth to Three.
Three gives birth to all things.
— Tao Te Ching—Chapter 42 —

It is more like Bucky Fuller's tetrahedron.[19] It's about the structural integrity formed when *three* points meet in dimensioned space. The tetrahedron is also the sacred geometry of infinity, energy, and the perfect balance of equilibrium found in post-quantum physics. It is the doorway into wholeness. We at first thought it was about opposites, about duality, about bridging polarity and painting our theories of gender, science and life under this light. Black and white comparisons kept us busy for hundreds of years. It has shaped the polemic universe we now take for granted. True or False. Body or Mind. Oppressor or Oppressed. Cognition or Feeling. Real or Imagined.

The world is indeed perceived in binary systems. It has caused un-told horror and helped create a rigid epistemology we now assume cannot evolve. We have options however. Why not experience duality like the Yin and Yang, Ku and Hina of our ancient selves?[20] Life *is* found in dual forms but as we gather evidence from all sectors of world scholars, mystics and practitioners, we are discovering that life moves within a *context of dynamic consciousness* that synergizes with Aristotle's highest intellectual virtue he referred to as phronesis. This is not simply a discussion of moral relativity or the third point in duality, it is a piercing into different planes of epistemology to discuss what inevitably shifts into non-duality because of its inherent wholeness. It has helped me step from entrenched patterns of thinking to include older ways and more experienced expressions of what intelligence *really* is and how it can be expressed. It's about time, don't you think?

REACHING FOR WHOLENESS

Relative and absolute, these two truths are declared to be.
The absolute is not within the reach of the intellect,
for intellect is grounded in the relative.
— Shantidevi —

The world is more than dual. It is whole. We have looked at parts so long we perhaps believe the gestalt of our knowing is not possible. With regard to research, we *still* believe statistics is synonymous with truth. It is a dangerous road to travel when we pack only empirical ways of being into our research backpack. Here is the point of doing research at this juncture of history: Empiricism is just one point in our triangulation of meaning and although it may begin the process of research, it by *no means,* is the final way in which to engage, experience or summarize it.[21] Research and life is more in line with three simple categories that have been lost in theory and rhetoric: Body, Mind, *and* Spirit. Thus begins the discussion of a triangulation of meaning. Ho'omakaukau? Let us begin.

BODY: THE GROSS AND PHYSICAL KNOWING OF LIFE
First Point in the Triangulation of Meaning

I believe we carry our values in our bodies.
We carry our culture in our bodies.
— Peesee Pitsiulak, Inuuit —

We're not talking gross as in yucky. Gross starts this Triangulation of Meaning because it describes what is outside, what is external, what is seen, what is empirical. It is the *form* that consciousness has shaped. It is one way to begin this discussion of research for meaning because it is what we are familiar with. It is Science in all its splendor. It is the part of your research that may be counted, sorted, emphasized because of statistical analysis. It is what you see, not the way in which you interpret what you see or hear. It is the A-B-C of experience you may jot down in memo form so you don't forget specifics. This is the description of what was in the room, the time of day, what was said or the written ideas on butcher paper informants shared. It is the information phase of gathering ideas. It is vital. It is the objective pathway we mistook for destination.

The Body idea in the Triangulation of Meaning is what Science has cornered. It is expressed through sensation via objective measurement and evaluation. It is a valuable and rigorous part in the Triangulation of Meaning and the center of most research processes. The gross/external part of the triangulation is the nitty-gritty of experience, the atomic process of physical movement, the force that moves objects. It is vital to not underestimate the beauty of research found at this level. The problem was that we assumed all the world could be described this way. In one sense all the world can be described in this way. We are simply acknowledging the world to be fuller, richer, and lived deeply also in the internal processes that empiricism only points to. Thus the world can be described via objectivity alone. It just would not be enough. Is not enough.

Table 1 draws out why detailing this portion of the triangulation is vital and yet only one-third of the whole. It will give you a clearer picture of what we are talking about. Table 1 gives us a glance at the future of rigor. Gross/external/ body knowing becomes part of a wholeness forming when combined with mind and spirit. Mature self-reflection finds objectivity moving in space/time toward a subjective reality that finally realizes the strength and beauty of its limitation and potential.

Study Table 1. Do you sense the simplicity here? The list is detailed now so we can be on the same page when we discuss the other two parts of the triangulation. This body-centered aspect in the triangulation is absolutely vital if we are to evolve. It is not the 'bad-guy' of research but a critical link to help us expand what it is we are engaged in. Valuing an empirical relationship with the world *begins* the discussion we may have with aspects of an idea, event or issue. It is simply not the end.

TABLE 1

The Triangulation of Meaning in its many forms

Body	Mind	Spirit	Source[22]
Objective	Subjective	Cultural	*Karl Popper*
Facts	Logic	Metaphor	*M. McCloskey*
Perception	Conceptualization	Remembering	*Yoga Sutra*
Empiricism	Rationalism	Mysticism	*Ken Wilber*
Information	Knowledge	Understanding	*Manu Aluli*
Sensation	Reason	Contemplation	*Ken Wilber*
Instinct	Intelligence	Intuition	*Halemakua*
Emotion	Feeling	Awareness	*Spinoza*
Force	Power	Liberation	*David Hawkins*
Its	I	We	*Buddhist inspired*
Life	Mind	Joy	*Upanishads*
External	Internal	Transpatial	*Ken Wilber*
Knowledge	Knowing	Enlightenment	*Maori inspired*
True	Good	Beautiful	*Plato*
Gross	Subtle	Causal	*Ken Wilber*
Tinana	Hinengaro	Wairua	*Maori*
'Ike (to see)	'Ike (to know)	'Ike (revelations)	*Hawaiian*
Hearing	Thought	Meditation	*Buddhist*
Duality	Non-Duality	Wholeness	*Ken Wilber*
Biology	Psychology	Spirituality	*Manu Aluli*
Seeing	Thinking	Being	*Ken Wilber*
Word	Meaning	Perception	*Patanjali*
Monologue	Dialogue	Presence	*Ken Wilber*
Empiricism	Epistemology	Hermeneutics	*Manu Aluli*
Dot	Circle	Sphere	*Mel Cheung*
Eye of the Flesh	Eye of the Mind	Eye of Contemplation	*Ken Wilber*

The body/external knowing of the triangulation is what we all can relate to because it is the template in which society and our institutions of higher learning operate from. It has been the bread and butter of research and science and the main assumption found in the notion of rigor. It is objective, tangible, and measurable. Now, don't you think it's time to evolve? After-all, one does not live on bread alone.

MIND: THE SUBTLE AND SUBJECTIVE KNOWING OF LIFE
Second Point in the Triangulation of Meaning

The great consciousness exists in my mind.
— Oscar Kawagley, Yupiaq —

Finally! Truth that objectivity is a subjective idea that cannot possibly describe the all of our experience. To believe that Science or objective and empirical-based research could describe all of life reduces it to its smallest part. Ken Wilber states it clearly: Physics is simply the study of the realm of least-Being. Claiming that all things are made of subatomic particles is the most reductionistic stance imaginable![23] Science and the belief in objectivity as the highest expression of our intellect, it turns out from those most experienced, works only in 'restricted fields of experience' and effective only within those fields.[24] What a revelation! Let me repeat that for the benefit of those in the back: *Objectivity is its own limitation.*

Enter mind, subjectivity, thought. Courage is needed to articulate these ideas with a robustness that will signal a leap in consciousness within our society. Even though insults will be hurled by mobs who have an investment in status-quo thinking, be prepared with ideas that scaffold what has become obvious: Our rational minds, our inside thoughts, our subjective knowing are *vital* to how we experience and understand our world. The question remains: How will the internal process of thought-made-conscious affect the process and product of your work?

Return to Table 1 and look again at synonyms found in the Mind category of the Triangulation of Meaning. They are not the EKG lines found on graph paper, they are the thoughts those lines represent. Thought is an inside and subtle experience inspired by a richness or poverty only you can imagine. Because thought shapes form, do you see how vital it is to develop our minds consciously and not get stuck on form? This is where we are heading as a planet—to become more mindful of what it is we must do, how we must heal, where we must go to invigorate our own process not fully encouraged within our institutions of learning.

The following four quotations are from my heroes. They are given here as an extension of what my own people have portrayed in their own reading of their world. As we begin to formulate authentic ideas within ancient streams of knowing, let the dialogue expand our connection to world-doers who have articulated the beauty found in their own knowing:

Maori Marsden (Maori) *Abstract rational thought and empirical methods cannot grasp what is the concrete act of existing which is fragmentary, paradoxical and incomplete. The only way lies through a passionate, inward subjective approach.*

David Hawkins (Psychiatrist) *To merely state that objectivity exists is already a subjective statement. All information, knowledge and the totality of all experience is the product of subjectivity, which is an absolute requirement intrinsic to life, awareness, existence and thought.*

Leroy Little Bear (Blackfoot) *Subjectivity is your starting point to reality.*

Greg Cajete (Tewa) *Native Science reflects the understanding that objectivity is founded on subjectivity.*

Subjective, thought, inside, logic, rationality, intelligence, conceptualization—these are some of the inside processes mind brings forward. They are the snapshots from our trip to meaning, heightened purpose and useful inquiry that will aid in healing ourselves and our world. The Mind part of this triangulation harnesses what is seen, counted and expressed into a meta-consciousness that explains, contextualized or *challenges*. It gives us the green light to engage in creative exploration needed to unburden ourselves from the shriveled promise objectivity has offered the world. We are being asked to *think* now, to develop truth in our bias, to speak our common sense, to deepen what intelligence *really* means.

This will change your research process and structure. Knowing of the relevance and maturation of conscious subjectivity will sharpen your rationality, help you speak through your gender so that you may lend what is beautiful about being alive, unique and one-of-a-kind. No kidding! Knowing mind, your mind and how it has helped shape your thoughts, will make you honest and help you write truthfully as an incest survivor, or a Pacific-Island scholar facing untold obstacles, or as a recovering addict working in prisons. Whatever it is. Whoever you are. It is all distinct, all shaped in mind patterns that if recognized will bring forth greater intelligence, not less. Self-reflection of one's thoughts and actions helps you understand that who you are, how you were raised, what you eat...all act as agents for your mindfulness or mindlessness. And all affect how you see and experience the world.

Mind as the second point in our Triangulation of Meaning helps us recover from the bullying and uniformity of "power-over" epistemology. It gives us breathing space to self-reflect in meaningful ways and engage with a rigor perhaps not captured in academic citations. Remember this! You will have to expand your repertoire of writers and thinkers if you wish to explore beyond the limitations of predictable research methodologies. It will be your mind that recognizes and describes new patterns needed for rationality, logic and the true rigor found in knowing something in depth. Follow mindfulness to its own intelligence and seek inevitably what most scholars refuse to admit exists: *spirit*. Yes, let us enter this grove with care and quietude.

SPIRIT: THE CAUSATIVE AND MYSTICAL KNOWING OF LIFE
Third Point in the Triangulation of Meaning

At this point, the rational, conceptual aspect of the mind
must let go, allowing a break-through
into direct, intuitive experience.
— Francesca Fremantle[25] —

Here it is, the third point in a spiral. It is what people misconstrue for religion and dogma. *It is not that.* To expand on ideas previously suggested earlier in this chapter, the spirit category in our Triangulation of Meaning is no less valuable, no more valuable. It is part of the whole, period. It is data moving toward usefulness moving toward meaning and beauty. It is the contemplation part of your work that brings you to insight, steadiness and interconnection. It is the joy or truthful insights of your lessons and the rigor found in your discipline and focus that is not so much written about but expressed none-the-less.

Spirit as a point in this triangulation is all about seeing what is significant and having the courage to discuss it. It is what Trungpa Rinpoche describes as "an innate intelligence that sees the clarity of things just as they are." This category that pulls facts into logic and finally into metaphor recognizes that one will eventually see more than what is presented. *You are being offered an opportunity to evolve.* Here is where the mystical aspects of this category encourages, inspires, calms. To know we are more than simply body and thought is to acknowledge how those ideas expand into wider realms of knowing and being. This is a spirit-centered truth that is older than time. Again, do not confuse the category of Spirit with religion.

Look again at Table 1. What do you learn from the Spirit category? Are these not the products and process of a conscious life? Is there any wonder billions of people wish to capture these values and ideas in ritual? The Spirit part of triangulating ourselves back to meaning is all about the purpose and reason of our lives. It will help you think of your research as something of value and keep you at the edge of your wonder with how it will shape who you are becoming. This third category encompasses the first two. It is an advancement of earlier ideas and gives a structure of rigor that positivism ultimately is shaped by.

Spirit in the Triangulation of Meaning is as it says: whole, contemplative, intuitive, metaphoric, joyful, liberating. Within research, it is answers you will *remember* in your dreams. It is questions you will frame differently after eye contact with a child. It is understanding an unexpected experience that will heighten the clarity of your findings. It is the 'Aha!' that came from stirring oatmeal after a night of transcription. Developing a respect for the qualities of awareness, joy and beauty will actually develop how you *think* and thus *see* the world. Do you see how all categories are really just one?

The spiritual category in this Triangulation of Meaning holds more than the extension of the first two categories. It is the frequency by which all connect. It is not simply a linear sequence. All three categories occur *simultaneously*. It is an idea who's time has come as it helps subjectivity mature into the fullness of its potential. Do not fear what is inevitable—that we are all part of the birthing of a new culture. Why not do it with a consciousness courageous in its purpose and quiet in its consistency?

Here is the point: research or renewal; mundane or inspiring; fragmented or whole. Do you see why Sir Karl Popper called the advancing of objectivity toward subjectivity into the inevitability of *culture* something we need to recognize? Culture is defined as best practices of a group of people. Here is the metaphor of this discussion: *that we change the culture of research.* We do this simply by engaging all *three* categories.

HA'INA MAI KA PUANA: THUS ENDS MY STORY

If knowledge is power then understanding is liberation
— Manu Aluli-Meyer —

I believe it is time to think indigenous and act authentic even at the price of rejection. To disagree with mainstream expectations is to wake up, to understand what is happening, to be of service to a larger whole. You may even begin to work on behalf of our lands, water and air. This is why we are heading into the field of hermeneutics—interpretation—via epistemology. We must first detail what we value about intelligence to even *see* there are other interpretations of life, brilliance and knowing. The idea that the SAT or other measurable tools of 'intelligence' are just *tiny* facets of intelligence is now timely. *Your* rendition of your own experience is now the point. Who are you then? What do you have to offer the world? Here is where hermeneutics enters with a bouquet of daisies. To realize that *all* ideas, *all* histories, *all* laws, *all* facts, and *all* theories are simply *interpretations* helps us see where to go from here. To understand this one idea has brought me to this point of liberation.

When ancient renditions of the world are offered for debate within a context of real-life knowing, there is a robustness that I find invigorating and breathtaking. Here is where interpretations matter and because indigenous folk are peopling places we were never found before, do you see why things are changing? We simply posit difference - a difference that knows place and encourages a harmony within that place. Of course we are far from perfect but we do bring something unique to the table. We bring dreams, food, elders, courage and the clarity of speech and purpose. After-all, there is no time to waste.

We are shaping long boards for a winter swell that is coming. It's time to learn new skills with our ancient minds. Time to deploy common sense back into our consciousness. Time to triangulate our way back to meaning. Time to laugh more and bear witness to the deeper truth of why we do what we're doing. Time to see how we can connect and help others. Time to work on behalf of our lands, water and air. Do you see how we are *all* on the path of sovereignty?

It's funny how the depth and practice of cultural specificity helps me be interested in the collective again. The wider collective. As if the path to wholeness first begins with fragmentation. It's my own body, mind and spiritual walk toward knowing that I have worked out in this chapter. And for this I'm grateful. Mahalo for sharing the space and making the time. May you find your own secret. May your bibliography be easy to gather. May you know your own brilliance. May it lead to collective joy.

Amama ua noa.

This article written for:
Linda Smith, Norman Denzin, Yvonna Lincoln (Eds.) (TBA) *Handbook of Critical and Indigenous Methodologies.* Sage Publishing.

References
Aluli-Meyer, Manulani (2004). *Ho'oulu - Our Time of Becoming: Hawaiian Epistemology and Early Writings.* Honolulu: Ai Pohaku Press.

Bodanis, David (2000). *E = mc2: A Biography of the World's Most Famous Equation.* New York: Berkley Books.

Bohm, David (1980). *Wholeness and the Implicate Order.* New York: Routledge.

Cajete, Gregory (2000). *Native Science: Natural Laws of Interdependence.* New Mexico: Clear Light Publishers.

Deloria, Vine (1999). *Spirit and Reason: The Vine Deloria Jr. Reader.* Colorado: Fulcrum Publishing.

Francesca Fremantle (2001). *Luminous Emptiness: Understanding the Tibetan Book of the Dead.* Boston: Shambhala.

Goswami, Amit (1993). *The Self-Aware Universe: How Consciousness Creates the Material World.* New York: Putnam Books.

Halemakua (2004). Unpublished writings of Halemakua. Hawaii Island.

Hartranft, Chip (2003). *The Yoga Sutra of Patanjali.* Boston: Shambhala.

Hawkins, David (2002). *Power vs. Force: The Hidden Determinants of Human Behavior.* Carlsbad: Hay House.

Marsden, Maori (2003). *The Woven Universe*. Te Wananga O Raukawa. Aotearoa New Zealand.

Nityananda (1996). *The Sky of the Heart*. Rudra Press, Oregon.

Tagore, Rabindranath (2004). *Sadhana: The Classic of Indian Spirituality*. New York: Three Leaves Press.

Talbot, Michael (1991). *The Holographic Universe.* Harper Perennial.

Tulku, Tarthang (1977). *Time, Space, and Knowledge: A New Vision of Reality.* Berkley: Dharma Publishing.

Wilber, Ken (2001). *Quantum Questions: Mystical Writings of the World's Great Physicists*. Boston: Shambhala.

End Notes

1. Universality in this ideal is not to be confused with uniformity—America's answer to diversity. Universality is a fundament spiritual truth exemplified in harmony, peace, awareness. This can only occur through respect and honoring of distinctness, thus the idea that 'specificity leads to universality.' It is best described in *Sadhana*, by Nobel laureate Rabindranath Tagore of India. It was also the one big idea that surfaced from my M.A. level class on Ethnicity and Education held at UH Hilo's Education Department in 2003.

2. Epistemology is the philosophy of knowledge. It asks questions we have long taken for granted: "What is knowledge? What is intelligence? What is the difference between information, knowledge and understanding?" It is *vital* to debate the issue of knowledge/intelligence because of the needs of our time.

3. Hermeneutics is the philosophy of interpretation. It helps us pause to ask the question: 'Who is talking and what interpretation do they bring and not bring to the discussion, idea or issue?" Hermeneutics makes the clear case that all ideas, all theories, all facts, all laws, or all histories are ultimately only *interpretations*. It is where philosophy is heading. The point here is that different ideas or priorities of knowledge (epistemology) are often dismissed given the nature of who is in control politically or ideologically.

4. This idea that we must learn from land and not simply about land was first learned through the writings of Greg Cajete. It has validated and informed our place-based pedagogy movement in Hawaii.

5. Aloha as the origin of our intelligence was first shared by hula teacher Olana Kaipo Ai.

6. The Yoga Sutra (Patanjali) cautions us to understand the difference between "word, meaning and perception" in order to get to the bottom of the world's problems and thus their solutions.

7. "We are all indigenous" came from the mind and writings of a beloved elder, Halemakua, a leader and teacher for our Hawaiian people and for many people around the world. I believe he meant that at one time we all came from a place familiar with our evolution and storied with our experiences. At one time we all had a rhythmic understanding of time and potent experiences of harmony in space. He believed we can tap into this knowing to engender, again, acts of care, compassion and right relationship with land, sky, water and ocean—vital for these modern times. To take this universal idea into race politics strips it of its truth.

8. For a discussion of this idea, please refer to Meyer, Manu (2003). *Ho'oulu: Our Time of Becoming.*

9. Books that bring out the causative agency of thought: Quantum Questions, $E=Mc2$; Self Aware Universe; Spirit and Reason, The Woven Universe, The Yoga Sutra, The Holographic Universe, etc.

10. The idea that "there are no causes within the observable world....the observable world is a world of effects" is detailed by Dr. David Hawkins in *Power vs. Force,* 2004.

11. Jean Houston in *Jump Time* summarized Einstein's famous idea that a new/different consciousness is needed to solve our current problems. Useful ideas were going to come from unknown places and differently trained individuals. She concurred that today the consciousness that solves a problem can no longer be the same consciousness that developed it.

12. True intelligence is self knowledge was put forth by Plato

13. Rabindranath Tagore, *Sadhana*.

14. Fractals are basic expanding and contracting patterns in nature. It was first described via Coherence Theory (Chaos Theory) as smaller and smaller elements of a larger and larger whole. A vein is a fractal of a leaf, a leaf is a fractal of a stem, a stem is a fractal of a branch, a branch is a fractal of a tree. It can then reverse itself back into the molecular level and then out into the forest, country side and world level. They represent a coherent whole we are not fully aware of. It is used here to infer that thoughts are also fractals in the world—change is directly linked to whether we think it possible. It begins first with an idea.

15. The idea that "words only point to truth, genuine knowledge must be experienced directly" came from Francesca Fremantle in *Luminous Emptiness: Understanding the Tibetan Book of the Dead.*

16. Audre Lorde inspired this dilemma found in post-colonial theory classes: Can you dismantle the Masters House (ie: imperialism, colonialism, etc) with the Masters tools? Answer: *Yes and No.* All outward realities are first inward expressions and thought-patterns. A new consciousness must be forged to approach old issues. False dualities of Master / Slave must also be reconfigured.

17. Heisenberg in *Quantum Questions: Mystical Writings of the World's Greatest Physicists,* Ken Wilber (Ed)

18. Ken Wilber, integral philosopher, was the first to introduce me to three points in philosophy and research. I discovered this in his epic work: *Sex, Ecology and Spirituality.*

19. I have always enjoyed the image of the tetrahedron learned from a lecture Buckminster Fuller gave in Honolulu before he died in the 1980's. He described the tetrahedron as "structural integrity" itself.

20. Yin/Yang is a Chinese way to organize Female and Male principles. Ku and Hina is a Hawaiian way. It gives us a way to recognize balance and to cultivate both aspects in our own character.

21. Empiricism is the belief that our five senses are the only modality in which to experience knowledge.

22. Unless noted specifically in the reference section at the end of this chapter, all descriptors in this list have been collected during a life-time of experiences and kept as journal entries without citation. Students have also given me their renditions and I have begun that list. The list itself is as self-evident as truth.

23. Ken Wilber, Page 26 in *Quantum Questions: Mystical Writings of the World's Greatest Physicists*

24. Heisenberg in *Quantum Questions: Mystical Writings of the World's Greatest Physicists*

25. Francesca Fremantle (2001). *Luminous Emptiness: Understanding the Tibetan Book of the Dead. Boston*: Shambhala.

26. Francesca Fremantle (2001). *Luminous Emptiness: Understanding the Tibetan Book of the Dead. Boston*: Shambhala. Page 59

27. Kumu Hula, Keola Lake said this during an interview for Meyer, Manu (Ed.D. Thesis) *Native Hawaiian Epistemology: Contemporary Narratives.* Harvard Graduate School of Education (1998).

28. Nityananda (1996). *The Sky of the Heart*. Rudra Press, Oregon.

AT THE THRESHOLDS

AT THE THRESHOLDS

Lucy R. Lippard

The dialogue and collaborations taking place for and around this exhibition are extraordinary enterprises. Though they probably won't lead immediately to tangible conclusions, they provide a beckoning threshold, inviting passage into another place, and offering some internal directives for the future. They may also help answer the question: Why are there so few Native writers on art? Why do so few Native artists put their thoughts into words? (I'll spare you the anthropological explanations—oral histories, no word in our language for art, etc.) Those who do write, and those participating in these dialogues, are on their way to forging the new language demanded by Apache artist Bob Haouzous when he threw down the gauntlet to his peers: "I don't think there are any Indian artists making important contemporary Indian art...because we don't have a cultural language to speak from."

What if that cultural language and that important art evolved together? The process could produce a distinctive kind of collaborative artwriting with an emphasis on tribal or pan-Indian wholeness rather than on splintered individualism. As Santa Clara Pueblo artist Roxanne Swentzell, puts it, "a birth into a choice."

In an uncompromising essay for the *Indigena* catalogue in 1992, Plains Cree artist Alfred Young Man wrote that "Native American self determination lives on through art." Yet Sara Marie Ortiz, from Acoma Pueblo, bravely challenges this today: "We say Self Determination through the arts instead of assimilation through the arts because it just sounds better. It's no different, though. In an eat-or-be-eaten economy... one eats or is eaten." With all the talk about sovereignty, an expanded Native art literature constitutes a necessary step over the threshold. When that step is taken, a couple of other questions can be considered. Is a Native perspective available to non-Indians? If it were, would that just constitute another colonial appropriation? Are non-Indian critics and curators part of the problem or just part of the equation?

Few people set out to be art critics. It's kind of an accidental vocation that emerges from a dual interest in words and images, from the challenge offered by working in the gap between the verbal and the visual. For several years I let it be known that I would mentor or read or edit or advise or help any young Native writers who wanted to be art critics. A couple of people (both artists' daughters) were vaguely interested, but in the end I had no takers. I didn't take it personally (maybe I should have?). I ascribed the reluctance to ambivalence about "art criticism" as a vocation. I dislike the term critic because it sounds adversarial, and almost everything I know about art I have learned from artists. So I call myself a "writer and activist" and leave out the "critic." At the same time, without "critical thinking"—the habit of questioning and scrutinizing everything we see and are told—we would be lost in the ether.

In any case, there's work out there to be done by Native writers on art that can't be done by anyone else. Every Native artist I know complains about being defined by an uncomprehending or arrogantly omniscient non-Indian world. But many museum catalogue texts are still written by non-Indians who don't have that Native perspective or by Native writers who don't have much of a grasp of contemporary art, whose musings can be moving, sometimes profound, but are by necessity generalized. Yet art is a *specific* endeavor and is best scrutinized by those who have created it or looked at an awful lot of it.

The few Native critics and curators working today are much in demand. Some have PhDs, although so-called art criticism is not an academic endeavor, not after-the-fact, but in the moment. It can be scholarly, but it's more important that it knows its way around the studios. In fact scholarship, though infinitely valuable, often requires a vocabulary and theoretical background that almost automatically make ideas incommunicable to a general audience. The artwriter is the bridge between the artist and the audience, but neither critics nor artists are trained in schools to identify their audiences, or their communities, and that's a crucial first step, for which many Native writers are well-prepared. Once an artist or writer is conscious of the gaps between maker and viewer, then steps can be taken to cross that particular threshold; in some cases it's just taking a few steps across a room, in others it's leaping an abyss.

The kind of straightforward artwriting I personally admire comes from the same kind of independence that produces art itself. One of the best statements I've heard on the exchange between critic and artist is what an anonymous Native artist told a non-Indian curator: "Keep talking while we keep working, but hold it down so I can hear myself think."

If non-Indian writers tend to depend on our own culturally approved taste, education, and background (which is "Western thinking," no matter how rebellious and sympathetic we think we are), Native writers who have a deeper knowledge are sometimes dependent on western contexts instead of swallowing them with a grain of salt. We're all in kind of a liminal place, not entirely sure of what our roles should be. Nancy Mithlo has described her own generation of Native writers as "thirty somethings who have enough confidence and training to openly question the mandates of an over-zealous market, but who find ourselves on a short rope when it comes to exposing the naivete of our patrons lest we find ourselves abandoned by the only transportation left. Too old to be overly optimistic, too young to be crassly cynical, we tread boldly into uncharted territory without the protection that age may afford and lacking a certain stupidity that may have been charming ten years earlier."

Is Indigenous America still "outside representation"? Are we all operating on what Jean Fisher calls the "faultline" between "the ungraspable real"—the cultural differences that remain illegible to white people, and "the imaginary sign (...which Indian peoples themselves are under pressure to accept as real)"? Contemporary Indian artists are aware of the delicate line they must tread between honoring their traditions and at the same time making their own art distinguishable from that of others, in the tradition of the mainstream avant garde. Native artists and writers acknowledge that indigeneity is an ideological space that can be worked in, and on. Aware that no single artist or style or subject can possibly "represent" Native America, they can reject the reduction of Native art to a simplistic spectacle of otherness. As scholar and photographer Jolene Rickard put it, "I must theorize a space for myself as a Tuscarora artist in a culturally diverse world."

Crossing the threshold means going somewhere, entering a different space. It's neither a stopping point, nor a waiting room. Perhaps it's that "Tsunami we so desperately need to create cultural renewal," as Hawaiian Native Rocky Jensen puts it. Certainly, as Santa Clara artist Rose Simpson says, "absolutely no one can do it for us, except ourselves."

A few passages in this essay are revised from a paper to be published in connection with the Denver Art Museum's *(Re)inventing the Wheel* symposium that took place in January 2006.

KILLER LANGUAGES AND PERNICIOUS ART MARKETS

KILLER LANGUAGES AND PERNICIOUS ART MARKETS:
A Plea for Self-Determination
of Indigenous Creativity

John R. Grimes

Indigenous people living today are the survivors of centuries of frequently catastrophic colonial contact with non-Indigenous, usually (not always) Euro-American cultures. Although the most overt forms of colonialism are now less common, Indigenous people around the world are still buffeted by civil wars, oppressive political regimes, famine, and disease, resulting in the dislocation and death of many thousands annually. In addition, the changing distribution of animal species, destruction of habitats, poisoning of resources, and rising sea levels that attend industrial pollution and global warming have a disproportionate impact on Indigenous communities, many of which still practice traditional subsistence activities. But even beyond such continuing assaults on their physical well being, Indigenous people face other, more insidious threats, resulting in the ongoing colonization of their cultures.

Various writers have attempted to summarize the salient differences between Indigenous people and their Euro-American colonizers. Indigenous culture is rooted in intuition, sociosensual[1] awareness, and consensus. Euro-American culture is "radically different. Based on dialectical reasoning, it intrinsically involves domination or conquest.... By its very nature... *[it] is confrontational.*"[2] In essence, Indigenous and Euro-American cultures operate according to profoundly different rules, with Indigenous people seeking consensus and positive feelings, while non-Indigenous people seek imposition, through argument, of a singular triumphant viewpoint. In a contest, the tendency of Indigenous people to seek consensus leads to an imbalance of power, as they typically yield to what has been called the "conquistadorial dialectic."[3]

Ironically, the force of this conquistadorial dialectic, now amplified and disseminated by mass media, the internet, and global consumerism, may be far greater today than at any time in the past. Throughout the world, the incessant assertion of non-Indigenous values, lifestyles, products, and language can be overwhelming to local cultures, especially those already weakened by previous colonial experience.

Among many Indigenous cultures, language has proven to be especially vulnerable. Mass media and the Internet undermine Indigenous languages by greatly privileging a small number of *lingua francas* – especially English, Chinese, Japanese, Spanish, French, and German.[4] Languages that displace others in this way are often referred to as "killer" languages, with English leading the list.

Of course, culture may exist without language, and to assert otherwise is to impose a cultural death sentence on individuals and communities who have already lost their native tongue. However, language is the essential means by which a culture delineates, from its unique perspective, the benchmarks, topography, and underlying dynamics of the cosmos. When, at the expense of its own, a community adopts a foreign language, it can eventually lose touch with this unique map of the cosmos, since any adopted language will not include the same referents, or organize them in the same way.

Thus, the survival of spoken languages can be regarded as an important indicator of Indigenous cultural health. According to many experts, a language should be considered endangered when it is being learned by less than 30% of a community's children. By this standard, a high proportion of the world's languages are at risk. It has been estimated that of the world's ca. 6,000 extant languages, and the much larger number of related dialects, ninety percent will become extinct in the coming century.[5] Most of these losses will be among Indigenous cultures.

Language is only one of the vital aspects of culture. Just as humans are individually creative, cultures have an essential creative character, each with a unique body of wisdom and practice with respect to meeting the challenges of a changing world. In other words, cultures have special ways of approaching and solving problems, ways that are informed by their accumulated experience, world view, and language. They are unique not only in their static character, but – perhaps even more so – by the ways that they creatively engage with the future-as-it-becomes-present, and the associated unpredictable problems and opportunities. Creativity is a culture's leading edge.

The nature and expression of creativity differs between Indigenous and Euro-American cultures. In the latter, creativity is a rarified, frequently elite commodity, produced by a few celebrity individuals, which is packaged and sold according to the demands of the marketplace. By contrast, in most Indigenous cultures, creativity is not an isolated activity, but part of everyday life. Moreover, most individuals – not just a few celebrities – participate in creative activities. Where group livelihood depends on cooperation and distribution of resources, creativity is not a privately-held commodity, but something to be shared.

Along with language, Euro-American concepts of creativity are an implicit part of mass-media exports. As part of the conquistadorial dialectic, Euro-American notions of creativity compete directly with aspects of Indigenous culture. Here too, the competition is skewed, since Euro-American-style creativity is part of a powerful economic engine, a commercial art complex that encompasses museums, galleries, auction houses, collectors, art historians, and critics. These individual entities act interdependently to identify, brand, market – then profit from – creativity, i.e. artists and artworks. Everywhere the commercial art complex extends, it forms a powerful attraction to individual artists, since it offers the possibility of financial success, and even celebrity status. But, like the killer languages that displace Indigenous tongues, the commercial art complex should be regarded as pernicious when it causes Indigenous cultures to forfeit intrinsic modes of creativity. When cultures trade these away, they undermine their own capacity for a strong and self-determined future.

Many Indigenous artists are quoted as stating their preference for being known as artists that *happen* to be Indigenous, rather than as Indigenous artists. On one hand, they express an understandable concern about being unfairly relegated to an inferior status, and distracting viewers – and potential buyers – from the inherent qualities of their art. But these assertions also seem to imply that the primary goal for Indigenous artists is to *fit in*, and to succeed in the mainstream art world, on *its* terms.

In fairness, it can easily be argued that achieving economic success and visibility can help reduce the lingering social and economic disparities between Indigenous people and the majority. But this is only true for a few individuals, unless it can be shown that the positive impacts are more widespread. Alternatively, it might also be argued that the commercial art complex engenders a form of assimilation, and ultimately undermines the integrity and sustainability of Indigenous culture. Here, there is no single correct perspective, but it seems imperative that Indigenous artists and their communities work together to find mutually beneficial ways of supporting and sustaining local culture.

And what of the commercial art market? It seems unlikely that there will be any rapid reform of it, as a whole, given the economic self-interest that it embodies. Among its constituents, however, museums should assume a high level of responsibility for how they directly and indirectly support or undermine Indigenous cultures. Unfortunately, museums – art museums, at least – are conceptually little changed from their counterparts of a century or two ago, and still function mainly as tools for projecting Euro-American ideology. Because of this, recent efforts to make museums more culturally inclusive are in the end merely symbolic, since inclusion still means adhering to essentially Euro-American sensibilities regarding the nature and value of art. Given a new paradigm – one that truly embodies and respects the spectrum of human creativity – museums could be a truly positive force in nurturing a new and more inclusive public appreciation of cultural diversity. Over time, this could reduce the pernicious impact of the art marketplace, and diminish the negative effect of the conquistadorial dialectic. One wonders if this is a wholly idealistic scenario, and if not, whether it could occur in any time period less than a century.

The Indigenous world cannot be passive, waiting for such change to come from the Euro-American world. Instead, Indigenous artists and intellectuals must set out to create a body of Indigenous art theory, a library of Indigenous art histories, and Indigenous approaches to creativity. The Institute of American Indian Arts (IAIA) is a nexus for such discourse, bringing together students, faculty, curators, artists, and visiting scholars from throughout the Native American and Indigenous world. At the IAIA Museum, we will seek to model *Indigenous* ways of being an art museum, and find new ways to present and interpret Indigenous art. The RELATIONS exhibition and dialogue is an opening chapter in this vitally important work.

End Notes

1. Christian de Quincey "Consciousness: Truth or Wisdom?" IONS Review, # 51 (March-June, 2000).
2. Ibid
3. Ibid
4. www.glreach.com/globstats/index.php3; Just two languages - English and Chinese – together constitute 50% of all internet use
5. David Crystal, Language Death (2000), p. 11.

GRAPHIC COMMENTARY

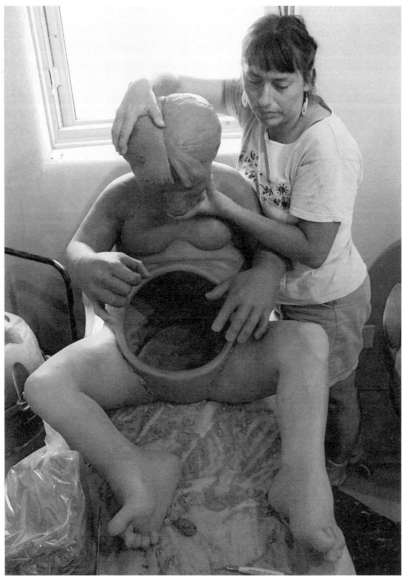

Roxanne: "I worked on this life-size clay figure of a woman half sitting–half lean-ing back. Her stomach is open to view what is inside...During the firing, a chair blocked the lever for shutting the kiln off at the right temperature. She had been on high all night! I have not looked inside yet as the kiln is too hot still but I'm sure she is completely melted and might have ruined my kiln also."

[Curator's note: above, *The Story of Our Births,* intended for RELATIONS exhibition]

Rocky Kaʻiouliokahikikoloʻehu Jensen, 2006

Othniel "Art" Oomittuk, 2006

Othniel "Art" Oomittuk, 2006

Jacob Fragua III, 2006

Roxanne Swentzell, 2006

Roxanne Swentzell, 2006

Harry Fonseca, 2006

Harry Fonseca, 2006

relations

matu

matu

inmi ma tiin-ma

shoet-nei-khi

shoet-nei-khi

daanaht'eke

daanaht'eke

stai-yahtru-tyaimesheeh

ittapiha

ittapiha

pilikana

pilikana

stah-we-tyaimesheeh

shideekende

pili loko

mitakuye oyasin

pili ma ka hanauna

pili ma ka hanauna

BIOGRAPHICAL NOTES

BOB HAOZOUS was born in Los Angeles, California in 1943 to Allan Houser (Chiricahua Apache/English) and Anna Marie Gallegos (Navajo/Spanish). He grew up in Apache, Oklahoma and northern Utah, and attended Utah State University before serving four years in the Navy. Following military service, he attended the California College of Arts and Crafts in Oakland, California, receiving a BFA in 1971. Three years later, Haozous won the Grand Prize at the Heard Museum's Sculpture II Exhibition. In 1999 and 2001 he helped organize the first Native American Pavilions at the Venice Biennale—a groundbreaking effort to inspire Indigenous artists to create a more meaningful contemporary statement of identity.

JOSEPH M. SANCHEZ is Curator at the Institute of American Indian Arts in Santa Fe, New Mexico. Born of a Hispanic/Pueblo Indian father and a Hispanic-German/Pueblo Indian mother in Trinidad, Colorado, he was raised on the White Mountain Apache reservation in Northeastern Arizona. He has worked with many artists including: Daphne Odjig, Norval Morriseau, Phillip Curtis, Guenter Uecker, John Paul Ledeur. He has curated exhibitions with many reknown artists such as Bob Haozous, Jean Tinquely, George Segal, Norman Bluhm, Jesus Morales, Harry Fonseca, Roxanne Swentzell and many others.

ROCKY KA'IOULIOKAHIHIKOLO' EHU JENSEN is a sculptor and historical illustrator, as well as the founder of *Hale Naua III*. He has mounted and participated in more than 125 fine art exhibitions. He serves as a cultural advisor to numerous organizations lending meticulous Native Hawaiian input. He is the recipient and honoree of several regional and national awards for his contributions to the cause of perpetuating the Native Hawaiian culture and arts. Along with his wife, Lucia, he has co-authored and illustrated several cultural books. Jensen's works have been exhibited in leading museums throughout the world and in numerous private and corporate collections.

OTHNIEL A. OOMITTUK, JR, sculptor, is an Inupiat born in Point Hope, Alaska, one hundred miles north of the Arctic Circle. At the age of nine, he moved with his family even farther north to Barrow. As a boy, he watched his grandfather carve masks from whale bone. Oomittuk began carving around 1997, when he was in his early thirties. He graduated from Western Oregon University, intending to be an art teacher, but his appetite for creation was wetted by courses in printmaking, photography and ceramics. Oomittuk has shown at the Heard Museum, Phoenix, the Portland Art Museum, and the IAIA Museum, among other national venues.

HARRY FONSECA is a painter of ethnic symbols related to contemporary storytelling concerning his 19th century Maidu ancestors. His paintings frequently depict coyotes, a subject he relates to the Trickster character. In 1978, fascinated by its multi-ethnic culture, Fonseca settled in Santa Fe, New Mexico.

ROXANNE SWENTZELL was born in Taos, New Mexico in 1962, part of the well-known Naranjo family of Santa Cara artists. She attended the Institute of American Indian Arts in Santa Fe, New Mexico, followed by the Portland Museum Art School in Portland, Oregon. Her highly emotive clay and bronze sculptures are found in museums and private collections around world.

NATALIE MAHINA JENSEN was raised on the island of O'ahu (Hawai'I). Natalie Mahina Jensen was educated and trained since childhood in Native Hawaiian featherwork—later specializing in the royal feather standard called *kahili*. Professionally trained in photography, she has expanded her field of expression, keeping her heritage as the focal point of her imagery.

ROSE SIMPSON is a current student at IAIA in Santa Fe, New Mexico. The daughter of a Santa Clara sculptor Roxanne Swentzell, Rose is a hip-hop artist, poet, painter, and sculptor. She performs with the band Chocolate Helicopter.

MICAH WESLEY is a painter and graphic artist, currently studying at IAIA. He has been shown in numerous exhibits and events including the Winter Indian Art Show in Collinsville, Illinois and the Red Earth Juried Art Competition in Oklahoma City.

SIMON ORTIZ is a writer, poet and storyteller. His books include *Woven Stone*, *From Sand Creek*, and *After and Before the Lightning*. As a major Native American writer he insists on telling the story of his people's land, culture, and community, a story that has been marred by social, political and economic conflicts with Euro-American society. He insists, however, upon stories that stress vision and hope through creative resistance to oppression.

SARA ORTIZ is an Acoma Pueblo writer currently residing in Santa Fe, New Mexico. A recent graduate of the IAIA, she is the youngest daughter of poet-laureate, professor and author Simon Ortiz.

ALEX JANVIER was born on the Cold Lake First Nations, just outside the town of Cold lake, Alberta in 1935. Proud of his Dene Suline heritage, it is a fundamental part of his artwork. He obtained a Fine Arts Diploma from the Alberta College of Art in Calgary in 1960. As one of Canada's most accomplished artists, Janvier has also been commissioned to paint more than a dozen murals in major buildings and schools across Canada. He has received numerous awards including the prestigious National Aboriginal Achievement Award in 2002, and he has been affiliated with the Royal Canadian Academy since 1993.

JACOB FRAGUA III is from the Pueblo of Jemez on the west side of the Los Alamos National Laboratories in New Mexico.

ANTHONY DEITER is a contemporary storyteller employing 3-D digital animation and other computer technologies to communicate the story of North America's Indigenous people, through references to his own history. As teacher, designer and artist working with visual and web site software, one of his personal mandates is to close the digital divide in Native American/First Nations communities.

PETER IRNIQ is an Inuit cultural teacher who has lived most of his life in the Kivalliq Region of Nunavut. He has served as Assistant Director of Nunavut Heritage and Culture, where he was responsible for developing programs and services to meet the needs of the new territory.

MANULANI MEYER works in philosophy, specifically epistemology, or the philosophy of knowledge. She is part of a movement to transform Hawaiian education, social services, higher learning and Justice. Her book; *Ho'oulu: Our Time of Becoming* is in its second printing. She is currently an Associate Professor of Education at the University of Hawaii in Hilo.

LUCY LIPPARD is a former art critic for "Art in America," "The Village Voice" and "Z magazine" as well as the author of 18 books on subjects ranging from Pop Art to Native American art.

ACKNOWLEDGMENTS

The editors would like to thank all of the individuals and institutions for their encouragement, advice and assistance in preparing this exhibition and RELATIONS publication. First and foremost, we would like to express our deep and heartfelt appreciation to the core group of participants – Bob Haozous, Rocky Ka'iouliokahihikolo' Ehu Jensen, Art Oomittuk, Harry Fonseca, Roxanne Swentzell, Rose Simpson, Micah Wesley, Simon Ortiz, Sara Ortiz, Alex Janvier, Jacob Fragua III, Anthony Dieter, and Peter Irniq. This important project just wouldn't have happened without their generous contributions of time and wisdom. In addition, we are grateful to Lucy Lippard for her written contribution to this publication, and also to Manulani Meyer, as well as Sage Press, for allowing us to include their seminal essay on Hawaiian epistemology.

Among the staff at the Institute of American Indian Arts Museum, we would especially like to recognize: Sallie I. Wesaw, Paula Rivera, Tatiana Lomahaftewa Slock, Audrey Dreaver, Jessie Ryker, Sandy Vaillancourt and Loni Manning who assisted with the preparation and editing of this book; Jary Earl, who very ably oversaw the complex and time-consuming financial matters inherent in working with a large number of consultants and vendors. Beyond these individuals, it is no exaggeration to say that every staff member directly supported this project in critical ways since its inception in the summer of 2005.

Outside of staff, the following individuals have provided important logistical support and advice for the exhibition and catalog: Eileen Torpey,

Rosa Leonard, Beth Grimes and Joe Mowrey. Janice St. Marie has done an exceptional job of designing and producing this publication, within very challenging time constraints.

Exhibition-related advertising has been funded in part by the City of Santa Fe Arts Commission and the 1% Lodgers Tax.

We would like to acknowledge the vital support and encouragement of the Trustees of the Institute of American Indian Arts, as well as Interim President Dr. Richard Tobin.

Finally, on behalf of the entire Institute and Museum, and all of the participating artists, we would like to extend our deepest gratitude to Lannan Foundation for their generous financial support of this project. Their continuing investment in Indigenous causes makes a truly positive, and important difference in the world.